Grammar of
the Shot

The newly revised and updated fourth edition of *Grammar of the Shot* teaches readers
the principles behind successful visual communication in motion media through shot
composition, screen direction, depth cues, lighting, camera movement, and shooting for
editing. Many general practices are suggested that should help to create rich, multi-
layered visuals. Designed as an easy-to-use guide, *Grammar of the Shot* presents each
topic succinctly with clear photographs and diagrams illustrating key concepts, practical
exercises, and quiz questions, and is a staple of any filmmaker's library.

New to the fourth edition:

- an expanded companion website at www.routledge.com/cw/bowen, offering
  downloadable scenes and editable raw footage so that students can practice the
  techniques described in the book, and instructional videos showcasing examples
  of different compositional choices;
- new and expanded quiz questions and practical exercises at the end of each
  chapter to help to test readers on their knowledge using real-world scenarios;
- updated topic discussions, explanations, illustrations, and visual examples.

Together with its companion volume, *Grammar of the Edit*, the core concepts discussed
in these books together offer concise and practical resources for both experienced and
aspiring filmmakers.

Christopher J. Bowen has worked within the motion media industries for over 18
years as a cinematographer, editor, director, and educator. Currently, he is an Associate
Professor of Film Production and Visual Media Writing at Framingham State University.
He is also an Avid Certified Instructor, Creative Director of his own media production
company, Fellsway Creatives, and author of the companion text, *Grammar of the Edit*.

Grammar of the Shot

Fourth Edition

Christopher J. Bowen

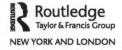

Routledge
Taylor & Francis Group

NEW YORK AND LONDON

Fourth edition published 2018
by Routledge
711 Third Avenue, New York, NY 10017

and by Routledge
2 Park Square, Milton Park, Abingdon, Oxon OX14 4RN

Routledge is an imprint of the Taylor & Francis Group, an informa business

© 2018 Taylor & Francis

Third edition published by Focal Press 2013

Library of Congress Cataloging in Publication Data
A catalog record for this book has been requested

ISBN: 978-1-138-63221-9 (hbk)
ISBN: 978-1-138-63222-6 (pbk)
ISBN: 978-1-315-20839-8 (ebk)

Typeset in Univers
by Keystroke, Neville Lodge, Tettenhall, Wolverhampton

Visit the companion website: www.routledge.com/cw/bowen

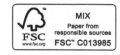

MIX
Paper from responsible sources
FSC™ C013985

Printed in the United Kingdom
by Henry Ling Limited

Contents

Contents

Introduction

For most of us living in the 21st century, the majority of our daily experiences are inseparable from interactions with digital media. We are constantly *communicating with* someone or something or being *communicated to* by someone or something: texting or speaking via smartphones; watching television or streaming media; using the internet; listening to the radio; playing networked video games; reading books, newspapers, and magazines; looking at billboards and advertisements; going to the movies; and on and on it goes. Our ability to understand these communications and gain further meaning from them is reliant upon our education and experiences: can we read, write, and speak a language, recognize images and sounds, decipher symbols, etc.?

This "education," whether it is from schooling or just living life, helps to determine how well we can compute what we take in, and there is a lot to take in. Collectively, over time, we have learned to codify our visual communications – from pictographs to written words, to paintings, photographs, and now motion pictures. What we depict has a recognizable meaning. Viewers know how to decode the images that they are shown. Understanding, or clear interpretation of what is viewed, stems from the established grammar or rules of depiction that have evolved over time.

It is this concept of grammar (meaning gleaned from structure) that motion picture creators rely upon so heavily. Fictional narrative films, documentaries, news reports, situation comedies, television dramas, commercials, music videos, talk shows, "reality" programming and the like, all use the same basic visual grammar to help to communicate to the viewer. As a filmmaker, when you "speak" the common cinematic language, you will be able to communicate your story to an incredibly diverse, worldwide audience. They will see it. They will hear it. They will get it.

This book, *Grammar of the Shot*, Fourth Edition, has been updated, enhanced, and expanded. Many of the figures that illustrate the concepts have been refreshed. Each chapter begins with an outline of that chapter's contents, and ends with a detailed review section highlighting the main concepts covered by that chapter. Value-added sections called Exercises and Quiz Yourself conclude each chapter. They present ways in which you can immediately put into practice the techniques and guidelines discussed in the chapter, and offer a gauge to see how well you absorbed the information. Many new topics have been added throughout and most recurring topics have been rewritten and restructured for clarity and flow.

This book is designed for those of you who are new to the area of visual storytelling but who wish to be well acquainted with the basic guidelines, conventions, and practices of the visual language of motion pictures. It will take you from the basic shape of the frame, to different types of shots, and to the ways to compose visual elements within those frames. You will be exposed to the basics of shot lighting, screen direction, depth elements, camera movement, and many general practices that make for a richer, multi-layered visual presentation. Most importantly, it will provide you with essential information to expand your visual vocabulary and help to jumpstart your motion imaging career in this non-stop world of motion media communications.

Acknowledgments

I wish to thank the supportive team of publishing professionals at Routledge/Taylor & Francis Group who helped to make this new and improved fourth edition a reality. I would particularly like to thank Simon Jacobs and John Makowski, who worked diligently to get this new edition off the ground. I hope our efforts continue to honor the legacy of Roy Thompson, who penned the first edition so many years ago. The goal we all share in producing this book is to get the pertinent information about recording motion media pieces into the minds and hands of the next generation of visual storytellers. I hope that this revised fourth edition continues to inform and inspire all of those readers who are just beginning their creative journey into the world of motion media production.

As an Associate Professor of Film Production and Visual Media Writing at Framingham State University, I benefit from being surrounded by fellow educators and a lively and engaged population of students in the communication arts. The environment fosters much innovation and many new approaches to teaching and learning about our discipline. I wish to acknowledge the support of my colleagues and the helpful contributions from all of my students over the years. The same goes for my experiences while teaching at Boston University and at the Boston University Center for Digital Imaging Arts. A collective thank you to everyone who has added to my growth as an educator and as a motion media producer.

As a media professional, I wish to thank my many collaborators and clients, who have helped me to continue learning and to explore new techniques in telling their unique stories.

I am also grateful to the fourth edition's proposal and manuscript reviewers for their helpful suggestions and critiques. A special thank you goes out to Katarina Damjanov, Adam Davis, David E. Elkins, Stephen Gordon, Jeffrey Hill, and Juli S. Pitzer.

Additionally, I would like to thank my on-camera talent for their time and cooperation:

Darby Andersson	Michael J. Bowen
Keegan Andersson	Nicole Castaldo
Shelissa Aquino	Wendy Chao
Zach Benard	Andrew Conley
Brian Boucher	Jacob Cuomo

Alexandra D'Ambrosio & Family

Mike Neilan

Tim English

Kelsey E. O'Connor

Deirdra Enos

Alyssa & Cameron Parmenter

Caitlin Harper

Elizabeth Proulx

Crystal Haidsiak

Colleen Reilly

Elaria Jacob

Rajiv Roy

Timi Khatra

Alexander Scott

Emily Klamm

Stacie Seidl

Hannah Kurth

Stacy Shreffler

Elizabeth Lospennato

Eliza Smith

Olivia Lospennato

Rachel Swain

John McNeil

Taylor Sweeney

Anthony Martel

Tucker and Ghost

Tamie Martel

The majority of images in this edition have been created by the author, but a significant set of new pictures have been donated by several photographers and a number of my students (both past and present) who have visual communication, photography, and design interests of their own. I would like to thank the following individuals for sharing their creative works and for also manufacturing topic-related images that help to illustrate the film language content in this book:

Darby Andersson

Elaria Jacob

Zach Benard

Brennan Marlow

Rachael Bissonnette

Anthony Martel

Nicole Casamento

Sarah Morgan

Andrew Conley

Mike Neilan

Amy DeCosta

Alyssa Parmenter

Miles Garnett

Rachael Swain

Nicole Girard

QiHui Zhang

The line art diagrams and the majority of the hand-drawn illustrations are also by the author. Several still frames have been contributed by the production team who made the independent feature film, *Consumer Beware* (2016). Thank you Zach Benard, Avarie Cook, Anthony Martel, and John McNeil (with special guest Connor Carson).

Finally, I acknowledge my family for their support and offer an extra special thank you to Emily Klamm, who has been there through the thick and thin of it all – again.

This book is for all people who wish to learn the basics about communicating visually through motion pictures. I hope you have fun and enjoy the ride. If you would like to learn more about the topic, find additional resources, or contact the author, please visit the author's website: www.fellswaycreatives.com.

For my #1 Mom

Chapter One
The Shots: What, How, and Why?

- Cinematic Language Defined
- Choose Your Frame Size
- Typical Shot Names and Descriptions
- Master Scene Technique and Shooting Coverage
- Script Analysis and Breakdown
- Shot Lists and Storyboards
- Phases of Film Production

You can find moving images just about everywhere these days. New techniques for micro processing, wireless transmission, and screen display technologies allow us to access time-based visual media on our smartphones, tablets, and laptops. You can see motion imagery playing around the world in taxis, on airplanes, on billboards, on the sides of buildings, at bus stops, in the aisles of "big-box" stores, at malls, in museums, and, of course, on television and in movie theaters. So many kinds of moving images, made by so many diverse groups of people for so many different purposes, are available via these numerous outlets. And we, the receiving audience, somehow comprehend what all of these images are saying. We may not understand the spoken or written language in these "movies," but we do understand, perhaps on an unconscious level, the inherent and intended meaning behind the use of this visual language: the grammar of the shot.

This use of visual communication — in our case, the worldwide cinematic language — forms the focus of this book.

Let's say you want to make a short film, or a funny web animation, or you need to interview someone for a school project. You, the filmmaker, are in a position of great creative power. You get to decide what the content of your video will be and how you will show it to a viewer. Your visual expressions (the pictures that show your story) need to be presented in ways that your audience can properly understand and interpret. If you do not "speak" the right language (use the appropriate grammar of the shot), then your message may not come across clearly. Think of this book as an introductory lesson in the visual language of moving imagery. It presents you with some of the core guidelines, commonly used tools, and accepted methodologies found in the art and craft of visual storytelling.

As we are discussing the grammar of the shot, it may help to determine, initially, what we mean by "grammar" and, later, for the majority of this text, what we mean by "shot." It should be understood that "grammar" in this sense of the word refers to the basic rules governing the construction and presentation of visual elements created for inclusion in a motion picture. These are the commonly accepted guidelines that describe how visual information should be displayed to the audience. Viewers (all of us who have grown up watching films, television, and web videos) have been trained over the years to observe, decode, and comprehend the various elements of the shots used in motion picture creation. In other words, we may not consciously acknowledge it, but we know what most images mean and how they make us feel. An adept filmmaker uses this dynamic between the shots and the viewer to tell better stories.

We will explore what basic types of shots are possible and what goes into their construction. We will also see what information and meaning the viewer can pull out of these shots when viewed in the context of your edited film. Remember that filmmaking is simultaneously a creative and a technical craft, and the extent of your success often depends on how well you communicate your vision to your audience. If you confuse them with faulty film language or improper visual "grammar," then they will most likely not respond well to your work. The meaning, message, and audience engagement may be lost. If, however, you purposefully construct your filmed imagery, then more efficient, aesthetically pleasing, and appropriately manipulative visual communication can occur during the viewing experience.

To keep things simple, we are, for the most part, using generic terms for discussion and explanation. For instance, the terms "motion picture," "motion imagery," etc. refer to any time-based media piece, work, show, animation, film, video, project, or program that is made up of a series of individual images that, when displayed to our eyes very rapidly, provide the illusion of movement. The term "camera" will refer to any device (simple or complex, old-school or cutting-edge) that can record these moving images. The term "filmmaker" refers to any person undertaking the creation of any kind of motion picture. At times, **camera person** or **camera operator** will be used to refer to anyone who operates the camera device that is recording the moving images.

What to Show Your Audience?

It may seem counterintuitive, but in filmmaking, if you are not sure where to begin, it can be very helpful to start at the end. Ask yourself some key questions:

- What is your goal?
- What are you setting out to make?
- What kind of story are you trying to tell and how do you wish to tell it?
- Who is the target audience?
- What purpose does this motion media piece have?
- What tools and other assets will you need to make it?
- Where and how will it be shown and viewed?

Understanding what your end result should be will help to inform where you can begin, and it will lead to many more creative and logistical questions (well beyond those posed above) for you to answer along the way. Media production is often a costly and time-consuming endeavor, so the best plan is to actually have a plan. Our main concerns in this book are with the visual elements of your motion picture, so let's begin your planning there.

Movies, television shows, music videos, commercials, and animations all rely heavily on their visual elements. For the most part, all traditional motion media products draw on the same basic guidelines within film's visual language. There are, however, certain types of shots and visual imagery treatments that are associated with specific media pieces (news, game shows, documentaries, etc.). These days, you will find that there is a lot of sharing, swapping, and intermingling of pictographic elements, especially within the realm of short "infotainment" videos found all over the internet and social media streams. As such, you have to decide very early on in the creative process what is important for the viewer to see and how these particular recorded objects, actions, and/or events should be shown to the audience.

Developing a visual plan – one that incorporates both the overall style and look of your project and the technologies and techniques that can help you to achieve that look – will prove very beneficial. **Cinematography** is the film production term associated with the art, craft, and practices of developing this visual plan, style, and overall look of a motion picture project. The decisions of what to actually photograph and how to photograph it can be the result of input from many people involved in the filmmaking process – from the writer to the director, to the **director of photography**, actors or producers, etc. (see a list of common film crew members and their job responsibilities in Appendix B). Regardless of who is making these choices, someone is doing this, and for your initial projects it will most likely be you, the filmmaker.

What to Show Your Audience?

Choosing Your Frame

The visual needs of your motion picture project can be guided by the script of your fictional narrative story (discussed later in this chapter), or are dictated by real-time documentary events, or driven by the content, style, and purpose of the show that you are producing. Knowing how you want to visually present your story can lead you to some of your first decisions regarding your visual plan: what camera and what lens will you use? In simple terms, these components work together to create your pictures. The **lens**, traditionally, gathers, focuses, and controls the amount of light entering the camera body. The camera body houses the light-sensitive "imager" (digital light sensor, emulsion film, etc.) that forms and records the image that you ultimately watch on a screen.

These two very important tools, the camera (referenced throughout this book) and the lens (primarily discussed in Chapter Three), work in tandem to reproduce a particular horizontal rectangle of reality that is out in front of the camera's position. This rectangle is only a small segment or cut-out window of the total sphere of the physical world around the camera. This cut-out has a defined and finite area and we call it the **frame** (Figure 1.1).

Whatever is inside this frame is recorded as a 2D representation of the actual world that exists in front of the lens. At present, because our video and film cameras can really capture only the two dimensions of width and height (frame left-to-right and frame top-to-bottom), they get displayed as flat images on a screen (projected movie, television set, computer monitor, tablet, or smartphone). The third dimension, depth (albeit present in reality), is only captured as an illusion on the actual 2D film or video. This concept is discussed in more detail in Chapter Two. We will not be discussing the technologies behind dual-lens, dual-camera, or digitally animated 3D production – that goes well beyond the scope of this book.

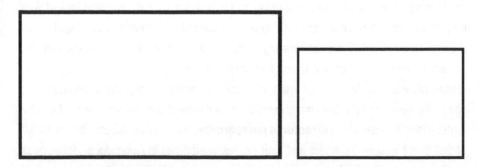

FIGURE 1.1   A high-definition (HD) 16 x 9 frame and a standard-definition (SD) 4 x 3 television frame. Think of these as your empty canvases where you will get to "paint" the various elements of your shots.

Not to get too technical at the outset, but the next topic, frame size and **aspect ratio**, really should be addressed early on so that you can begin shooting your project with a solid understanding of the visual frame. It is the camera's format (the area of width and height of the imager) and the type of lens used that dictate the shape and amount of space that you get to record and what the audience may ultimately watch within the 2D rectangular frame on their screen. We look to lenses later, but we should address frame sizes now. Your choice of camera (**video format** or **film gauge** with variable masking) will lead to many other decisions in both the **aesthetics** of your motion picture (the grammar of your shots) and the **workflow** (or media pathways) used to complete it.

Aspect Ratio

The dimensions of a camera's frame (the active recordable image area) or the width-to-height relationship of that frame is often expressed as a ratio of that width to that height. This ratio is called the aspect ratio and, depending on the format of the medium, may be written 4:3, 16:9, 1.85:1, etc. The first example, 4:3 (said "four to three" and sometimes written "4 × 3" or "four by three"), means that if the height is three units tall, then the width is equal to four of those same units. It can also be represented by the ratio of 1.33:1 (said "one-three-three to one"). This is the aspect ratio for **standard-definition** (SD) television in North America (NTSC, NTSC miniDV, and DVD) and Europe (PAL, and DV-PAL). This was the "standard" for 20th-century TV, but SD has been rapidly phased out of both production and broadcast by HD (see below) – although you will still find it as a frame size selection (or resolution) on certain digital cameras that can record very high frame rates used to achieve extreme digital video slow-motion playback effects. The aspect ratio of all **high-definition** (HD) video is 16:9, or 1.78:1.

Figure 1.2 shows several frame sizes and their aspect ratios from television and motion picture history. The size has evolved over the decades as technologies and marketing trends have changed. At present, theatrical motion pictures, residual standard-definition content, and high-definition television all have different aspect ratios, which makes it rather confusing and complicated to get the images of one format to fit into the shape of another, but we will not worry about that now. We will simply select a single frame size and work with that. As SD has become a thing of the past, and professionals as well as amateurs have adopted Hi-Def or HD (of one flavor or another), we are going to use the widescreen 16:9 HDTV aspect ratio for our examples in this book. If your project calls for using any gauge of film, NTSC-DV or PAL-DV, or even Instagram square images, you have nothing to fear – the concepts discussed here, and the examples, will all translate

Choosing Your Frame

into the shape of your particular frame. The beauty of film language is that no matter what camera or aspect ratio you choose, the shot grammar is still applicable, as many of these guidelines have remained relatively unchanged for the past 100 years.

A Brief History of Aspect Ratios

Theatrical motion pictures in North America have been widescreen (1.85:1) for a long time now. European widescreen theaters projected 1.66:1 images. Glass-tube standard-definition television sets of the 20th century (roughly 1.33:1 or 4:3) were more square-like in shape and less rectangular than Hollywood features and today's widescreen HDTV (roughly 1.78:1 or 16:9). There were several reasons for these differences, but the gist of it was that classical Hollywood 35mm motion picture film had, for many years, used an aspect ratio around 1.33:1. This is overly simplistic, but when television became very popular in the late 1940s and early 1950s, the broadcasters needed material to play, and Hollywood could offer several decades of motion pictures to be displayed – thus the 1.33:1 television aspect ratio.

Television became more popular, and in order to compete with that popularity the movie industry began to create very wide- or large-screen aspect ratio film formats such as VistaVision (1.5:1), Cinemascope (2.4:1), and, more recently, IMAX® (both 1.43:1 and

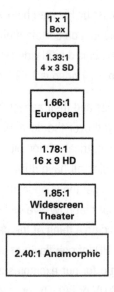

FIGURE 1.2 Comparison of various frame sizes from the history of film and video. Note the tendency to move toward a wider rectangular frame.

1.9:1). The less costly 1.85:1 was also popularized, and thus the standard North American widescreen aspect ratio was born. The problem was that the 1.33:1 frame size of television was too small to show the wider 1.85:1, 1.66:1, and certainly the 2.4:1 movies.

A process called **pan and scan** was developed so that a smaller screen size could be extracted from the larger, wider original film's aspect ratio to show the television audience. The big downside to this was that the original composition – basically all of the hard work of the filmmaker's visual plan – was destroyed. **Letterboxing** (maintaining the original aspect ratio of the picture by placing black bars at the top and bottom of the frame) improved this, but TV audiences were never truly won over by this approach. Happily, the native widescreen aspect ratio of HDTV more closely matches that of the feature films and there is not as much need for this "cutting-off" of the original frame (Figure 1.3).

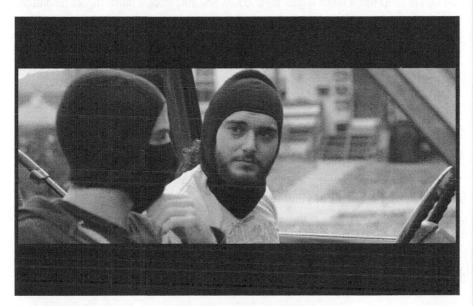

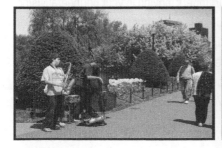 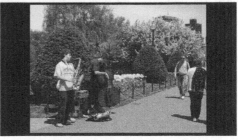

FIGURE 1.3 An example of a widescreen letterbox and an older standard-definition pillarbox inside a 16:9 HD frame. (Still frame from *Consumer Beware* courtesy Zach Benard, Avarie Cook, Anthony Martel, and John McNeil)

Choosing Your Frame

TABLE 1.1

	Format				
	SDTV (NTSC)	HDTV	FULL HD	UHD	4K CINEMA
ASPECT RATIO	4:3	16:9	16:9	16:9	1.9:1
PIXEL DIMENSIONS	720 x 486	1280 x 720	1920 x 1080	3840 x 2160	4096 x 2160

As digital video technologies advance, and references to aspect ratio decrease, the references to a particular format's pixel dimension increase. Pixel dimension, in this usage, is not related to the size or shape of an individual pixel (picture element) but to the overall resolution of the image. How many pixels comprise the given "frame" of the camera's light sensor and subsequent video media file? As an example, full HD has a pixel dimension of 1920 x 1080 while the more recent ultra-HD (UHD) has 3840 x 2160 – yet both formats have a widescreen 16:9 aspect ratio (Table 1.1). They have the same-shaped frame, but UHD has a much higher pixel count and therefore a much higher resolution with better image fidelity, clarity, and detail. Further discussion of this technical point goes beyond the scope of this text.

Further Exploration: Why Do We Like Widescreen So Much?

It can be argued that widescreen aspect ratios are a better choice for image capture because their display on the screen is more suited to audience appreciation. Longer and more horizontally rectangular in shape, the widescreen imagery appeals to our eyes (and brains) because the **field of view** (what we get to watch) is closer to what our eyes naturally see when we look at the world.

Try this: stand in a well-lit room and stare straight forward. Hold your arms up out at your sides, shoulder high but slightly behind you. With palms forward, point your fingers straight ahead and wiggle them quickly. Do you see your fingers moving? If not, slowly move your arms forward. Stop when you see your fingers moving in your peripheral vision (or what you see at the extreme left and right sides of your field of view). Now, drop your left arm down toward your waist and raise your right arm straight over your head. Looking directly in front of you, do the same finger wiggle and slowly move your arms out in front of you until you can see your fingers moving. You should find that you are able to see a field of view that is much wider than it is tall. We see in widescreen.

Of course, on an interesting technical, cultural, and visual media sidenote, apps such as Vine and Instagram have re-popularized the square frame for still photo and video recording. This goes to prove that what is old is new again and all of our technological and aesthetic developments have given us plenty of frame size choices. This will be a good time to discuss content placement and object size within the frame shape and size you have chosen for your video project.

An Introduction to Shot Types: The Basic Building Blocks of Motion Pictures

You now know the shape and size of your frame, but you still have to figure out how to fill it. Visual communication in cinematic language starts with the most basic pictorial building blocks: the **shot types**. In filmmaking, the terms "shot," "shoot," and "shooting" can be used in several ways, but they typically refer to the act of recording (or capturing) action with a camera. In our immediate context, a **shot** is the recording of subject matter from a particular point of view at one time. Its imagery shows a discrete unit of photographic coverage of a person, place, or event in a motion picture as seen from a unique distance and angle.

Typically, a shot (as we are using the term) is gauged by the power of magnification of its subject – meaning how small or how big the subject looks on screen. The audience relate to the subject according to its apparent proximity: an object, appearing small on screen, is far away and less important, while that same object, seen as big, is closer and more personal. The "size" of the shot (or magnitude of the apparent size of the recorded subject within the frame) also helps to show more or less information to the audience – or should we say different kinds of information. A successful filmmaker uses this connection between the viewer and the shot's perceived meaning and its visual information to create effective cinematic experiences.

Perhaps the terms **long shot**, **medium shot**, and **close-up** are already familiar to you. These are the three groups of basic shot types, so let us take a look at an example of each shot type now. Although you may photograph or illustrate any subject matter in the world from any vantage point for your movie or animation, for clarity of discussion here we will first explore the shots through the simple framing of a standing human subject (static, **locked-off** shots). We will then build in complexity of content, composition, and execution in the remainder of the book.

The Long Shot/Wide Shot

The long shot or **wide shot** (often abbreviated LS or WS) is a wide, encompassing shot that shows a large area (width, height, and depth) of the **film space**. Physical (or spatial) relationships between or among subjects, objects, and their actions are clearly visible

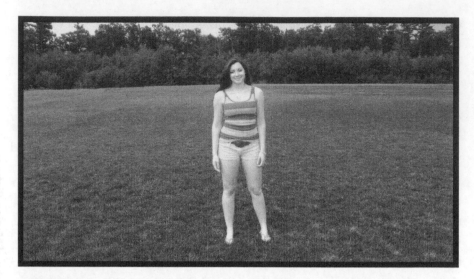

FIGURE 1.4   A long shot/wide shot of a standing human subject.

from this apparently distant vantage point. The environment or location is the "star" and any persons or objects appear smaller within it. The long shot can establish place, time, and mood for the audience (Figure 1.4).

The Medium Shot

The medium shot (MS) is the shot type that nearly approximates how we, as humans, see the environment most immediately around us. Typically, there would be several feet of space between you and another person, which would most likely result in your viewing each other in medium shots — roughly from the waist up. A moderate distance then (let us say 3–5 feet) may lead to a medium shot. Other factors, such as actual object size and the focal length of the lens on the camera, can also come into play, but we'll explore those options later in the book. What it really comes down to, though, is how much of a person, object, or environment is included in the frame. A viewer watching a medium shot should feel comfortable with the proximity because the subject is near but not in his or her "personal space" (Figure 1.5).

The Close-Up

The close-up (CU) is the intimate shot in filmmaking. It provides a greatly magnified view of some person, object, or action. As a result, it can impart rather specific, detailed information to the audience. It also brings the subject inside the viewer's personal space — in a good way if the viewer likes the subject, and in a bad way if he or she does not (Figure 1.6).

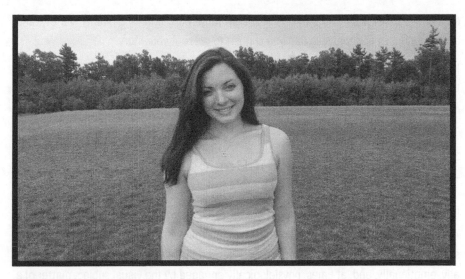

FIGURE 1.5   A medium shot of a standing human subject.

These three major types of shot – LS/WS, MS, and CU – will be the basic building blocks that you can use to start capturing your moving images. It will be up to you, the filmmaker, to decide which shot type you use to cover the various persons, objects, or actions in your visual story. To help you to choose, you may find it useful to ask yourself, "If I were watching this motion picture, what would I want to be seeing right now?" Remember that it is the audience who ultimately watch all of your shots edited together, and their

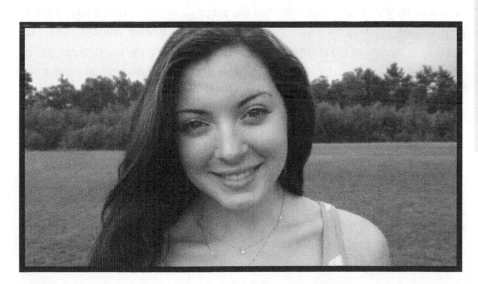

FIGURE 1.6   A close-up of a standing human subject.

An Introduction to Shot Types: The Basic Building Blocks of Motion Pictures experience of viewing your movie is based, in large part, upon the quality, variety, and appropriateness of shot types that you choose to present your story.

Next, we will list and describe several other derivations of these three basic shot families. So don't worry, you will have plenty of shot variety available to you for making your movies.

The Extended Family of Basic Shots: The Powers of Proximity

99.9% of produced motion imagery is meant to be viewed by some audience of some kind in some way. A filmmaker should always be thinking about how to best show the story to the viewer. It has been commonly accepted that the audience can be intellectually, emotionally, and, at times, physiologically engaged by the visual subject matter of a motion picture. The perceived nearness or proximity of objects on screen (based on their magnitude within the given frame) plays into this audience manipulation. A key responsibility you have is to present the viewer with images that are engaging, informative, and efficient. The extended family of basic shots provides you with a larger vocabulary of visual expression to help to meet your storytelling needs.

The illustrative examples presented here are an introduction to the variety of shots that you will be able to create in each category. In order to keep things simple, the illustrations will depict a lone human subject in a plain environment. The recording camera will be placed roughly at the same height as the subject's eyes. For comparative training purposes, we will keep the subject centered in our frame, looking straight to lens. This is a subjective view of the talent, and is sometimes referred to as "direct-to-camera" or "direct-to-lens" shooting. It breaks the implied **fourth wall** of the cinematic space and is often used in non-fiction television programming. As you continue to read this book, you will learn about other interesting and genre-specific ways to frame your subjects.

The following is a list of the basic shots (Figure 1.7):

- the extreme long shot/extreme wide shot
- the very long shot/very wide shot
- the long shot/wide shot/full shot
- the medium long shot/knee shot
- the medium shot/waist shot/mid-shot
- the medium close-up/bust shot

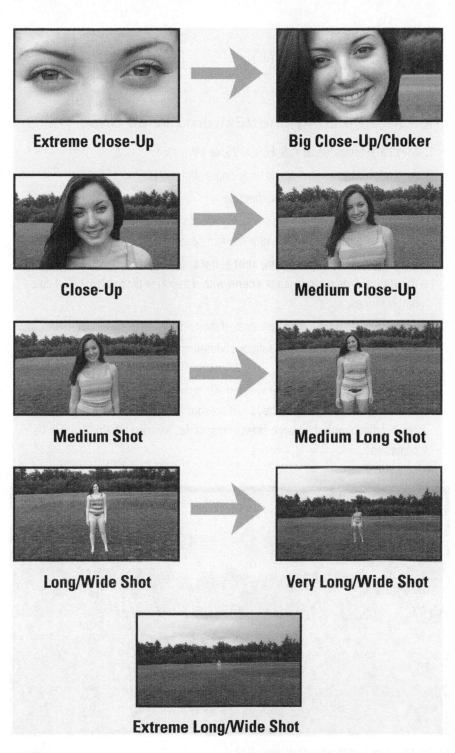

The Extended Family of Basic Shots: The Powers of Proximity

FIGURE 1.7 Examples of the nine shot types.

- the close-up
- the big close-up (UK)/choker (US)
- the extreme close-up.

The Extreme Long Shot/Extreme Wide Shot

1. May be abbreviated as XLS, ELS, XWS, or EWS.
2. Also referred to as an extreme wide-angle shot.
3. Traditionally used in **exterior** shooting.
4. Encompasses a wide and deep field of view, forming an image that shows a large amount of the environment within the film space.
5. Often used as an **establishing shot** at the beginning of a motion picture or at the start of a new sequence or **scene** within a motion picture (typical of epic battle scenes, etc.).
6. Shows where: urban, suburban, rural, mountains, desert, ocean, battlefield, etc.
7. May show when: day, night, summer, winter, spring, fall, distant past, present, future, etc.
8. May show who: lone stranger walking into town, massive invading army. Most often, the human figures in the XLS, if present at all, are so small that details are not distinguishable; large-scale, not specific, location information will be conveyed.

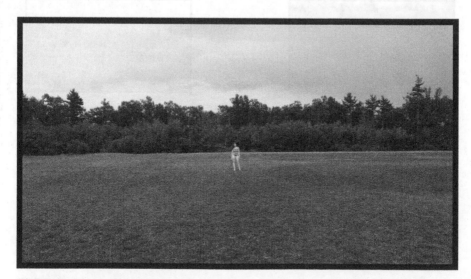

FIGURE 1.8   Example of an extreme long shot or XLS/ELS.

The Very Long Shot/Very Wide Shot

1. May be abbreviated as VLS or VWS.

2. Also in the wide shot family.

3. May be used in exterior or **interior** shooting when enough width and height exist within the studio set or location building, such as an open warehouse, airline hangar, or sports arena.

4. The environment within the film space is still very important as it fills much of the screen, but the human figure is more visible and limited clothing detail may be observed.

5. May be used as an establishing shot where movement of character brings the figure closer to the camera.

6. Shows where, when, and a bit more of who (Figure 1.9).

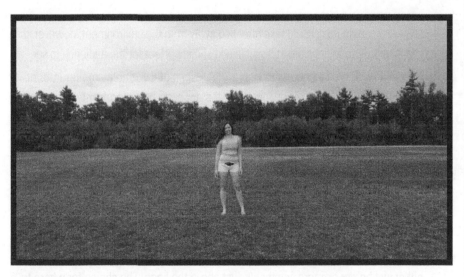

FIGURE 1.9 Example of a very long shot or VLS.

The Long Shot/Wide Shot/Full Shot

1. May be abbreviated as LS or WS.

2. This is usually considered a "full body" shot, wide but in close to a figure with head and feet just visible in the frame.

3. May be used in interior or exterior shooting.

The Extended Family of Basic Shots: The Powers of Proximity

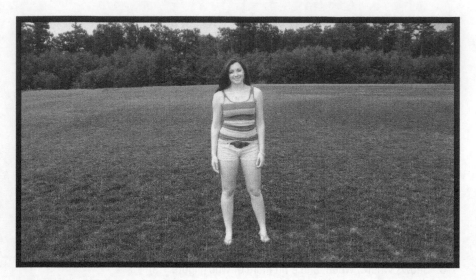

FIGURE 1.10   Example of a long shot or LS.

4. Larger human figures should take attention away from the environment; however, the character's surroundings are still visible and still important for the audience to see.

5. May still work well as an establishing shot, especially within a smaller interior space or a contained exterior space like the doorway to a storefront.

6. Shows where, when, and who: the gender, clothing, movements, and general facial expressions may be observed more easily (Figure 1.10).

The Medium Long Shot/Knee Shot

1. May be abbreviated as MLS.

2. This is the first shot in increasing magnitude that cuts off a body part of the human subject – traditionally framed such that the bottom of the frame cuts off the leg either just below or, more commonly, just above the knee. The choice for where to cut may depend on costuming or body movement of the individual in the shot. If you cut off above the knee, it is sometimes referred to as the "American shot" or "cowboy" because in American Western movies there was interest in being able to show the firearm in the holster strapped to the thigh of a cowboy character.

3. May be used in interior or exterior shooting.

4. The human figure is prominent; details in clothing, gender, and facial expressions are visible.

5. Shows more of who than where and can still show when (Figure 1.11).

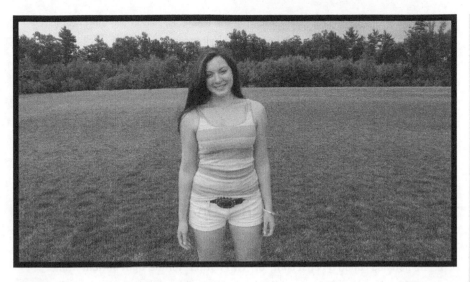

FIGURE 1.11 Example of a medium long shot or MLS.

The Medium Shot/Waist Shot/Mid-Shot

1. May be abbreviated as MS.
2. May also be called the "waist shot," as the frame cuts off the human figure at or just below the waist.
3. May be used in interior or exterior shooting.

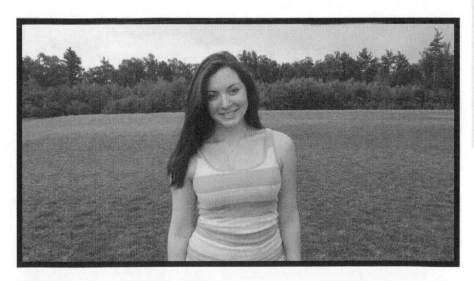

FIGURE 1.12 Example of a medium shot or MS.

The Extended Family of Basic Shots: The Powers of Proximity

4. The human figure is most prominent in the frame: eyes and the direction in which they look, clothing, hair color, and hairstyle are all plainly visible.

5. Subject movement may become a concern, as the tighter framing restricts the freedom of gesture; be careful not to **break frame** (have an actor's body part touch or move beyond the established edge of the picture frame).

6. Certainly shows who and may still provide generic detail about where (inside or outside, apartment, store, forest, etc.) and when (day or night, season) (Figure 1.12).

The Medium Close-Up/Bust Shot

1. May be abbreviated as MCU.

2. Sometimes called a "bust shot" or "two-button" for the tight bottom frame cutting off at the chest, roughly where you would see the top two buttons on a shirt. Definitely cuts off above the elbow joint. Adjust the bottom frame slightly for men or women, depending on costuming and physique.

3. May be used in interior or exterior shooting.

4. The subject's facial features are rather prominent: where the eyes look is obvious, as is emotion, hairstyle and color, make-up, etc. This is one of the most commonly used shots in filmmaking because it provides so much information about the character while speaking, listening, or performing an action that

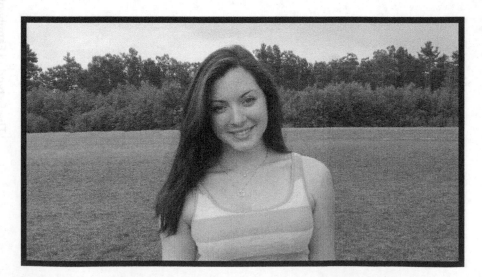

FIGURE 1.13 Example of a medium close-up or MCU.

does not involve much body or head movement. Ideal for news broadcasts and **"talking-head"** interviews in documentaries.

5. Audiences are supposed to be watching the human face with this framing, so actions or objects in the surrounding environment should hold little to no importance. Reducing your **depth of field** (**DOF**) and blurring out these background elements will help to keep them from being distracting. (For more on this practice, see Chapter Three.)

6. Depending on general lighting and costuming, you may discern general information about where and when (Figure 1.13).

The Close-Up

1. May be abbreviated as CU.

2. Sometimes called a "head shot," as the framing may cut off the top of the subject's hair and the bottom of the frame can begin anywhere just below the chin or, more traditionally, with a little upper shoulder visible (costuming and hairstyle dependent).

3. May be used in interior or exterior shooting.

4. A very intimate full face shot of a human subject showing all detail in the eyes and conveying the subtle emotions that play across the eyes, mouth, and facial muscles of an actor; health conditions and facial hair in men and make-up use in women are clearly visible.

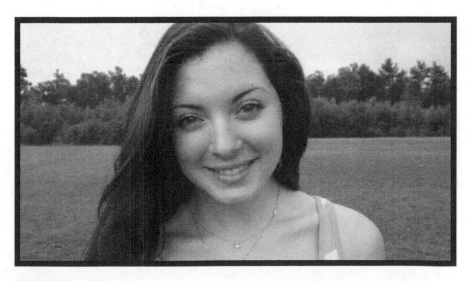

FIGURE 1.14   Example of a close-up or CU.

The Extended Family of Basic Shots: The Powers of Proximity

5. Audiences should be totally focused on the human face with this framing, especially the eyes and/or mouth while speaking.

6. Shows who, but not so much where or when (except as indicated by lighting or possible visible aspects of the background elements) (Figure 1.14).

The Big Close-Up (UK)/Choker (US)

1. May be abbreviated as BCU – although many filmmakers simply refer to it as a "tight close-up" or a "choker."

2. The human face occupies as much of the frame as possible and still shows the key features of eyes, nose, and mouth at once: however, the top of forehead and bottom of chin are cut off.

3. May be used in interior or exterior shooting.

4. Such an intimate shot puts the audience directly in the face of the subject. Because every detail of the face is highly visible, facial movements or expressions need to be subtle; very little head movement can be tolerated before the subject moves out of frame. An emotional connection is easy to make with this "in-your-face" framing.

5. This shot is about who and how that "who" feels: angry, scared, loving, etc. (Figure 1.15).

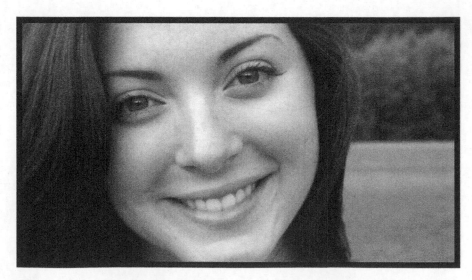

FIGURE 1.15 Example of a big close-up/choker or BCU.

The Extreme Close-Up

1. May be abbreviated as ECU or XCU. It may sometimes be called an "Italian shot" due to its use in some of Sergio Leone's Italian Western movies.

2. Purely a detail shot: framing favors one aspect of a subject such as his or her eyes, mouth, ear, or hand only *or* a solitary object or magnified portion of a larger object.

3. May be used in interior or exterior shooting. Lacking any points of reference to the surrounding environment, the audience have no context in which to place this body part or object detail, so understanding will stem from how or when this shot is edited into the motion picture. It may be helpful if the greatly magnified content of the XCU is first shown in its normal form in a wider shot so that context may be established for the viewer.

4. This type of extremely magnified imagery can be used in documentary work, such as medical films or scientific studies, music videos, commercials, and experimental art films, and may be used sparingly in fictional narrative, depending on the established visual style of the project (Figure 1.16).

Now you understand the names (like medium shot), the abbreviations (like MS), and the order of magnitude of film space, objects, and subjects that these shot types present. As you will see, the different shots exist to engage and inform the viewer, yet how you use them can vary. For instance, a very long shot can act as an establishing shot providing the audience with information about a story's location in physical space and in time, and it

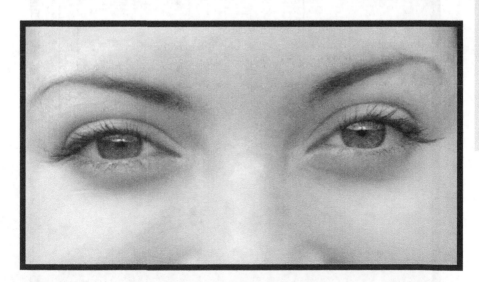

FIGURE 1.16 Example of an extreme close-up or XCU/ECU.

The Extended Family of Basic Shots: The Powers of Proximity

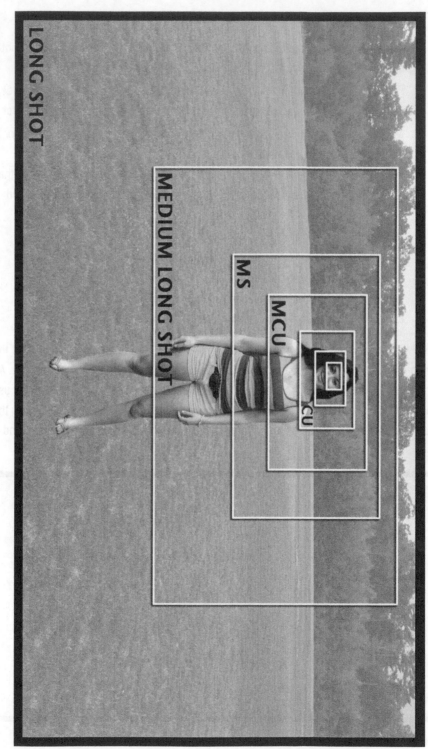

LONG SHOT

MEDIUM LONG SHOT

MS

MCU

CU

FIGURE 1.17 The closer shots – from LS in to ECU.

can possibly show your subjects within that wider space. However, the VLS also typically keeps the subject at a far distance from the camera. This distance can withhold information from your audience (e.g., who are those little people way in the background?) and can serve a thematic purpose in the story (like creating the sense of isolation and loneliness when you see that character so small, far away, and alone on screen).

The same thing can be said for an XCU. The extreme close-up details an object (provides information), but if the audience don't know who or what that XCU is part of, then they are actually missing information. Additionally, one school of thought holds that the

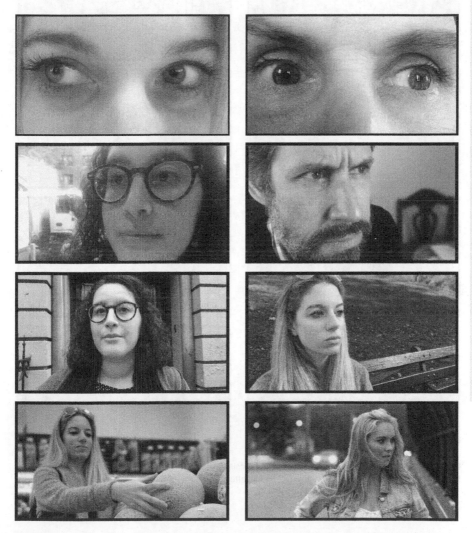

The Extended Family of Basic Shots: The Powers of Proximity

FIGURE 1.18 A series of examples from each shot type family.

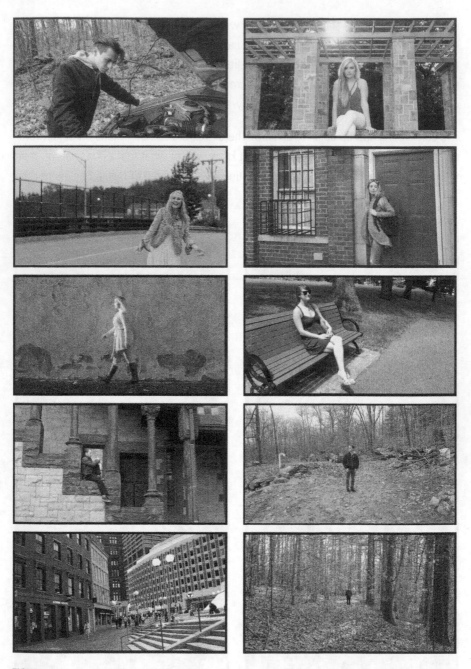

FIGURE 1.18 Continued. (Photo credits: A–G & L – Nicole Casamento; H, J, & K – Mike Neilan; I & P – Anthony Martel; M & O – Darby Andersson; R – Rachael Bissonnette)

size of an object on the screen is directly related to its importance to the story at that point in the narrative. Again, this is a situation where one shot may be showing information but also have another intended (thematic) meaning. These are the sorts of things that a clever filmmaker can do with visual language in motion media productions.

Why Do We Even Have Different Shot Types?

These shot types were not all originally part of the visual language of film production when it began in the late 1800s. The first motion pictures often just documented actual events from real life, like workers leaving a factory or a train pulling into a station – almost exclusively filmed in a wide shot. Filmmakers then began to tell short stories from scripted material, but these too were mostly photographed from a distance with a wide-angle view of the action. Much like a staged play in a theater, the audience only got to experience the action from one vantage point. The technical sophistication of the camera (and lenses) and the storytelling practices evolved quickly and it wasn't long before an expanded visual vocabulary was being formed. New shot types, like the close-up, and new editing techniques soon allowed for greater flexibility in showing the audience a more visually complex and emotionally engaging story.

What eventually developed was an approach to filmmaking that is still used by many today: the **master scene technique**. A story is broken down into scenes, or events that take place at a certain time and in a certain place. The filmmaker initially records the entire scene from one, often wide, camera angle called the **master shot**. The actors say all of their lines and do all of their actions chronologically from the beginning of the scripted scene until the end. The filmmaker then repeats the actions and records shots that show the event's details – traditionally from the outside in or from wider shots to closer shots. The result is a selection of shots that depict all of the events in the scene from different angles and with different subject sizes within the frame. This is called shooting **coverage**. The actions within the scene have been "covered" by these recorded shots that have varied camera positions, framings, and shot compositions.

On larger productions, a script supervisor takes notes on all coverage shots on each character for each scene. These notes, the script, and the video and audio media files of this production footage are later handed over to the editor. The editor takes all of these different views of the repeated action of the scene (the coverage) and stitches them together according to the script and notes – traditionally from wider to tighter shots. In its most simplistic assembly, it might go something like this:

- a master (wide) shot that opens the scene to establish the location and the subjects' placement within that environment – they begin their dialogue here
  - CUT TO
- a medium shot that provides more detail of the subjects gesturing and speaking
  - CUT TO
- a close-up that reveals the intimate detail of the emotional state of one subject at the most dramatic moment of the scene (typically near the end).

This process gets more interesting and elaborate when you add more shot types and subject/camera movement, etc. (See Chapters Two, Three, and Six for more information.)

The master scene technique, complete with shooting coverage using a variety of shot types, is a very thorough approach to filmmaking and has been used for around a century. It provides a "safety net" of sorts, virtually ensuring that all events in a scene can be fully assembled from the recorded shots – especially in "continuity-style" film production. You will be learning more about preparing your visual material for the editing process in Chapter Five.

Pulling Images from the Written Page

When you read a novel, you get to create the look of the characters and the locations in your imagination. The descriptions on the written page help you to conjure the imagery in your head. Making motion pictures involves a similar process. Whether you are creating a short film, an animation, a music video, or a how-to video, you are most likely going to start with a written script that either contains the exact content or outlines the major material that needs to be covered for the project.

A script, or a screenplay, is the written story, laid out on the page in very precise formatting for the type of motion media project being planned. This formatting varies for fiction filmmaking, television show production, documentaries, commercials, etc. and there are numerous resources to help to teach you this process and several apps (both free and expensive) that format for your show's needs. The majority of these script formats stick to the bare bones of brief location descriptions, character/narrative action descriptions, and character dialogue. Many of these formats do not encourage the inclusion of camera angles, shot types, or general cinematic language. These visual elements ideally come from the creative interpretations and cinematic visions of the project's director and director of photography.

Script Breakdown for Cinematographers

The script for a project, even if just rough ideas for scenes or segments, provides the basic framework of your story around which you build your visual plan. Understanding the story you are trying to tell helps you to figure out what shots you can use to show that story to your audience. This is often referred to as the **script analysis** or **script breakdown** for the picture. There are others associated with the production who need to conduct a different flavor of script breakdown (especially the assistant director, who needs to account for *everything*), but the cinematographer should be thoroughly familiar with the story, the intent of the piece, the emotional tones throughout, and every technical consideration relating to the image creation process.

You read over the entire script at least once and get a feel for the whole piece. Then it would be wise to read each scene or show segment again and determine from where it would be best to show the action. You analyze the content of the scene (dramatic dialogue, factual information, band performing a verse from their song, etc.) and you break down the imagery into the necessary coverage for shooting that specific moment in your video.

Larger projects may require significant pre-planning, which may include special equipment, location and set needs, lighting schemes, thematic color usage, lenses of a specific focal length, etc. Small projects can certainly benefit from this pre-planning as well, but the limited time and/or budget may force you to go less indepth with each area. The important point to take away is that having a written plan (of some significant substance) will greatly facilitate the ease with which the production phase of the project can flow. If questions arise, you have your master "idea" notebook (physical or digital) as a reference.

Shot Lists

It helps to document the shot choices you decide upon during the script breakdown, so you should create what is called a **shot list**. The shot list does what its name says: it lists the shots you need to record – for each scene, each film set, each location, etc. Creating a **lined script** may help with the formulation of the shot list. Lining a script is most often done by the show's director and necessitates physically drawing lines down the page of the script. These vertical lines encompass all of the actions and dialogue of a scene that will be covered by a particular camera angle/shot type. Some lines will be shorter and some longer, depending on the pre-envisioned, edited scene that the director is seeing in her or his mind while reading the script. The longest line down the page is typically the

Pulling Images from the Written Page

wide shot (sometimes called the **safety**) that covers the entire set, all of the characters, their actions, and their dialogue from the beginning to the end of the scene. Shorter lines may just be a single action or a single line of dialogue. The top of each vertical line is notated with the scene number, camera "set-up" letter, and the type of shot (CU, MS, WS, etc.).

With the scene-by-scene breakdown and lining of the script completed, it makes sense to list your shots according to their chronology in the story. The first thing we see in the movie is Scene 1, the next major action at a new location is Scene 2, etc. To be clear, the actual shooting of the film rarely follows the chronology of scenes in the script. It may be wise to prepare shot lists for scenes that occur at each set or location. The shooting schedule is made around actor and location availability, etc., so Scene 24 may be recorded on the first day of production and Scene 3 may be recorded last. The goal is to record all of the scenes' coverage on your shot list. Keep in mind that other **genres** beyond fiction filmmaking can benefit greatly from shot lists. The elements of non-fiction motion media, such as interviews, cutaways, inserts, B-roll, establishing shots, etc. also need to be pre-planned and accounted for during production.

Each individual shot type on your list that you need to record will most likely require a different physical camera placement. This unique camera position/framing is called a **camera set-up**. As each scene has a number, the first camera set-up for that scene, usually your master wide shot, would be noted as "Scene 1" or simply "1." The second set-up of that scene would then receive a letter starting with "A" as in "Scene 1, A" or, more typically, just "1A." The third camera set-up would be "1B," etc. The English alphabet has 26 letters, so you should be safe using this method, but on larger productions, repeats like "AA" or "BB" may be required.

If you have to record the action of a single set-up many times to get it just right, then these multiple recordings are called **takes**. The first attempt at shooting the first set-up of the first scene in your movie would be "Scene 1, Take 1" or "S1T1" or simply "1-1." If there was a flub, then you would reset and shoot "Scene 1, Take 2" or "S1T2" or simply "1-2," and on it would go until it was recorded satisfactorily. Moving the camera to achieve a new shot set-up will lead to "Scene 1A, Take 1." Some folks like to use a word instead of the letter, such as "Scene 1 APPLE, Take 1" or "Scene 8 CHARLIE, Take 3." Your goal should be to get the material recorded correctly in as few takes as possible to save time, energy, and money. Nobody wants to see "Scene 52ZZ, Take 117."

Storyboards and Animatics

Beyond the script and shot list, another resource that will help you to be efficient is a **storyboard**. If the written screenplay is the descriptive text version of your story, then the storyboards are the blueprints for your visual plan. You actually illustrate (draw) what each framing (shot type choice) will look like when you physically compose the visual elements for the set-up. Everyone on the film production crew will have a picture of what the visual goal will be when the time comes to record it (Figure 1.19). On today's sets, with laptops or tablets handy, the use of animatics has become more popular. Animatics are animated storyboards that can show framing but also animate the movements of subjects and cameras during each shot and may include scratch track voice-over and roughed-in music. Regardless of how crude or advanced your pre-production "boards" are, their purpose is the same: to pre-visualize the final product and help everyone to get the shots set up correctly.

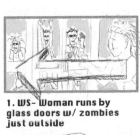

1. WS– Woman runs by glass doors w/ zombies just outside

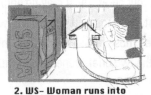

2. WS– Woman runs into short hallway

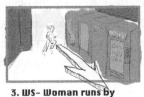

3. WS– Woman runs by soda and candy machines

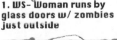

4. MLS– Low Angle Dutch Woman rattles locked doors and turns around in a panic

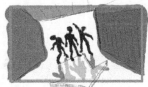

5. WS– DUTCH TILT, zombies in silhouette stumble up darkened hallway

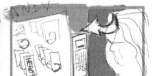

6. MCU/OTS – Woman turns head toward candy machine and sees the candy bar hero

FIGURE 1.19   An example of a storyboard.

Phases of Film Production

All of this important preparatory work should be accomplished before you begin the recording process. This initial planning phase of filmmaking is called **pre-production**. The script is written or acquired, your visual style is determined, you select your camera and other equipment, form the shot list, draw the storyboards, and do hundreds of other things like scheduling, budgeting, etc. This means that once you begin **principal**

photography (the actual recording of the main shots of your story), you are in the phase called **production**. Production continues until you have recorded all of your elements for the final version of your motion picture. All elements (picture and sound) are passed off to the editorial team and the **post-production** phase of filmmaking takes place. The shots are edited together to show the best story possible given the production materials submitted. The last steps in this chain are the distribution and exhibition stages: getting your finished product out to the world for people to see and enjoy.

Let's Practice

The following is a very simple short fiction sample script that you may use to practice shot selection, storyboard creation, and coverage shooting using the shot type families (in Chapters One and Two). It is referred to as a "contentless scene," meaning that it is purposefully vague and does not follow strict screenplay formatting so that you may interpret freely and maximize your creativity. It may be helpful if you first read the script, the make some decision about who these characters are, what their story is, and where and when it should take place. Those decision will then inform your shot selection and how you approach recording the two brief scenes. Have fun.

CHARACTER A

Hey.

CHARACTER B

Hey.

CHARACTER A

How's it going?

CHARACTER B

Good.

CHARACTER A

Cool. Cool. Um, listen – I'm really sorry about the –

CHARACTER B

Yeah. It's no big deal.
What are you going to do about it, right?

CHARACTER A

Right.

CHARACTER B

Well, I've got to get going.

CHARACTER A

Yeah. Yeah. Me too.

Character B exits – cut to new location. Character B enters followed by Character A.

CHARACTER A

Hey. Wait up. You forgot this.

CHARACTER B

That's not mine.

(A few hints about this particular script: it should happen in at least two different locations; Character A must be sorry about something that can be represented visually, in some way, in the scene; Character A must try to present Character B with some "forgotten" item, in either a literal sense or in a figurative or symbolic fashion.)

Remember that although the script does not call out locations or specific items, your shot list should allow for such things as establishing shots, detail shots, inserts/cutaways, and a variety of shot compositions, as outlined in Chapter Two.

Chapter One – Final Thoughts: The Pictures Speak

Humans like stories – to tell them and to be told them. At the foundation of film's power for visual communication are the basic shot types. These moving pictures tell some sort of story to the audience. We have all been educated over the years to understand what these different images are telling us. It is the job of the filmmaker to use this filmed language to translate the stories written down on the page into images up on a screen.

Related Material Found in Chapter Seven – Working Practices

At the end of each chapter in this book, you will find a concluding section like this that lists the numbers for corresponding working practices that are relevant to the chapter that you are just completing. The working practices are discussed and illustrated in Chapter Seven with a practical application in mind for the working filmmaker. You *do not* have to skip forward to read these elaborations now. You may cover them as you get to Chapter Seven or at any point you wish. We simply list these working practices now for your convenience.

#1, 12, 38, 39

Chapter One – Review

1. Visual "grammar" or film language is used, with consistency, around the world to record imagery for motion media products.
2. Filmmakers should plan, record, and edit the shots that will best convey their intended story to the viewing audience.
3. Cinematography refers to the art, craft, and practices of developing a visual plan, style, and overall look for a motion picture project.
4. The format of your camera initially determines the size and shape of your frame.
5. The aspect ratio describes the dimensions of width to height in your active recording area (e.g., 4 x 3, 16 x 9, or 1.78:1).
6. The pixel dimension of an image is its width in pixels to its height in pixels (e.g., 1920 x 1080, meaning 1920 pixels across the screen and 1080 pixels from top to bottom of the screen).
7. The three basic shot types are the long/wide shot, the medium shot, and the close-up.
8. The extended family of nine basic shot types is comprised of the extreme long shot, the very long shot, the long shot, the medium long shot, the medium shot, the medium close-up, the close-up, the big close-up, and the extreme close-up.
9. Sometimes, the larger an object is in the frame, the more significant it is to the story at that time.
10. The audience typically gauge their involvement with the film world via the sense of proximity that they get from the subject's size on the screen (meaning the perceived nearness to the viewer).

11. Traditional approaches to the master scene technique encourage recording coverage shots of the dialogue exchange between characters from different angles and with different "magnifications" (or shot types) of the subjects. This variety in footage will aid in editing the scene in the most engaging, efficient, and emotionally manipulative ways possible.

12. The written script or screenplay presents the bare bones of the story with brief descriptions of location and action and thorough inclusion of dialogue content. Filmmakers break down the scenes on the lined script into the shots that will best cover the action, and from all the pre-planning they create a shot list.

13. Having a storyboard, or drawings that represent the shot types needed, is very helpful when you go to shoot the actual scene.

14. Pre-production, production, and post-production are the three main phases in the filmmaking process.

Chapter One – Exercises

1. Using your smartphone, tablet, or video or stills digital camera, practice capturing images of a person in all nine basic shot types. You may end up using these images or video clips in Exercise 3 below (refer to Figure 1.7).

2. In a similar fashion, practice location/object photography without any human subjects. Choose your own objects and your own locations, but shoot an example of each shot type.

3. Shoot and edit a shot type "training" video. Pretend you've been hired to teach people who know nothing about the nine basic shot types: what they are called, what they look like, and how they may be used in a short fictional narrative story. You should include illustrative video examples of the shot types (refer to Figures 1.8–1.16 for what to shoot, or use the images/video you shot for Exercise 1 above). Also, have clear examples of them "in use" in the short movie you produce for this exercise. Titles/keyed graphics and voice-over will help to clarify the educational points that you need to make. Appropriate music can help to move the video along too.

4. Create a shot list and storyboard for the script found at the end of this chapter.

5. Record the shots for the script based on your pre-production work from Exercise 4 above.

Chapter One – Quiz Yourself

1. If you need to clearly show the emotion in the eyes of your subject, which shot type might be best and why?

2. You are creating an animated cartoon that takes place in a dark, decaying, futuristic city. You want to generate a wide view of this moody environment to show on screen at the beginning of this story – which kind of shot would be good to use?

3. "XCU" is the abbreviation for which shot type?

4. Going from the widest shot to the most close up, which shot type is the first shot to cut off (frame out) the feet of a human subject?

5. What is the aspect ratio of HDTV?

6. Why might human beings respond well to widescreen motion picture imagery?

7. Why should you bother creating a shot list?

8. What is a camera set-up and how many would you need if you had to record an LS, an MS, and a CU of only one subject?

9. What is principal photography and during which phase of filmmaking does it occur?

10. Which camera set-up for Scene 9 is happening if you hear "Scene 9 Bravo, Take 2?"

Chapter Two
The Basics of Composition

- Headroom
- Shooting Style: Subjective versus Objective
- Look Room/Nose Room
- The Rule of Thirds
- Camera Angles
- The Two-Shot
- The Over-the-Shoulder Shot
- The Power Dynamic Two-Shot
- The Three-Shot/Group Shots

Composition, as we are applying the term, is the purposeful arrangement of artistic parts selected for the "art form" being practiced. You can compose notes in music, steps in a dance routine, figures in a painting, elements on a web page, subjects within a film frame, etc.

Now that we understand how basic shots pictorially cover persons, actions, or events of varying magnitude/proximity, we have to look at how you can fill that frame with objects and information – meaning where, specifically, do you place the person's head in a close-up shot or where, specifically, do you place that tree in a wide shot? And it is not only where you place these compositional elements but also why you place them where you do. The arrangement of these visual elements and their placement within the overall frame is a big part of visual communication and should be a part of your visual plan for expressing your story. Object positioning helps to establish traditional film aesthetics and can convey particular meanings to the audience. This is the power of picture composition. In this chapter, we will explore ways to compose basic shots and see what those compositions can do to enhance a viewer's understanding of your visual story.

As the filmmaker, you decide what to capture in your motion picture frame, so let's go ahead and place a camera in your hands. Okay. Now what? Well, first determine the shape of the frame for that camera's format. Knowing the active recording area and aspect ratio, you now understand the boundaries of width and height that are going to help you to plan for the various compositional choices ahead of you. Next, figure out what you would like to record, point the camera at that thing, and capture the images.

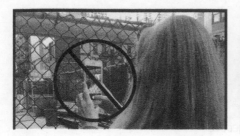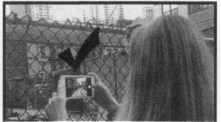

FIGURE 2.1 Just because you may hold your phone vertically for most functions does not mean that you hold it that same way to record video. Keep your video camera aligned to the horizontal (or landscape) framing. (Photo credits: Nicole Casamento)

Did you think about how you arranged that thing in relationship to other things in its environment or in relationship to the edges of your frame? Did you think about where you placed the camera or how you held it? Most people do not, especially if they are using the camera function of their smartphones. If widescreen is how we like to see, then why do so many people record smartphone video with a vertical frame rather than a horizontal frame? It boggles the mind. For motion media productions, it would be wise to hold your camera (phone or otherwise) in the "landscape" or horizontally widescreen orientation.

A new creative dilemma has presented itself. You know the subject to be recorded, but you have to be equally aware of how to appropriately place that subject within a purposefully oriented frame. It is this conscious placement of objects within the width, height, and depth of the frame that helps to underscore meaning, provides **subtext**, and, in general, empowers your imagery with an internal sense of beauty, balance, and order. This is the art of composition.

Simple Guidelines for Framing Human Subjects

Let us start with something simple that you will have to record many, many times: a medium close-up of a human subject. Perhaps you've already done this a thousand times, taking still pictures of your friends and family. We shall see that what at first seems rather simple will, in fact, require you to make many creative choices – choices that will help to make your images stronger, better equipped to help to show your story, and more understandable to your motion media audience.

Here is a medium close-up (Figure 2.2).

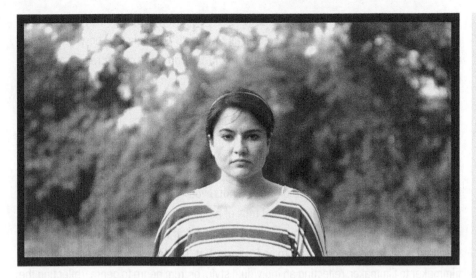

FIGURE 2.2 Generic medium close-up of a standing human figure.

What do you notice about the image in Figure 2.2? Does it look like one of those candid photos you took of your friends? The compositional elements are pretty simple, but where is the person's body located within the frame? Where is the head? Where do the person's eyes look? How much other visual information do we get from the rest of this image? A quick observation will tell you that the body is aligned down the middle, the head is very close to center frame, and the eyes are looking directly at the lens, which represents you, the audience member. This got the job done, an image was captured, but, depending on the type of motion media project that you are producing, there are other choices you could make regarding this composition. We will first discuss the placement of the head.

Headroom

Within a given shot type (LS, MS, CU), there is a generally accepted guideline as to where the head of a person should be placed within the frame. This guideline applies much more to MS and CU shots because in these tighter shots you mostly see the person's torso and head and much less of the environment. When communicating, human beings naturally tend to look each other in the face and, specifically, in the eyes. This "face focus" allows us to gain insight into the physical and mental health of an individual and to get a handle on his or her emotional state. Therefore, when the audience watch a human subject on screen, they will most often look at the person's face, particularly at the eyes and the mouth. Filmmakers know this to be true and they count on it when composing shots of people.

The placement of the head within the frame is very important, which is why we have the guideline of **headroom**. Headroom specifically refers to how much or how little space exists between the top of the subject's head and the top edge of the recorded frame. Because screen space is at a premium, it would be a shame to waste it, so we often set the top of the frame to cut off just above the talent's head in a tighter shot (Figure 2.3). In wider shots, you should also consider how much screen space above the talent you allow (Figure 2.4). Unless the story or event calls for some extra room above the head, you should let it go in favor of more information at mid-frame.

Later, when we review examples of closer shots, you will see how it is appropriate to also cut off (or "frame out") the hair and tops of people's heads as long as you keep their eyes and mouths well within the screen space. There is no exact measure or industry standard on what headroom needs to be for each shot. The amount allowed can vary from filmmaker to filmmaker, reflecting an individual style, or from genre to genre, reflecting the needs of the particular motion media project, but most will be very similar. In general, try not to give too much headroom as it wastes screen space and can throw off the overall balance of the composition.

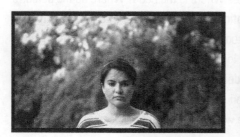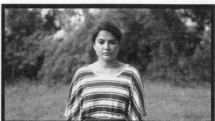
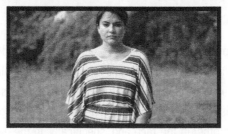

FIGURE 2.3   Medium shots with too much, about right, and too little headroom.

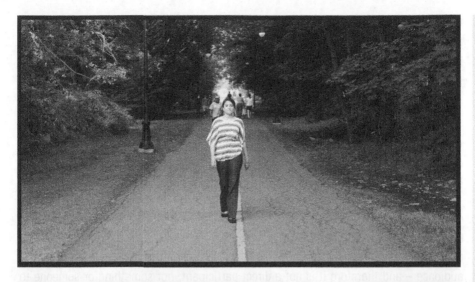

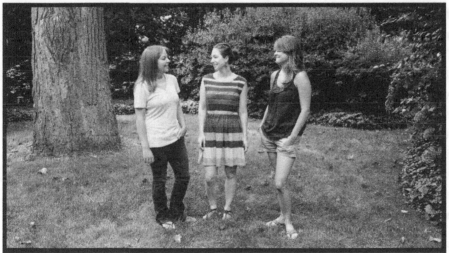

FIGURE 2.4 Wider shots (VLS and LS) demonstrating proper headroom.

Subjective versus Objective Shooting Styles

Now let us address how the subject's eyes are looking straight at you (Figure 2.3). What might it mean if the person being recorded by the camera looks directly into the lens? How does it make you, the viewer, feel when you are addressed directly by onscreen talent? Of course, it may depend on the kind of project you are watching or shooting, but it may make you feel "connected" to the person on screen or it may make him or her seem to be some sort of authority figure. If you were photographing a news reporter on location, then it would make sense for him or her to look straight into the camera's lens and deliver the factual report. The reporter makes a direct connection with you, the home audience, by looking you square in the "eye" and speaking directly to you. You see this all of the time with game show, talk show, and talent show hosts and sports analysts, and it is often used in music videos. These television programming genres have an accepted visual style that a subject may look directly into the lens and address the viewer. It can make that viewer feel as if she or he is a passive member of the live studio audience or has a direct, personal connection to the onscreen talent in some way. This style of camera work is often referred to as **subjective shooting** or **direct address**.

A subjective recording style is not typically present in scripted fictional narrative film projects (although exceptions do occur). With a fictional story, you have actors playing roles in a pretend world. The camera is almost always an observer – a proxy for the audience – and therefore it is not a direct participant, not something or someone to be addressed. The talent is not supposed to look directly into the lens – and often not even near it. If an actor looks into the lens, or addresses the camera, it is called "breaking the fourth wall." This expression gets its origins from the theater stage, where the audience always see the actors from the same direction, through this fourth "invisible" wall. If the camera were in a room recording the actions of a performer, the camera may see the back wall and the two side walls. The wall behind the camera – that is, the wall that should be physically in place where the camera is positioned – is the "fourth wall." It is the place from where the actions are being recorded and, ultimately, the place where the viewing audience are privileged to sit and observe the story. All onscreen talent behave as though the camera is not even there. This style of camera work is often called **objective shooting**.

For ease of demonstration, let us continue our medium close-up examples as though we are composing our shots for a fictional narrative film project where an objective shooting style is the goal. So let's take our subject's eyes off the **lens axis**: the imaginary line that refers to the path that light travels along to the optical center of the lens (Figure 2.5). This is a good start. The talent is no longer directly addressing the lens/audience, but the face and body are still straight to the lens. Depending on the lighting and the focal length of the lens that you are using, this can cause a flattening of the facial features and is not always that interesting for the viewer. (Lighting is covered in Chapter Four, and for more on lens talk see the end of Chapter Three.)

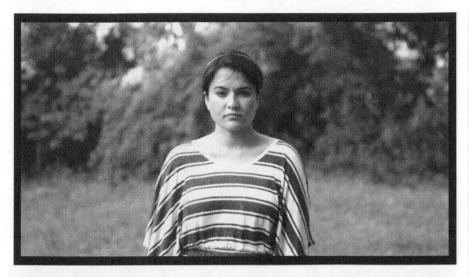

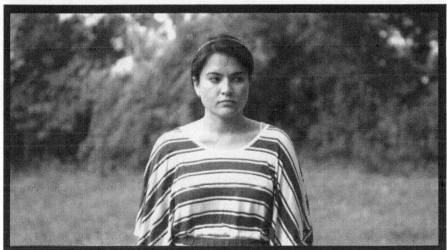

FIGURE 2.5   The talent looking into the lens (subjective) and away from the lens (objective).

Let us put a small shift on how the subject is standing in relation to the camera (Figure 2.6). Now it appears that this person is looking at someone or something just out of frame right. It is safely assumed at this point in the 21st century that the audience understand that there is film space existing outside the visible frame of the motion picture on the screen. (**Open frame** is the name of this film concept and you will read more about it later in this book.) She is engaged by an unknown element within the film world.

Simple Guidelines for Framing Human Subjects

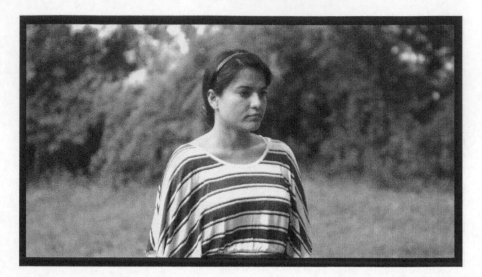

FIGURE 2.6   The subject turns her body and eyes off the lens axis, resulting in an objective shooting style.

Someone watching this moving image will be curious about what she is seeing and will want to see that thing as well. This is one of the key strengths of an objective filmmaking style. Rather than being told information directly by the talent, the audience are invited to get involved, to observe, to wonder, and to anticipate. Unlike subjective shooting, where the audience feel like passive recipients, the objective shooting style encourages their active participation in the unfolding events by having them become involved in the story via the visual construction of the shots and how they are edited together. Remember that for many fiction film experiencers, the camera acts as their eyes and ears. Through imagination and suspending disbelief, the audience use the camera as their proxy or avatar inside the pretend film world. (For more information on the topic of motion picture editing, please check out the companion text, *Grammar of the Edit.*)

Look Room/Nose Room

Our composition of this individual (Figure 2.6) is getting better, but the center framing may not work so well for our story. Notice how the face in the center of the screen is looking off to the side – at someone or something yet to be shown in another shot. A centralized framing like this is very solid and is often used in news reporting and hosted programming (with subjective or direct address), but perhaps it is too uniform or compositionally neutral for narrative fiction. Let us shift the image's balance and create more **look room** for our subject (Figure 2.7).

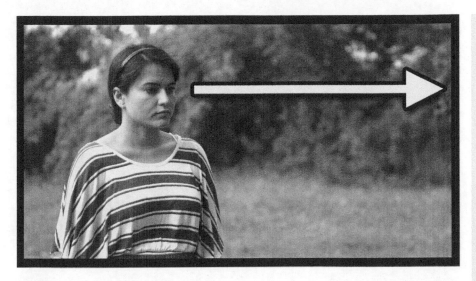

FIGURE 2.7 Placing the head and body on frame left allows the subject to look across the empty space. The frame's left and right halves (mass and void) are now balanced.

Look room (also called **looking room** or **nose room**) is the empty space that we have provided within the frame, between the talent's eyes and the edge of the frame opposite the face. It is this empty area or **negative space** that helps to balance out this new frame where the weight of the object (the talent's head and body) occupies frame left and the weight of the empty space occupies frame right. In this case, the word "weight" really implies a visual mass, whether it is an actual object, such as a person's body, or an empty space, such as the void filling frame right. This frame is now composed of two balanced masses.

The actor's **gaze** across this negative space causes the audience to also want to see what the actor is looking at. The look room has a direction (in this case, frame left to frame right) and an accompanying energy or implied movement. This direction is often called a talent's **eye-line**. The eye-line and look room are tied together. Think of the look room as the space provided within the frame that accommodates the direction and implied movement of a subject's eye-line, gaze, or attention. As you will see throughout this book, the audience get invested in the subject on the screen and want to follow the eye-line of that subject across the frame (and across the edit point into the next shot).

Now that you understand look room and eye-line, what would happen to the grammar of the shot if we moved a subject's head to the opposite side of the screen but kept the face and eyes looking in the same direction as our previous example (Figure 2.8)?

Simple Guidelines for Framing Human Subjects

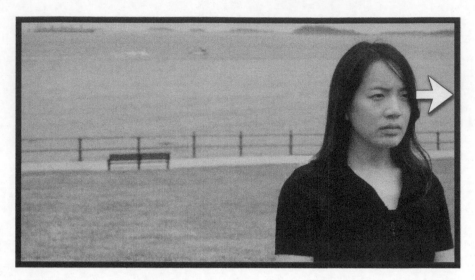

FIGURE 2.8 No look room creates a void behind this subject crying out to be filled.

The look room in this composition (Figure. 2.8) is severely cut off on frame right and we have a large, empty space on frame left. Our weighted objects – the body and the void – still exist, but their placement just does not feel correct. We have not achieved a visual balance. The actor's face is too close to the near "wall" of the frame. Despite the empty space, the image feels congested and claustrophobic, or maybe it conveys a sense of being trapped. The eye-line is truncated. Of course, this might be stylistically appropriate if the subtext for your character at this point is "up against it." Also, you get the sense that the empty space occupying the majority of frame left is crying out to be filled with someone or something. That negative space behind the head can conjure feelings of suspense, dread, or vulnerability. The audience might expect that void to be filled by something, and they would shout at the screen, "Look out behind you!" So, unless that is your creative intention and it fits the mood of your story, it might be best not to compose your shot with such minimal look room.

Of course, our original MS example with the head at the center of the frame is not wrong – it's a stylistic choice. But it may not always be as visually engaging to keep your objects of interest at the center of the frame. That may work well for still photographic portraiture, news broadcasting, and selfies, but it lacks a certain punch for motion picture imagery recorded with an objective shooting style – especially when it comes to dialogue scenes. You will become quite adept at arranging important objects in your frame and balancing your compositions as you study and practice your visual grammar. We will further discuss the implications and consequences of eye-line in more detail later in the book, but right now let us introduce you to another set of guides that will help you to place these objects within the composition.

The Rule of Thirds

We moved the subject's body off toward frame left in our MS example (Figure 2.7) in order to generate a more balanced frame of "weighted" objects. The image achieves this sense of balance because it now follows a very common guideline of visual grammar known as the **rule of thirds**. The rule of thirds is very easy to remember and very simple to execute. Take your frame and divide it up into thirds, both vertically and horizontally (Figure 2.9). Other art forms, such as painting, sculpture, and architecture, also have similar guidelines (often mathematically based) for the division of sections, such as the **Golden Ratio** or the **Fibonacci sequence**, etc. Feel free to explore those on your own to help to expand your understanding of image composition and visual communication (see web and book references in Appendix A).

Of course, these lines seen in our illustrations will never physically live on your frame (unless you want them to). You have to know their approximate placement on your particular viewfinder in your camera (although many digital video cameras do have a built-in grid overlay that you can make appear in your viewfinder or monitoring screen, often found under display settings). So, when searching for a rule of thirds composition, you may choose to frame your pictorial elements of visual interest along the one-third horizontal lines, along the one-third vertical lines, or at the crossing points where two of the lines intersect.

In Figure 2.10, the heads of our subjects (what most audience members want to look at) are placed roughly at the upper left and upper right crossing point of the one-third grid lines. The object in Figure 2.11 has been purposefully placed at the lower right intersection

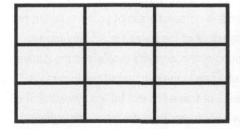 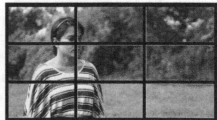

FIGURE 2.9 Markings along the one-third lines inside a 16:9 frame: the overlay grid of horizontal and vertical lines divides the video image into thirds.

Simple Guidelines for Framing Human Subjects

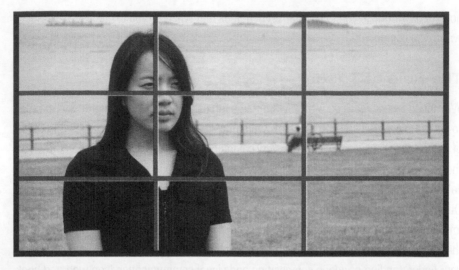

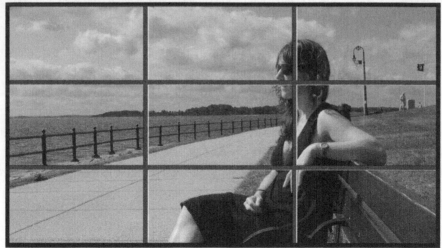

FIGURE 2.10 Subjects placed along the vertical one-third lines with heads at intersection points.

of thirds, inviting the audience to explore the (in-focus) deep background of the frame. It is certainly possible to also place your subjects in different areas of your frame, but be cautious of extreme alignments or having the edges of the frame cut off important portions of your object of interest. The composition of the woman's profile and the distant harbor might serve as a good starting frame of a pan to the right out to sea (Figure 2.12), but otherwise her bisected head along the edge of frame left is a bit too awkward. The cut-off faces in Figure 2.13 may be "artsy" shots appropriate for music videos or experimental films, but the lack of information or their divergence from the norms of cinematography may cause the audience to question the image as a possible mistake.

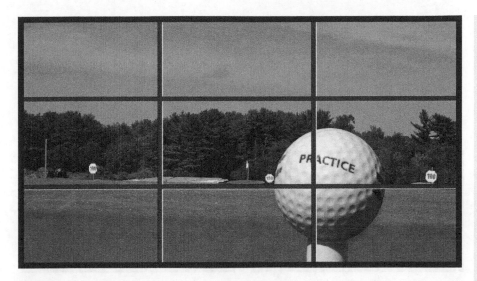

FIGURE 2.11   This object was purposefully placed at the lower right intersection of thirds.

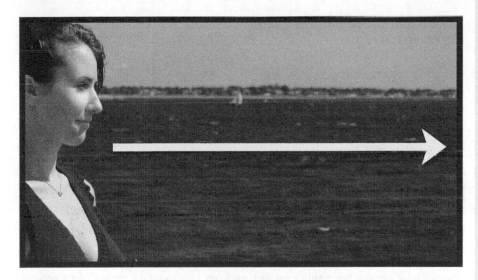

FIGURE 2.12   The back of the talent's head is outside the left frame edge, causing a bit too much look room across the image to frame right.

Simple Guidelines for Framing Human Subjects

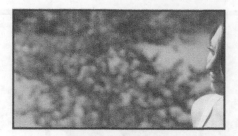

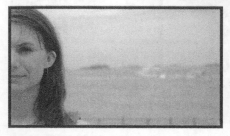

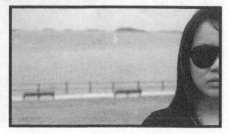

FIGURE 2.13 Cutting the face in half may be considered "artsy" or "experimental" or useful in music videos, etc.

Camera Angle

So now you should feel comfortable composing simple subjects within your frame. The rule of thirds, good headroom, and appropriate look room provide you with some basic techniques for creating a well-balanced frame for use with an objective shooting style. Although we have stopped our subject from looking directly into the lens and the head is turned at a slight angle, we are still photographing the talent from a frontal camera placement. This makes some sense because you usually wish to place your camera at the most advantageous position to record the important details – in this case, the expression on the actor's face and the look in both of the eyes. There are times, however, when you need to move the camera around the actor and record the action from a different angle.

We will now explore the **angles on action** from two separate circles that surround our subject. The "angle on action" refers to the angle from which you photograph a person, object, or event. The position of the camera and the view of our subject that that position offers to the audience will affect how much visual information is conveyed. It can also allow the viewer to glean certain meaning from the shot. First, we will work our way around the subject along a horizontal circle, where the actor is the center and our camera traces the circumference (Figure 2.14). Then we will explore a vertical circle, where the actor is the center and our camera will move above or below a neutral height to show our subject from a high or low angle (Figure 2.15).

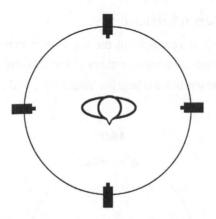

FIGURE 2.14 Bird's-eye view of the camera's horizontal circle around the subject.

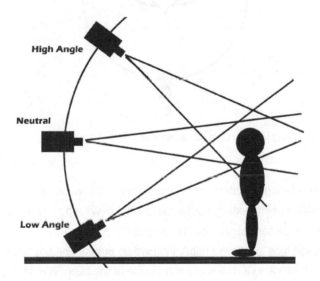

FIGURE 2.15 Side view of the camera tracing a path along a vertical circle around the subject. It is used to create high-, neutral-, and low-angle shots.

Horizontal Camera Angles

When you photograph a person directly from the front of his or her face, it often yields a rather flat, uninteresting image (depending on lighting, which we will look at in Chapter Four). An easy fix to this is to ask the talent to angle his or her face or body away from the camera lens. Keep in mind, however, that the camera can also be moved around the subject. Let us imagine that the talent is at the center of a circle, like the hub of a bicycle wheel laying flat. The camera, facing inward from the rim, can then move around that circle's center, showing the subject from any horizontal angle.

The 360-Degree Method

As there are 360 degrees in a circle, let us use the degrees to help to describe how far along the circumference we can move the camera and what kind of shot that would create. We'll split the circle into positive and negative values up to 180 degrees (Figure 2.16).

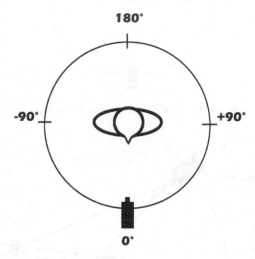

FIGURE 2.16 The camera's horizontal circle around the talent, divided into degrees.

With the camera facing the talent at the zero degree mark, we would have a full frontal shot: flat and often uninteresting, but factual as in a news report. If the talent remains stationary and the camera begins to move around the subject along the arc of the circle to the talent's left side (or camera right), then we go through the positive degrees (+45, +90, +135) until the camera comes to the backside of the talent and sees only the back of the head at +180 degrees (Figure 2.17). The same type of arc can be made around the circle on the talent's right side (or camera left) and the degrees would progress the same but in negative values (–45, –90, –135, –180) (Figure 2.18).

The Clockface Method

It might be easier to think of the degrees of the circle like the face of an analog clock where the subject is at the center of the hands and the camera is at the outer ring of numbers. In this case, you could use the callouts of six o'clock for full frontal, three o'clock for left profile, nine o'clock for right profile, and 12 o'clock for full back of head – which is sometimes called a reverse (Figure 2.19).

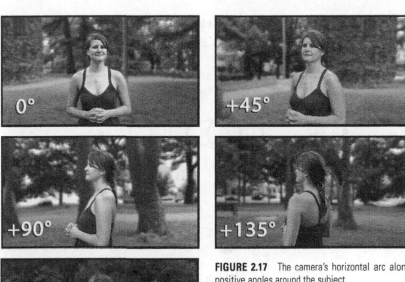

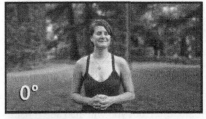

FIGURE 2.17 The camera's horizontal arc along positive angles around the subject.

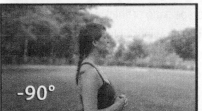

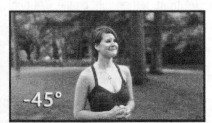

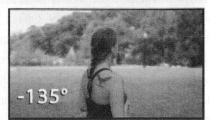

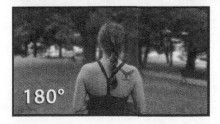

FIGURE 2.18 The camera's horizontal arc along negative angles around the subject.

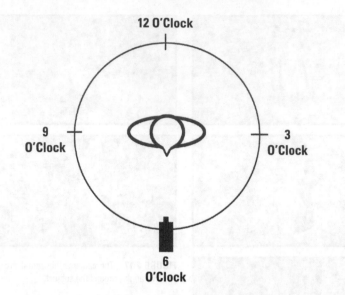

FIGURE 2.19 The numbers of the clockface can represent camera positions around the subject.

The Camera Position Method

Many people simply use a family of rough camera positions around the talent, such as frontal, 3/4 front, left or right profile, 3/4 back, and from behind (also called a reverse) (Figures 2.20–2.24).

The Frontal View

Remember from our earlier discussion that frontal shooting is used a great deal in nonfiction production (news reporters and talk show hosts, etc.), but you will also see it used often in fictional filmmaking when the subject is speaking or thinking, walking toward the camera, or driving (as seen straight in through the windshield). The difference lies entirely in the shooting style: subjective or objective. The frontal view provides the audience with the entire face and both eyes. Much character information is visible (Figure 2.20). However, the overall image (depending on the style of lighting and lens used) can sometimes seem flat and lacking a dynamic dimension.

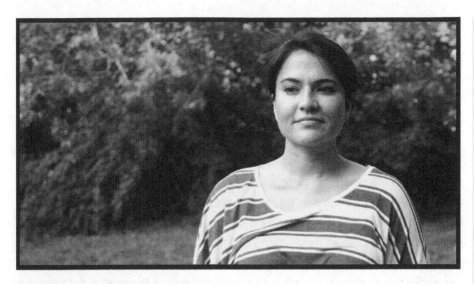

FIGURE 2.20   The frontal camera angle.

The 3/4 Front View

The 3/4 front view, or 3/4 profile as some call it, is probably the most common angle on the talent in fictional filmmaking. It provides the audience with a clear view of the front of the talent so that facial expressions, hand gestures, and the like may be plainly seen. It also provides the frame with an increased degree of dimension. In closer shots of the human face, it brings out the contours and depth of the facial structures (nose, mouth,

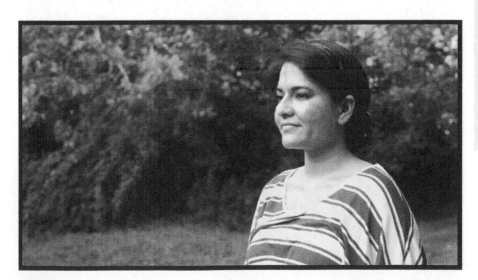

FIGURE 2.21   The 3/4 front left camera angle.

cheekbones, brow, jaw, ear, etc.) and it still shows both of the subject's eyes. Note that the subject has swiveled around to achieve the 3/4 frontal view, and we have also placed the head and eyes along the line of thirds, yielding appropriate headroom and ample look room (Figure 2.21).

The Profile View

The profile shot shows a person directly from the side. It quickly reveals the prominent facial features of nose, lips, and chin, and can also help to identify a character if he or she is known for a particular hairstyle, hat, or headdress (think superhero or cartoon character). In works of art and coinage, the profile was and is used to represent the portrait of a strong leader. The chiseled facial definition of this leader looks out and surveys all that she or he commands. Unfortunately, only half of the information is visible. The viewer can admire this personality, but will not be privileged enough to see what the character might really be thinking or feeling.

It is said that the eyes are the windows to the soul. Not showing your audience the eyes (and full facial expressions) of an actor (as with a profile shot) can generate feelings of duplicity, distrust, aloofness, or secrecy. Certainly, the audience will have diffculty in making an emotional connection to someone they cannot fully see.

Thematically, in your story's visual plan, if this is the desired result you seek, then by all means use the profile shot; otherwise, you may wish to reserve it for special compositions

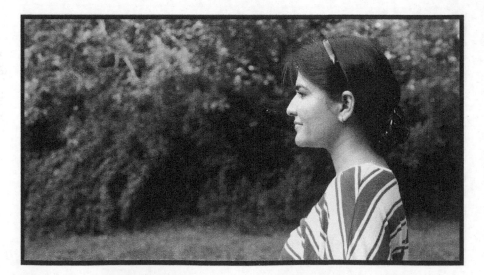

FIGURE 2.22   The left profile camera angle.

or for special characters (Figure 2.22). However, when you add another subject to the shot, as you will see later in the **two-shot**, the profile view becomes a common and efficient way to show both characters interacting within one frame.

The 3/4 Back View

When used in tighter shots, the 3/4 back shot looks more like what is called an **over-the-shoulder (OTS) shot**, which we see later. The camera gets to peek over the shoulder of our main subject and shows the audience what the subject is looking at (Figure 2.23). They get to see the film world from the character's **point of view** (**POV**). Granted, the face of the actor is hidden from view, so we do not know what he or she may be thinking or feeling from this particular angle, but the filmmaker probably has other angles of this character to cover the scene. The 3/4 back view still has the feeling of an objective shot and asks the viewer to share the experience along with the character in the story. The participating viewer is invited to do the thinking and feeling as if he or she were the character.

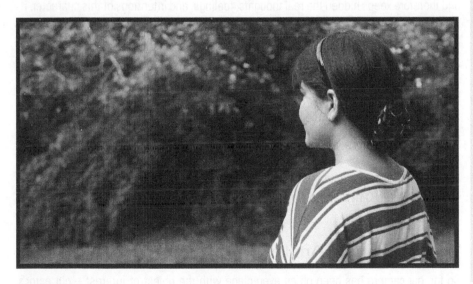

FIGURE 2.23   The 3/4 back camera angle.

The Full Back View

The full back view is 180 degrees from the front view. It is sometimes called a reverse, especially if used in a wider framing of the subject. Although you do not see the face of the subject, the usual guidelines of framing apply: headroom, look room, the rule of thirds, etc. As you may have already guessed, this type of shot totally obscures the subject's face

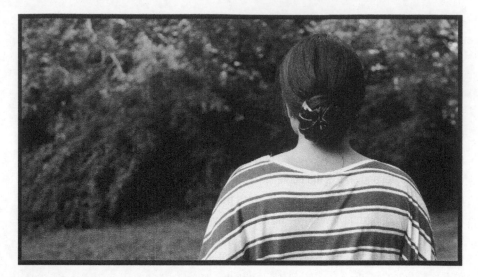

FIGURE 2.24 The full back camera angle, sometimes called a reverse.

and therefore keeps hidden the real thoughts, feelings, and intentions of this character. If, however, this is a known character placed in a suspenseful situation in the narrative, then this type of shot takes on a very subjective point of view, as though someone or something were following our hero from behind and is just about to strike. Scary stuff! (Figure 2.24)

When you add movement to the full back view (as in a tracking shot, discussed in Chapter Six), it becomes another strong method to have the subject lead the audience into a new scene or location, or to reveal new story information as the camera follows behind. On tighter shots, this view can generate mystery or suspense as the camera follows closely behind the subject without showing much of the environment to the curious audience, who feel like they are walking closely behind our hero.

Vertical Camera Angles

So far, our camera has been on an even plane with the object of interest – our actor's head, most often. In other words, if the head is four feet off the ground, then our camera and its lens are also about four feet off the ground (Figure 2.25). We commonly refer to this value as the lens height. The lens height can also rise above or drop below the height of the subject, as we will see in the next section (Figure 2.26).

As a special note, it might be important to mention **camera support** – or what holds the camera in its position/angle while recording. Figure 2.25 illustrates a camera on a tripod,

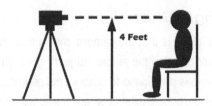

FIGURE 2.25 Camera height and angle of coverage traditionally fall at the same height as the subject's head for a neutral angle on action.

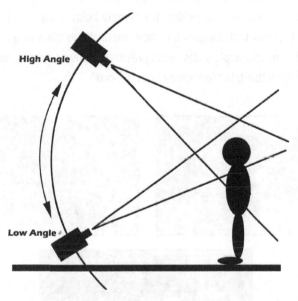

FIGURE 2.26 Vertical camera angles: high and low. The camera is physically placed above the subject and the lens is angled down or the camera is positioned below the subject and the lens is angled up to record.

the most common means of video camera support that can ensure a stable and steady recording process. Going "handheld" is easy to do, but often difficult to do well. Remember that just because you are 5'6" tall does not mean that the camera being held in your hands at 5'2" off the ground is the best lens height for your shot. The camera/lens height has nothing to do with your comfort level as camera operator. Place the camera in the appropriate position so that you can get the shot needed by the story, and adjust your body position accordingly. Also, typically, to achieve some strong high-angle shots, you may need to employ a jib arm or a boom arm. These camera support methods (and more) are covered in greater detail in Chapter Six, but for now, please continue to think about camera placement around your subject and the resulting lens angle on the action to be covered.

Camera Angle

The Neutral-Angle Shot

The general guideline to follow is that the camera and its lens should be looking at the subject from the same horizontal plane as the subject's eyes. This generates a neutral angle on action. The camera is positioned to observe the people, objects, or events from the same height as where the people exist or where the action takes place. The audience will relate to the characters as equals. Whether the subject is standing, sitting up in a tree, or laying stomach down on the ground, it is a good idea to place the camera at a similar height to maintain a neutral view (Figure 2.27). Once you raise the camera position above your actors or actions, or drop the camera below them, you begin to create a privileged point of view that deviates from how we might normally observe others in real life. These high- and low-angle shots usually result in a power dynamic within the frame and within the story itself. Let us explore both options.

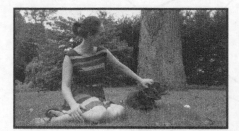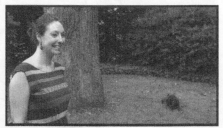

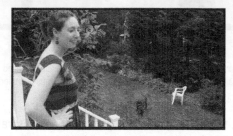

FIGURE 2.27 A neutral-angle view of the subject. Regardless of subject height (distance from ground), the camera lens observes from the same elevation.

The High-Angle Shot

Shooting from a high angle means that you are covering a shot of a person or action from a higher vantage point. The camera is physically higher than the subject or the scene being recorded. Unlike a neutral shot, the lens is angled downward. Depending on the context of the shot in your story, there can be different implied meanings.

The High-Angle Shot of an Individual

The grammar of a high-angle shot of a character in a movie may be interpreted by the audience to mean that who they are seeing on screen is small, weak, subservient, or diminutive, or is currently in a less powerful or compromised position – perhaps both physically and thematically within the narrative. Through **foreshortening** and through "compressing" the character into the floor or ground underneath him or her, the camera's frame "contains" the subject and makes him or her appear physically small and "trapped" (Figure 2.28).

Alternatively, you will also find that a *slightly* higher camera angle down on a subject yields a more pleasing line of the nose and jaw (think about why most people hold their phone camera up high when taking a selfie for their social media streams). As a filmmaker, you will often strive to make your talent look as good as possible and this small angle down might do the trick.

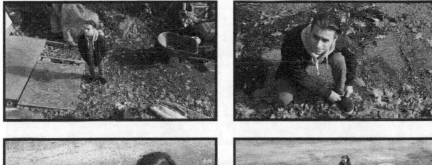

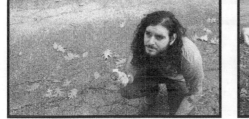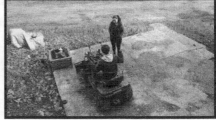

FIGURE 2.28   A high-angle view of the subject. The floor or ground enclosing the figure within the frame can invoke a claustrophobic or trapped feeling. (Photo credits: Zach Benard and Anthony Martel)

Camera Angle

The High-Angle Shot as a POV

What can it mean if the high-angle shot represents a point of view from another character in the story? Literally, it simply shows that one character is physically up higher in the film space, looking down on the other character. Thematically, this shot could mean that the higher character has the upper hand or does not think much of the other, lower character at this time. This POV may come from many entities such as a king, a giant, a judge, a dragon, or an alien spaceship. An up/down power dynamic is created. Of course, this scenario would require an **answering shot** or reverse set-up back up to the higher character, which we'll discuss in the next main section on low angles.

The High-Angle Shot of an Environment

Whenever there is a vast expanse of geography to show within your frame (think extreme long shot or very long shot), it can be helpful to have the camera elevated above the space.

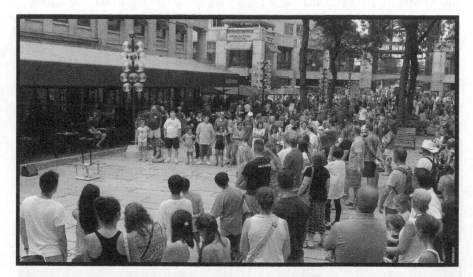

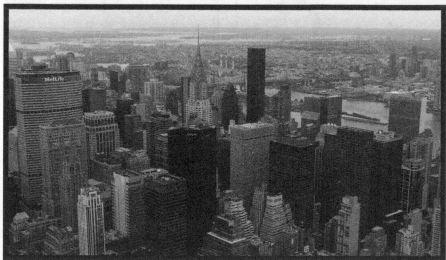

FIGURE 2.29 A high-angle view of an environment shows more information in an objective style. (Photo credit: B – Mike Neilan)

You can establish the layout of the location and the events going on within it if you have a higher-angle view. The extent of the parade, the concert, the crowded beach, or the epic medieval battlefield can be shown more clearly from above, but still within the "human scale" of observation (Figure 2.29).

If the camera were to be neutral in one of these environments, meaning placed down among the actual viewers of the parade or concert, then it would put the film's audience in the scene as one of these experiencers. Only the immediate vicinity would be visible. Drop the camera lower and angle up and you now have a victim – a child or someone vulnerable – observing the scene from a very low and compromised position within the crush of the crowd.

If you place the camera very high, directly above the action, then you move into the realm of the **bird's-eye view** or **God view** (Figure 2.30). This angle down on action is not something that a typical viewer is accustomed to seeing in his or her real-world experiences and therefore it will stand out in your visual style – for better or for worse. Watching from directly overhead really compresses the standing or seated subject into the ground, to the point of almost appearing 2D. This unnatural vantage point can create feelings of being observed by otherworldly entities (ghosts, angels, aliens, etc.). If, however, the figures are laying down face up (in bed, on a couch, etc.), then this angle directly overhead seems a little more natural. It can provide a view of prone faces that other, more neutral angles could not achieve.

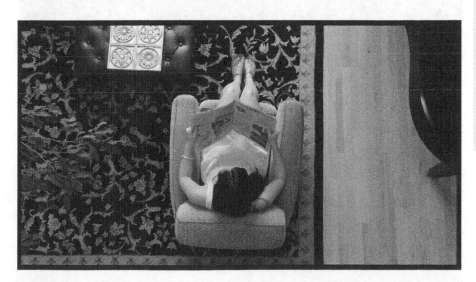

Camera Angle

FIGURE 2.30 A bird's-eye view of a seated subject.

Aerial shots are also used in very high-angle location cinematography, especially as establishing shots over cityscapes, mountain ranges, jungles, etc. You will also see use of these shots in non-fiction programming such as sports coverage, news, exploration shows, real estate videos, etc. Vehicles such as airplanes, hot air balloons, helicopters, and blimps are employed to help to achieve these high-altitude pictures. As technologies have improved and pricing has dropped, drone videography has become very popular among amateur motion media producers. If these types of very high-angle shots fit within your project's visual design, then by all means find a way to achieve them, but please be aware that safety guidelines and legal regulations will need to be followed for your region of production.

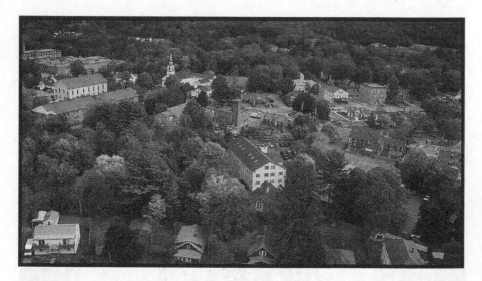

FIGURE 2.31   A high-angle view from a drone camera. (Photo credit: Miles Garnett)

The Low-Angle Shot

Let us now go in the opposite direction and drop the camera and lens below the neutral point and shoot from a lower angle up onto our person, location, or action.

The Low-Angle Shot of an Individual

As you may have already guessed, this angle on action usually generates the reverse feeling in your audience to that of the high angle. On a psychological level, the character seen from below appears larger, more looming, more significant, and more powerful. It is part of the accepted film grammar that a shot from below implies that the person or

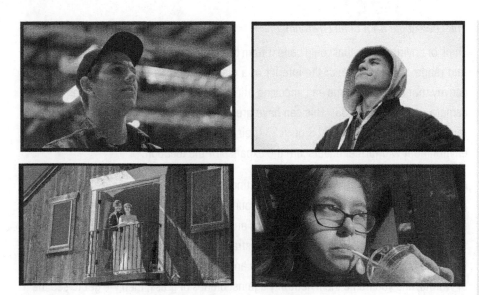

FIGURE 2.32   A low-angle view up onto subjects who may appear heroic, imposing, or simply elevated. (Photo credits: A – Mike Neilan; B – Anthony Martel; C – Alyssa Parmenter; D – Elaria Jacob)

object that you observe from that angle has a substantial presence, is considered "larger than life," or may, at that point in the narrative, have the upper hand (literally and figuratively) (Figure 2.32). Of course, this character may also simply be physically higher in the film space – running down a fire escape, climbing a ladder, etc. A significant part of this implied meaning comes from the proximity or magnification of the figure being recorded. Long shots to medium close-ups of characters will really enhance this underlying theme. The subject becomes statuesque.

The Low-Angle Shot as a POV

The low-angle shot as a POV also implies that the person (camera) doing that low-angle observing is smaller, weaker, or in a more compromised position (think of a jungle adventure story where someone who has fallen into a pit trap is looking up at the person who set the trap – clearly a situation where the film space and narrative allow for the use of these shots). The low-angle POV may also indicate awe or respect on the part of the observing character (think of a commercial starring a small child who idolizes a 7'2" basketball player). Again, it should be pointed out that sometimes a character is just at a lower elevation than other characters for the purpose of compositional balance in the frame. All of these views help to visually create a different energy and a different mood within the story and the viewing experience.

Camera Angle

The Low-Angle Shot of an Environment

Think of environments that could benefit from being seen at a low angle: perhaps a mountain range, a city skyline, or the interior of a giant cave. As a filmmaker, if you want to convey that a space is large and imposing, then it can be helpful to show it from a lower camera angle (Figure 2.33). This can have greater effect if you incorporate your characters in the frame, as in an XLS or VLS. Their diminutive size compared to the looming environment will further underscore the expanse of the location.

At this point, it would be wise to draw a distinction between a low-angle shot and a shot that has a neutral angle but is taken from ground level. The angle of tilt of the actual camera lens determines what the shot becomes and what the viewer experiences because of that angle. Remember, that comic-book illustrations and animations typically follow film language grammar, so if you are making an animated cartoon web series about a family of worms, and you frame them neutrally against blades of grass, then we get to see them as equals – on their plane (Figure 2.34).

In children's cartoons, the camera often stays neutral to the height of the subjects (talking babies, cats, mice, etc.) and actually frames out the heads/faces of the adult humans, allowing the audience to make a connection with these smaller characters. But, if a giant boot heel looming over the worm family suddenly imperils them, then the camera could assume a low-angle position shooting upward to the large foot overhead. This would

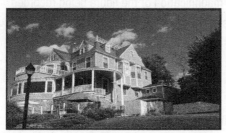
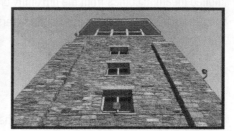
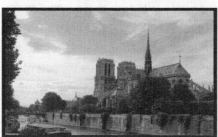
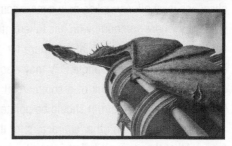

FIGURE 2.33 A low-angle view of an environment. The architecture seems to rise in grandeur over the location. (Photo credits: C – Sarah Morgan, D – Brennan Marlow)

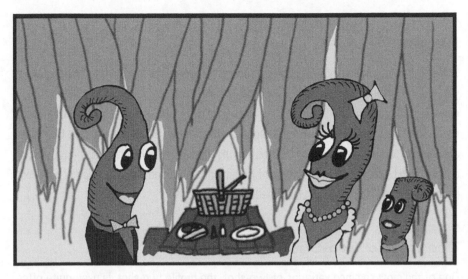

FIGURE 2.34   A neutral-angle view of the worm family picnic. The camera lens height matches their head heights.

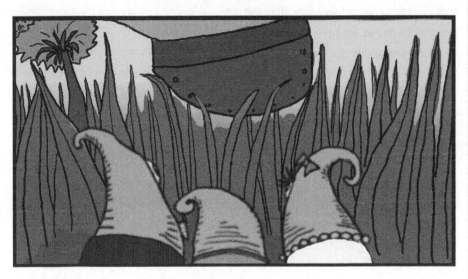

FIGURE 2.35   A low-angle view of the threatened worm family. The camera lens drops below their head height and angles up toward the boot heel overhead. Look out!

yield a more diminutive POV from the worm's endangered position below (Figure 2.35). Similar treatments of the low angle could be used for babies or dogs or people among giant beings, etc. when you wish to stress the size differences.

The Two-Shot: Frame Composition with Two People

So far, our basic shot types have been composed around one person. What happens when you need to include two people in a single frame? Well, as you have probably already guessed, you follow similar guidelines as used for the single subject. Headroom, look room, the rule of thirds, balance of weighted objects, etc. all apply to a shot that must encompass two people having some interaction. The nature of the physical interaction, of course, also helps to dictate what type of framing must be used and what type of two-shot (also shown as 2-shot) will be composed.

The Profile Two-Shot

One of the most common varieties of two-shot, the profile two-shot, is used quite often to help to set up a dialogue between two people in a scene. A long shot or medium long shot will most successfully cover all of the action during the meeting of the two characters. As the figures are smaller and the environment is more prominent, the setting can be established and larger body movements may be covered, particularly if one character must hand something over to the other character: the object could also be seen in this framing. There are innumerable scenarios where a profile two-shot may be appropriate. Some examples are a meeting of two friends (Figure 2.36), a confrontation between two feuding characters (Figure 2.37), or a romantic dinner for two over a small, candle-lit table (Figure 2.38).

When using a tighter framing to compose a profile two-shot (sometimes called a **50–50**), you alter the implied meaning of the encounter by enclosing the characters in a much smaller space. A medium close-up or a close-up will force the characters' faces together in an unnatural way, unless there is an obvious aggressive intention or an intimate overtone. On the basis of our previous examples, the confrontation (Figure 2.40) and the romantic dinner (Figure 2.41) may be good candidates for the medium close-up profile two-shot, but the meeting between the two friends may not be well served by that framing (Figure 2.39). Forcing the faces of two characters together in a tight frame, when there is no real reason to do so, can make the viewing audience feel subconsciously uneasy. For comedic purposes, you could also unite two unlikely characters together in a tight frame, particularly if your hero is encountering a "close talker." We get to feel his discomfort.

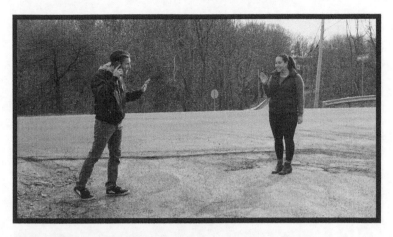

FIGURE 2.36   A profile two-shot as composed for the long shot. (Photo credit: Anthony Martel)

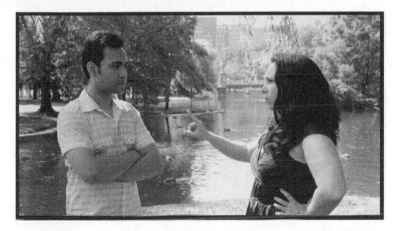

FIGURE 2.37   A medium shot brings the feuding characters very close together in this profile two-shot.

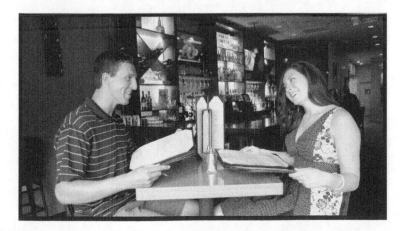

FIGURE 2.38   A profile two-shot as composed for the medium long shot.

The Two-Shot: Frame Composition with Two People

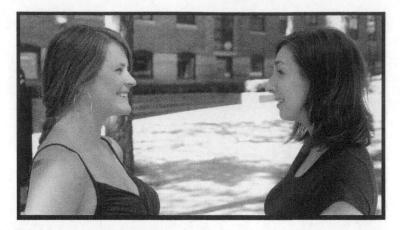

FIGURE 2.39 A casual meeting between two friends on the street seems a bit close in this MCU.

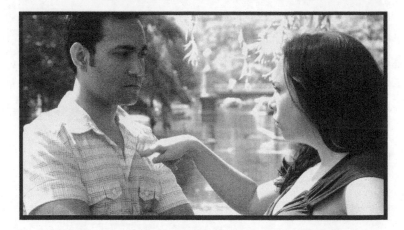

FIGURE 2.40 An aggressive confrontation works well in this tighter MCU.

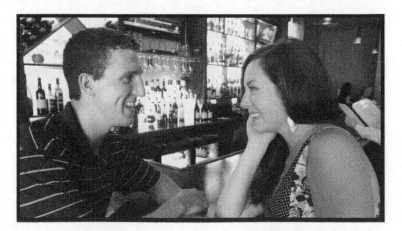

FIGURE 2.41 An intimate occasion like this romantic dinner for two feels right at home in this MCU.

The Direct-to-Camera Two-Shot

Whenever two people stand or sit side-by-side and face the camera, you generate a more subjective shot. Their attention is toward the lens (but not into it, as in subjective shooting style) and not necessarily always toward one another. An example of a truly subjective direct-to-camera two-shot would be two news anchors or sportscasters sitting side-by-side, addressing the viewing audience directly via the camera lens. A less subjective example would be two characters walking side-by-side down a city sidewalk approaching the camera (often called a **walk & talk**) (Figure 2.42), or perhaps two characters sitting in the front seats of a motor vehicle (Figure 2.43).

These subjects in a fictional narrative have their bodies and faces "opened up to" (which means facing) the camera, but they do not ever look directly into the lens. The audience are privileged to observe what they do, what they say, and how they react, yet never feel directly addressed by the talent.

Either way, the framing for this type of shot must be wide enough to accommodate the shoulder widths of the two people. The 16:9 widescreen aspect ratio of HD video will certainly help with this, but an MS or MCU may be the closest shot types that could be used to adequately frame a direct-to-camera two-shot. Attempting to frame any tighter will mean overlapping one body in front of the other. This establishes a visual "favor" for the character in the unobstructed forward position. In this case, favor may establish a more dominant character in the story, or it may just prove a convenient way of seeing a more intimate view of faces within one shot. Sometimes, it is simply easiest to have the shorter talent in front and the taller one behind (Figure 2.44).

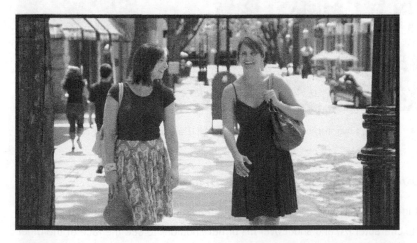

FIGURE 2.42 The medium long shot allows for ample room to move in this open-to-camera two-shot.

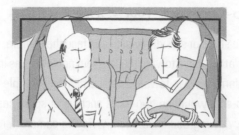

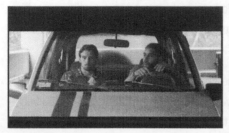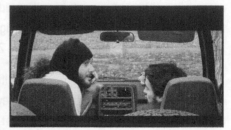

FIGURE 2.43 A very common type of direct-to-camera two-shot. The car's interior dictates the distance between and placement of the two characters facing the same camera. Here we see the storyboard frame, a frontal view, and a reverse view. (Photos from *Consumer Behave*, courtesy Zach Benard, Avarie Cook, Anthony Martel, and John McNeil)

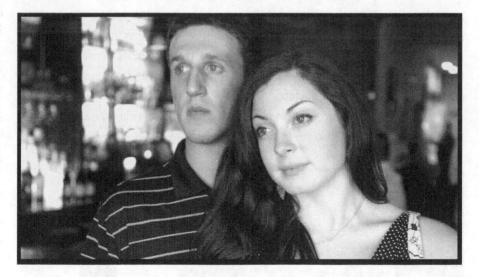

FIGURE 2.44 Achieving a two-shot open to camera in this tight MCU requires overlapping the subjects' bodies.

The Over-the-Shoulder Two-Shot

This shot looks like its name: while recording a dialogue scene, you place the camera behind one character (A) and shoot over his or her shoulder to see the face of the other character (B). The backside of Character A's head and shoulder form an "L" shape at either

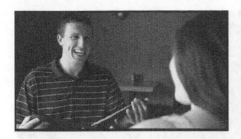 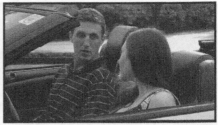

FIGURE 2.45   Examples of over-the-shoulder shots for Character A. Note the "L" shape of head and shoulder in the foreground.

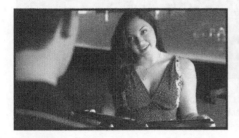 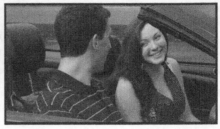

FIGURE 2.46   Examples of over-the-shoulder shots for Character B. Note the "L" shape of head and shoulder in the foreground.

left/bottom or right/bottom of frame, depending on which side you have placed him or her (Figures 2.45 and 2.46).

This is a form of overlapping composition and is most often edited into a scene after the audience have first viewed an establishing shot and, perhaps, a wider profile two-shot. These preceding shots serve to establish the location and the positions of the two characters involved in the dialogue.

An OTS shot allows the audience to focus more attention on the visible subject, what he or she says, and his or her reactions to what the other character says. Of course, you would eventually shoot the matching OTS shot from Character B's shoulder onto Character A's face so that you could alternate back and forth in the edit if needed. In both previous versions of the two-shot, the audience could choose which character's face they would look at and when, but with the OTS shot the filmmaker decides that for them – for emphasis and/or for further character and story development.

An over-the-shoulder two-shot may be composed appropriately within a variety of shot types, ranging from the long shot to the medium close-up, and may or may not contain multiple characters (see the OTS reference on p. 55). Sometimes, as in Figure 2.47, the

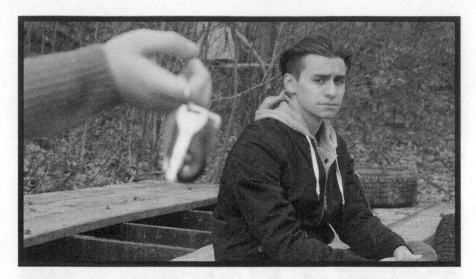

FIGURE 2.47 Camera height has dropped slightly in this modified over-the-shoulder shot. The foreground object is important to the story line as is seeing the look on this subject's face. (Photo credit: Anthony Martel)

camera height is dropped and it shoots from behind the waist, hips, or thighs of a character, especially if he or she is carrying something of visual or dramatic interest at his or her side (a letter, gun, bouquet of flowers, etc.). The most commonly used framing, however, is the MCU (Figures 2.45 and 2.46). It allows for proper composition of the body, equal headroom, and the maintenance of the screen direction of the eye-line or look from one character to the other. The wider aspect ratio of 16:9 may allow for a tighter framing of an OTS shot, but it might run the risk of compromising good composition in favor of more facial detail; you won't know until you try it with your camera, your chosen lens, and your particular actors. A standard "clean" single close-up may be more appropriate.

The Dirty Single

If you wish to get a small slice of Character A in a shot of Character B, but you do not want a full OTS shot or a "clean" single, you may compose what is called a "dirty" single (Figure 2.48). This slice of Character A in the shot helps to keep the viewer oriented. As with any of these shots that incorporate a bit of head or body of the non-favored subject, you have to be extra careful with their placement and movement. Even the slightest gesture or head nod could disrupt the shot's composition. Be clear in your need for relative stillness when you discuss the shot with your talent.

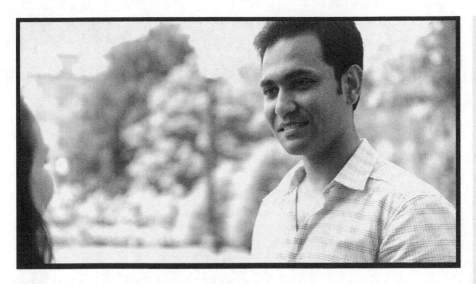

FIGURE 2.48   Just a slice of Character A is visible along frame left in this "dirty" single.

Additionally, as a filmmaker, you may have to ask your talent to stand unnaturally close to each other to achieve the two-shot framing you are seeking. This holds especially true for the over-the-shoulder shot or anything tighter than 50–50. For the actors, it may feel strange, but in the recorded image the distance will look appropriate to the viewing audience. Also, depending on the scene, the players, and your camera placement/lens, you may have to ask the actors to stand or sit further apart, higher, or lower in order to make the shot composition look correct for your needs. Just be aware that in cinematic language, proximity and grouping establish a unity between characters. The family of two-shots is an integral part of your standard scene coverage and the OTS shot may often be the best choice for recording different angles of the same conversation between two characters.

The Power Dynamic Two-Shot

We call this an "up/down" in a two-person profile shot. One character (A) is placed higher in the frame while the other character (B) is placed lower on the opposite side of the frame (Figure 2.49). Even though the camera angle is neutral in this special two-shot, a power dynamic is created. As you will read further in Chapter Seven, the subtext of this shot tells us that the higher character has the upper hand. The OTS coverage will clearly call for the use of high-angle and low-angle answering shots, further underscoring the significance of this composition within the story.

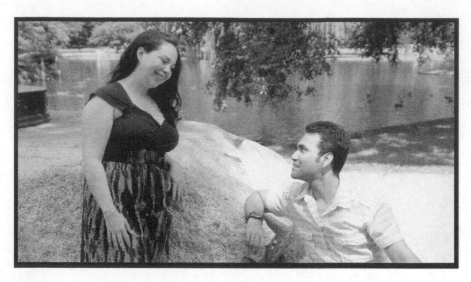

FIGURE 2.49 The character whose head is placed higher in the frame has control of this scene.

The Three-Shot

Much as the standard two-shot works for two people, the "linear" **three-shot** can show three people standing side-by-side-by-side — especially with the widescreen aspect ratio of HD (Figure 2.50). The shot types capable of comfortably generating this framing range from the XLS up to the MCU. Think of three contestants on a game show, three news anchors at the desk, or three friends walking down a school hallway. You may use similar

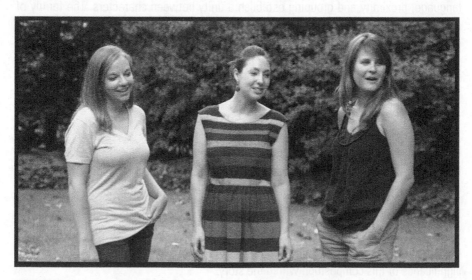

FIGURE 2.50 The three figures fit comfortably in this "linear" three-shot.

guidelines for headroom and the rule of thirds. This shot could apply to both subjective and objective shooting styles.

If you were to put one person in the back seat of the vehicle shown in Figure 2.43, then you would have created another flavor of direct-to-camera three-shot. A triangle of connectivity is now present and the audience can play with the energy generated by bouncing attention from one to the others in this composition (Figure 2.51). You will find that both physical and implied geometric shapes (lines, triangles, squares, ellipses, etc.) are used quite often in visual communications. We discuss these more completely in the next chapter.

OTS three-shots are also possible when you are shooting coverage for a three-person dialogue, but generating two-shots can pose problems for the editor. A linear OTS three-shot relies heavily on figures overlapping within the frame and can look rather "stagey" (Figure 2.52). A high- or low-angle OTS three-shot will create a similar power dynamic as the diagonally arranged two-shot version (Figure 2.53).

When your scene requires five or more characters to be recorded at once, you move into the realm of the **group shot**. Figuring out how to place small groups of known characters around the set or location, such that a viewing audience may see and discern the

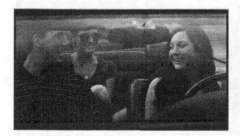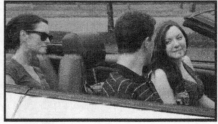

FIGURE 2.51   The triangle shape created by the three heads generates implied energy lines for the audience to follow.

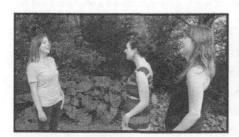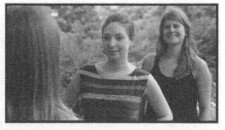

FIGURE 2.52   Tight framing and tight talent blocking can generate this OTS three-shot.

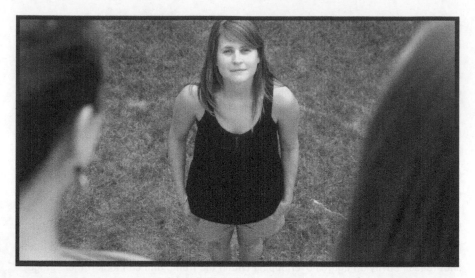

FIGURE 2.53 Camera angle and triangular composition provide extra meaning to this OTS three-shot.

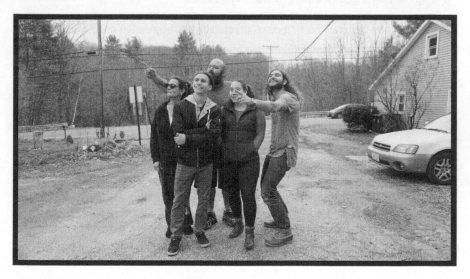

FIGURE 2.54 Layering subjects into the depth of the shot will help to show more faces in a small group shot like this. (Photo credit: Zach Benard and Anthony Martel)

identity of each character throughout the scene, can be a challenge. A practice called **blocking** can help with this. Blocking, in film terms, usually refers to how a director places the talent around the set or location in relation to the current camera position and the lens' angle on action and field of view. Where can you put the bodies and still have the lens see the majority while still allowing the lens to pick up the faces of the actors? It may be near impossible to see them all clearly so remember that the audience will most likely seek out and pay attention to the face that is most visible (and, potentially, most well lit and in focus). The term **staging** (often used interchangeably with blocking) can refer to the purposeful arrangement of set dressings, furniture, doorways and windows, etc. Group shots can benefit greatly from rehearsal time on set such that staging, talent and camera blocking, and lighting decisions can be made in a timely fashion.

Chapter Two – Final Thoughts: Wrapping Up the Basics of Composition

The basics of frame composition are relatively simple. We have demonstrated them using several simple shot types covering one person placed "creatively" within the frame. As with the various two-shots introducing a second subject into the frame but still following similar framing guidelines, so it goes for the three-shot as well. The basics of composition will apply to any of the wide variety of shot types and to any objects that you need to record. Whether you are creating a shot of a vase with flowers, a cat, or a lone planet floating in space, you should consider the same guidelines of composition: headroom, look room, the rule of thirds, camera angle, etc. Once you know the shot types, the basics of framing, and the power behind camera angles, you are on your way to using our shared film language to make well-balanced images for your motion pictures – whatever the project may be.

Related Material Found in Chapter Seven – Working Practices

#11, 14, 16, 24, 26, 36

Chapter Two – Review

1. Provide appropriate headroom for each shot type.
2. Decide whether a subjective (to camera lens) or objective (not to camera lens) shooting style is more appropriate for your project.
3. Create ample look room/nose room for your subject to balance the weight of the frame.
4. Follow the rule of thirds and place important objects along one-third lines within the frame, both horizontally and vertically, and at their intersections.

5. Choose a horizontal camera angle around your subject for more meaningful coverage (the 3/4 front view being the most popular).

6. Shoot from a neutral, high, or low vertical camera angle to inform the audience about a character's "power dynamic."

7. Profile and direct-to-camera two-shots work best from long to medium shots, but over-the-shoulder two-shots may work best from the medium close-up.

8. A "dirty" single contains only a small portion of the other character in the scene. Such shots are good for audience reference but may pose a continuity problem for the editor.

9. A power dynamic can be generated while using a neutral camera angle on a profile two-shot if you place one character higher in the frame.

10. The three-shot can add a triangular energy pattern to your composition.

Chapter Two – Exercises

1. With whatever camera you have access to, practice framing a single human subject in all shot types, paying particular attention to your angle on action, the rule of thirds, headroom and nose room, etc.

2. Shoot still picture storyboards of two people having a conversation:

    A) across a table from one another;

    B) walking side-by-side down a street or hallway (either leading them or following them – for extra information on this, you may wish to skip ahead to Chapter Six).

3. Find two actors of different heights and record them in a standing profile two-shot and then try to figure out the best approach for getting matching over-the-shoulder shots of each. Or simply have one actor stand and one sit and capture their matching OTS shots.

4. Think of at least three scenarios where two characters can be visible within the frame of a medium shot, a medium close-up, and a close-up. Stage and block those scenarios with two friends or family members and record the results of each, progressively making your frame tighter and tighter.

Chapter Two – Quiz Yourself

1. If you wanted to make a character in your story look subordinate or diminutive, where might you want to put the camera in relation to his or her body?

2. In a scene involving only one character, why might you choose to compose a frame shooting over that person's shoulder?

3. Why might you want to record a character in profile?

4. The cartoon that you are animating starts when a little girl gets lost in a big city. In drawing and placing your shot's compositional elements, how could you visually indicate her feelings of being alone and small?

5. At what level, or height, would the majority of neutral shots of people be recorded? Why?

6. What possible scenarios would benefit visually from uniting the heads of two people in a profile CU?

7. What is the difference between a "clean" single and a "dirty" single?

8. What do the terms "blocking" and "staging" refer to when you are setting up the elements of a shot?

9. What does the term "negative space" refer to in relation to a film frame's composition?

10. What is an "objective shooting style" and when might a motion media producer wish to employ it?

Chapter Three
Composition: Beyond the Basics

- The Illusion of 3D
- The Lines: Horizontal, Vertical, Diagonal, Curved
- The Depth Factor: Foreground, Middle Ground, Background
- Depth Cues: Overlapping, Object Size, Atmospherics
- Lens Talk: Focal Length, Primes, Zooms
- Lens Talk: Focus

Up until now, we have kept most of our compositions relatively basic: one or two subjects in a simple environment. By this point, you should feel comfortable with your camera's aspect ratio, the families of shot types, the rule of thirds, headroom, look room, and camera angles on action. Chapter Three builds on these basic components of cinematic language and introduces new and compelling ways to compose your shots – increasing their visual information, their meaning, and, for some, their beauty.

The Illusion of the Third Dimension

The basic shot examples presented so far have been composed with a rather two-dimensional subject framing. The images (except for the very long shot and the extreme long shot) do not really take advantage, in a serious way, of the depth of the film space behind the subjects. We would like to start blocking, staging, and framing objects within our video frame to generate and accentuate the third dimension in our shots. There are many ways to use compositional elements to create the illusion of 3D space within a still photograph, an animation, or a video frame. Many popular methods include the use of lines, foreground and background objects, depth cues, atmospherics, focus, wide and long lenses, and lighting (the latter will be discussed in Chapter Four).

The basic motion picture camera captures a flat, 2D image and movie theater, television, tablet, and computer screens display a flat, 2D image. So how is it that when we watch television and, more noticeably, movies on very large theater screens, the elements of the frame seem to occupy a 3D space? Well, the simple answer is to say that this phenomenon is achieved through visual illusions and tricks for the human eye and brain. There are many more in-depth physiological and psychological reasons, but this is not the appropriate place to explore those topics fully. Feel free to do your own research on the human visual system and how we interpret light, color, motion, depth, etc.

We will, however, briefly discuss how our human visual system differs from the visual system of a traditional camera. On the most simplistic level, it comes down to how many lenses are used to create the image. We have two eyes on the front of our heads, and our eyes are spaced several inches apart. This configuration results in binocular vision ("bi-" meaning "two" and "-ocular" referring to the "eye"). Binocular vision allows us to establish depth in our visual space by enabling us to see the same objects from two separate vantage points. Each eye, offset by those several inches, sees the same objects from a slightly different horizontal position and therefore "captures" a slightly different picture. The brain then unites those two separate pictures and generates one view of the world in front of us rendered in 3D perspective (Figure 3.1).

Each eye's vantage point helps to create the illusion of 3D depth. Test this yourself by holding any 3D object about 1.5 feet in front of your face, making sure that it is askew and not perfectly flat to your vision, then alternately open one eye and look at the object and then close that eye and open the other eye to see the same object. Note how the two views of this close object are slightly different.

Remember that a keen filmmaker will be familiar with how the audience process visual information and will use it to her or his advantage when planning the project's motion imagery.

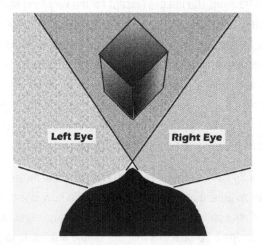

FIGURE 3.1 Bird's-eye view of a person looking at a box. Each eye's vantage point helps to create the illusion of 3D depth. The left and the right eyes see slightly different versions of the same close-up object. This difference in angle on objects does not apply as much to things further away from us.

There are consumer-level 3D video cameras on the market today. Most have two lenses and record two separate images, much as human eyes do. The appropriate computer video-editing software and display technologies will render a more "realistic" 3D viewing experience for the audience, although it is all still only seen on a 2D screen. Typically, you must wear special glasses to see the illusion properly.

Of course, traditional film and video cameras have only one eye – the single lens – so they are unable to record the same type of 3D space as the human visual system. Filmmakers must generate the illusion of multi-dimensionality. The following sections will give you some tools and techniques to help you to explore ways to be a great 3D illusionist with your own motion media shots.

The Use of Lines

In artwork, the use of lines – both straight and curved – helps us to render patterns and shapes, direct attention and energies, and delineate sections. The filmmaker has to make many decisions about lines and how to incorporate them into the imagery of the motion picture. Just as in other works of art, lines within a film frame can do different jobs and generate different ideas and feelings for the audience. The following topics touch on some of their purposes and effects.

The Horizon Line

We are going to leave our human subjects aside for the time being and focus our attention on recording an exterior environment. Shot-wise, we are talking about the long shot family, especially the extreme long shot (XLS) and very wide shot (VWS). Depending on the surrounding topography of your shoot location and your camera angle, this shot should result in capturing a large field of view of the world: the ground, the sky, and many things within those zones. For illustrative purpose, we will keep the environment rather bare and start with just a **horizon line** (Figure 3.2).

The horizon line helps to keep the audience grounded in an understandable spatial relationship with the environment depicted in the frame. In other words, it allows them to perceive a clear up/down and left/right orientation in the film world. Typically, a major goal is to keep your horizon line as level as possible and in alignment with – or parallel to – the top and bottom edges of your physical film frame. You will see that Figure 3.2 accomplishes this goal, but let us add actual objects to further discuss horizon line and composition (Figure 3.3).

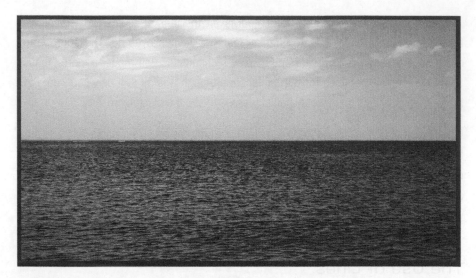

FIGURE 3.2   A simple horizon line bisecting the vertical plane of the frame.

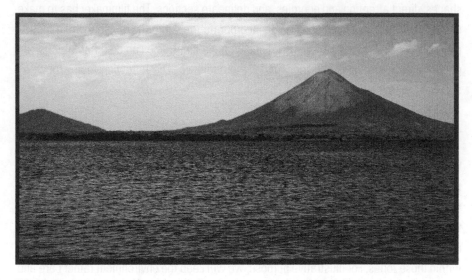

FIGURE 3.3   Adding visible objects to your horizon line frame helps to establish place, time, and physical scale.

Now we can begin to appreciate what the level horizon line is doing for our picture composition. Figure 3.3 shows a frame cut directly in half: the horizon line bisects the frame, separating top from bottom. There is headroom for the volcano, sky, and clouds, but does the image follow the rule of thirds? Does it have to? The horizon line may be placed across your frame wherever you see fit, but its placement will allow you to highlight more sky and less ground or less sky and more ground. If we tilt the camera lens angle down,

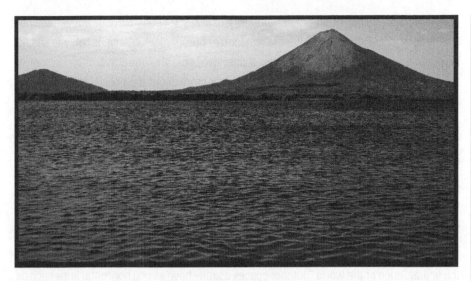

FIGURE 3.4 By tilting the camera lens down, the horizon line appears to rise vertically in our frame. It now falls along the upper one-third of the frame, resulting in less headroom for the volcano and sky and showing more ocean.

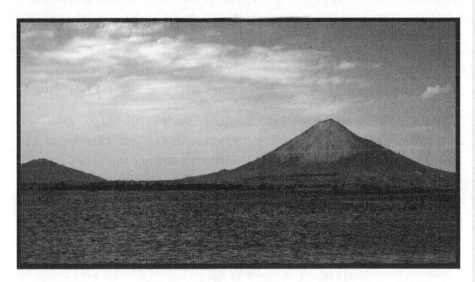

FIGURE 3.5 By tilting the camera lens up, the horizon line now falls along the lower one-third of the frame, resulting in more visible space for the volcano and sky and less ocean.

we push the horizon line up in our frame (Figure 3.4). If we tilt the camera lens angle up, we push the horizon line down in our frame (Figure 3.5). Each of these examples shows the horizon line following the rule of thirds. For many people, the composition of Figure 3.5 is more pleasing pictorially, but it truly depends on what fits the visual needs of your story.

Designing shot composition around the story is a key responsibility of any filmmaker, animator, or visual storyteller. After the rectangular border of your frame is set, you should be planning the placement of the horizon line. Dropping the line toward the bottom of the frame will expose more night-time sky in your story about the possibility of invading aliens: the audience feel that they might be out there. Raising the line toward the top will expose a vast expanse of open ocean in your story about the possibility of sea serpents: the audience feel that they might be lurking just under the surface of all of that visible water. Perhaps your story is about a long-struggling farmer during a drought. You can play it both ways with this: push the horizon up to show more dry, scorched, barren fields, or pull it down to show the cloudless sky baking the thirsty earth below. Either way, the audience are feeling the farmer's plight.

Keep in mind that a horizon line exists in interior film spaces as well; it just may not be the actual "edge of the world." Interior spaces usually have strong horizontal lines such as where the floor meets a wall, window sills, tops of laboratory benches, tables or desks, etc. The idea would be to keep these horizontal lines flat and level. Any narrative significance would have to be dependent on the size of the set and the art direction, etc. Horizontal lines in general can imply stability, repose, and order.

Vertical Lines

When your horizon is level, then all vertical lines in your image should rise up straight, parallel to your frame's left/right edges and perpendicular to the top/bottom (Figure 3.6). Filmmakers use strong vertical lines for many purposes in their compositions. Just look around yourself and, depending on your location, you are bound to see several strong vertical lines: doorways, corners of walls, edges of windows, edges of buildings, lamp posts, telephone poles, and trees, to list just a few possibilities. They are often associated with strength, height, loftiness, or even rigidity and staunchness.

A single vertical element can divide the frame into sections of different sizes depending on where you place it. This serves to partition areas of your film world or separate characters from one another – both literally and figuratively. Doorways, or "frames" within your film frame, can do the same thing. Multiple vertical elements, like the posts in a fence, could symbolize the bars of a jail cell. Your wide horizontal rectangle of a frame can easily be cut down, blocked off, and recomposed by using verticals to create smaller squares and rectangles (Figure 3.7). Beware of placing a single vertical background line directly behind your subject, as it can appear strange on the screen and detract from the overall composition.

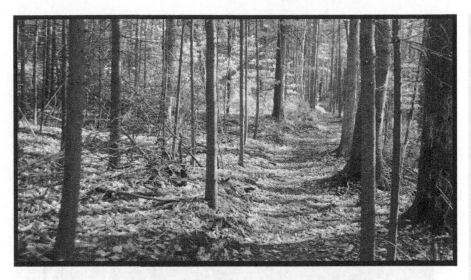

FIGURE 3.6   Bold vertical "lines" like these trees accentuate height, strength, and solidity.

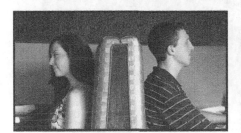 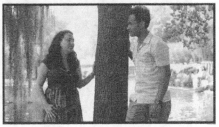

FIGURE 3.7   Vertical lines, objects, or structures can cut the frame into smaller pieces. They can physically and thematically separate subjects in the narrative.

Dutch Angle

You will most often strive to keep your horizon line stable and level, thus ensuring an even viewing plane for your audience. A shift in your horizon line is also likely to cause shifts in your vertical lines: any tall building, tree, door frame, etc. will look tilted or slanted, not upright and even. When horizontal and vertical lines go askew, it causes a sense of uneasiness and a slight disorientation in your audience. If this is done unintentionally, then you get people confused. It this is done on purpose, then you have created what is called a **Dutch angle**, a **Dutch tilt**, a **canted angle**, or an **oblique angle** on action.

When a character is sick or drugged or when a situation is "not quite right," you may choose to tilt the camera left or right and create this non-level horizon (Figure 3.8). The imbalance will make the viewer feel how unstable the character or environment really

The Use of Lines

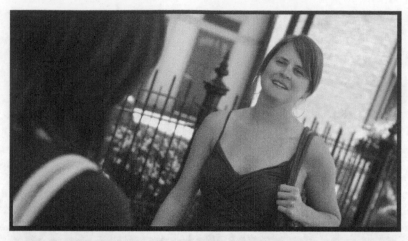

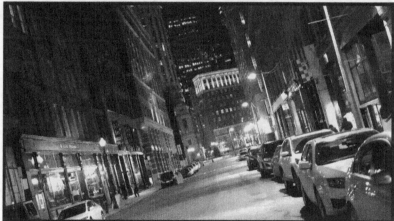

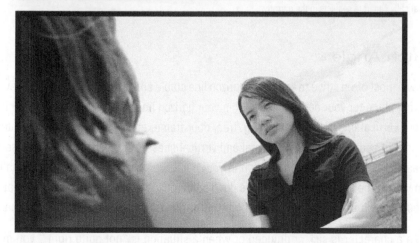

FIGURE 3.8 Examples of Dutch-angle or canted-angle shots. Note how the slanted horizontal and vertical lines skew the balance of the image. Something is not quite right within the story at this point. (Photo credit: B – Brennan Marlow)

is. Think of a murder mystery aboard a boat in rough seas: things tilt this way and that, everyone unsure, everyone on edge. Once again, visuals underscore the story when the horizontal and vertical lines are as askew as the personalities of the murder suspects.

Diagonal Lines

The grid-like horizontal and vertical lines do a good job of partitioning the two-dimensional frame, but we need to begin our exploration of how lines help us to achieve the illusion of depth. To get us started, let's look at Figure 3.9. The line shape could represent the slope of a hill. Depending on whether your energy is moving up the "hill" or down it, the symbolic meaning of the ball shape within your story can be different. What if the line shape indicates a flat path along the ground like a sidewalk? If we employ visual perspective and foreshortening, the ball now seems to be rolling away to or coming from a more distant point in the depth of this 2D frame. Implied "direction" and "movement" have been added due to the use of perspective. (For more information on movement, see Chapter Six.) This example helps somewhat in understanding diagonal lines and how their varying thickness adds depth to an otherwise flat third dimension in our film frame.

If we switch our example back to a horizon line and add two diagonal lines from the bottom of the illustration that converge at the horizon, then we have made something new (Figure 3.10). Does this look familiar? Those of you with a studio art background may know that this example employs an artistic technique called the **vanishing point**. These

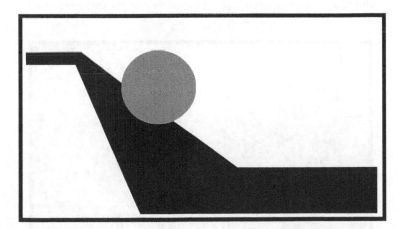

FIGURE 3.9   This small circle and bent line could indicate a "ball" rolling down a "hill." Or maybe it is a "ball" rolling away along a flat "sidewalk" into the depth of the image? Foreshortening and perspective add to the illusion of 3D in a 2D plane.

The Use of Lines

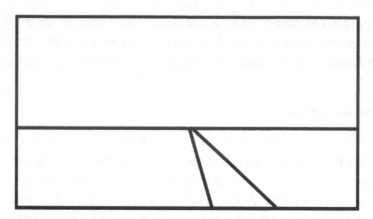

FIGURE 3.10 Two diagonal lines converge at a third horizontal line. Where they meet is called the vanishing point.

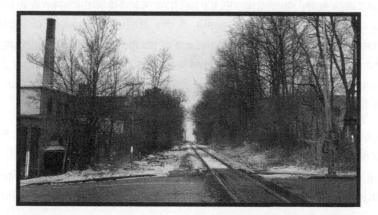

FIGURE 3.11 A railroad track provides a good example of diagonal line perspective and the illusion of 3D.

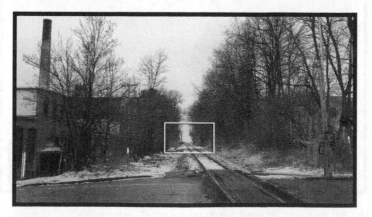

FIGURE 3.12 The box indicates where the parallel tracks converge and appear to vanish at the horizon line.

diagonal lines may represent a road, a stream, a sidewalk, or, in our example, railroad tracks (Figure 3.11). Railroad tracks have a consistent width and therefore should be parallel to each other for as long as the tracks cover the ground. In reality, when observed across a large distance, the tracks seem to get closer and closer together until they appear to merge at the horizon. This place along the horizon where parallel lines appear to merge together is the vanishing point (Figure 3.12).

This illusion, as perceived by our human visual system, signifies "distance" to our brains. When observed in reality, in drawings or paintings, and in a filmed image, we infer the existence of depth. This is related to foreshortening (as mentioned with high-angle shots), and is most noticeable on linear shapes (buildings, roads, even people) but is less effective on amorphous shapes of unknown mass (ocean, sky, rocks). The key thing to realize here is that the use of diagonal lines can bring that illusion of depth to your frame. So, whenever you can employ diagonal lines within your composition (a road, a hallway, a line of people waiting for the bus), you are creating the impression of 3D space in the 2D film frame.

Staircases and their railings can generate a great deal of visual interest and energy when incorporated into your composition. They can rise up or down diagonally or recede into the depth of your shot straight on. Much like roads, paths, rivers, etc., they lead the eyes of the viewer in or out of the depth of your frame and they are useful for up/down power dynamics as well (Figure 3.13).

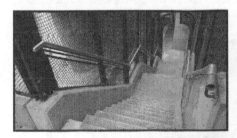 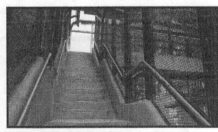

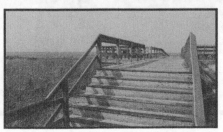

FIGURE 3.13 Examples of how stairs and railings can create depth in your shot composition. They help to lead your eye up, down, and out to a more distant point.

The Use of Lines

This does not mean that you must always use diagonal lines, however. Yes, they are compositionally bold elements within your frame, and yes, they can create depth, but what if your goal is to create a shot that has no depth? Your character is feeling trapped or not capable of moving in a dynamic direction at a certain point of the narrative. Composing him or her in a flat space (such as up against a wall) could help to visually underscore his or her state of being, reflecting the story's subtext and psychological messaging (Figure 3.14).

To achieve the shot in Figure 3.14, the camera had to be placed at the height of the subject and perpendicular to the wall itself. This frame, flat onto a wall, has no real sense

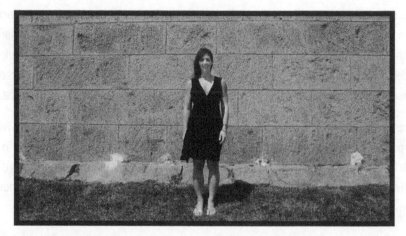

FIGURE 3.14 The subject, framed up against a flat wall, seems boxed in or trapped by the environment. Lacking indicators of depth, this shot can convey thematic meaning about the character in the story.

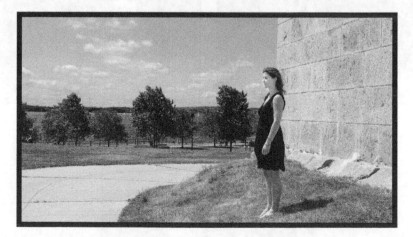

FIGURE 3.15 By recording the same subject by the same wall from a different camera angle, we now unlock the diagonal lines, which lead the eye into the depth of the "3D" shot. The meaning of the shot and the character's mental and emotional state may now be different: free and open.

of depth. The full frontal angle on action shows only some horizontal lines on the wall. The person is enclosed by the environment and can only move left or right, or potentially toward the camera. In this instance, the perceived absence of depth may enhance the depiction of the mental or emotional state of the character. The composition of the shot underscores the state of being for the character recorded within it.

A slight shift in the camera's angle on action (horizontal repositioning) yields a different image with a different meaning (Figure 3.15). It shows the same subject in front of the same wall, but now a diagonal line exists, as does a distant horizon. With the frame opened up in this way, the character has more options for movement – left, right, near, or far – and she is pictorially and thematically freer. Depth is created because the diagonal and horizon lines draw the viewer's eye away from the character and out into the deep space of the film world. So, in addition to helping to create the illusion of depth, the presence of strong diagonal lines in a composition helps you to direct the attention of the audience into that depth – to explore deeper inside your frame for more visual information about your story.

Curved Lines

Performing similar tasks to diagonal lines are curved lines, either enclosed like circles and ellipses or open like arcs and S curves. Adding curves to your compositional arrangements can help to lead a viewer's eyes into or out from the depth of your film frame, separate

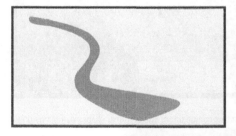
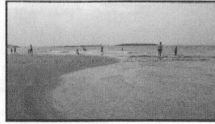
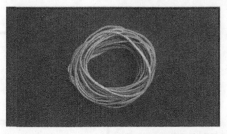

The Use of Lines

FIGURE 3.16 Relaxed or uniform curved lines help the eye to stay calm and ask us to follow them.

sections of your frame, conjure feelings of unity, or establish directions of movement or the implied flow of energy.

Curves may be fluid and smooth and subtle. These work well to help the audience to feel relaxed by showing some natural connectivity (Figure 3.16).

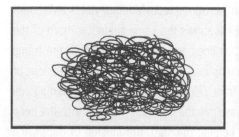 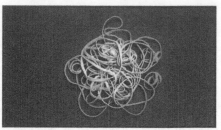

FIGURE 3.17   A viewer may just feel confused while looking at these messy curved lines.

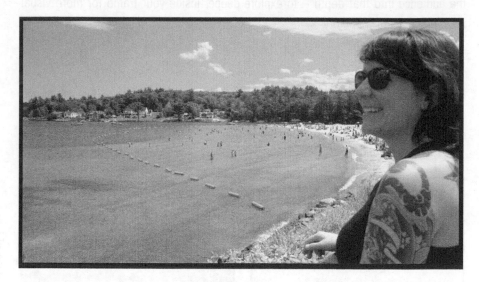

FIGURE 3.18   A viewer may sense the curved "lines" in this composition. The elliptical shapes can gently draw the eyes around the elements of the frame.

FIGURE 3.19   Do you see a familiar pattern in these "random" shapes?

Curves do not have to be physical lines either. They can be constructed, artfully, in your compositions by arranging people, objects, colors, and contrast (covered in greater detail in Chapter Four). The audience will "extract" the shape you "embed" in your shot (Figure 3.18). Humans are quite good at seeing patterns and shapes in our environment, and image makers (artists, filmmakers, video game designers, etc.) count on this when they construct their images (Figure 3.19).

The Depth of Film Space: Foreground, Middle Ground, and Background

We have seen that diagonal and curved lines framed within a shot can help to draw a viewer's eyes from objects close to the camera to objects further away from the camera, or deeper into the film space. To help us to understand this space better, let's divide it into three sections based on proximity to the camera's lens: **foreground** (FG), **middle ground** (MG), and **background** (BG). Together with the borders of the frame, these zones help to form the film's 3D space: height, width, and depth.

Foreground

As the name implies, the foreground is the zone between the camera's lens and the main subject being photographed. It is the space before, or in front of, the main area of interest. Nothing has to occupy this space and often it is simply filled with empty air. A creative filmmaker, however, can choose to place something in that space. Of course, a foreground element should enhance the composition of the shot and, if it is stationary, it should not obscure the zones behind it unnecessarily.

The object may serve to help to set the environment (e.g., a tree branch), it may be an abstract shape (e.g., part of a lamp post or a park bench), or it may also carry meaning for the narrative (e.g., a stop sign at a crossroads) (Figure 3.20). Whatever the object and whatever the purpose, you should be judicious in choosing your treatment of foreground elements because they may distract your viewer from observing the more important details that are staged deeper in your shot.

This type of overlapping or obscuration would work if your story involves someone "spying" on a character and the shot using excessive foreground elements is a POV (Figure 3.21). If an object in the foreground, typically blurry and underexposed, were to move across the screen momentarily and entirely obscure the subject in the middle ground, then you have what is called a **natural wipe**. This can be arranged by the filmmakers or just happen on

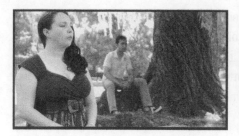
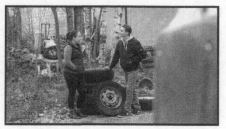

FIGURE 3.20 The foreground elements help to set up depth cues in the shots. (Photo credit: B – Anthony Martel)

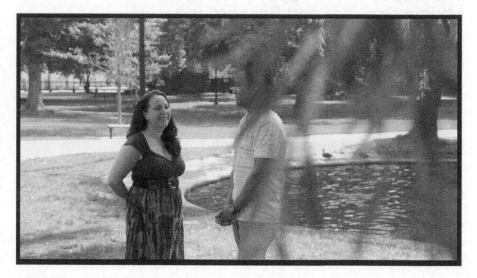

FIGURE 3.21 If used as a POV shot, the foreground elements create a sense of mystery or of spying.

set, but this momentary blackout, as it were, can be used as a convenient cut point to a new coverage shot while editing. (See Chapter Six for subject and camera motion.)

Middle Ground

Regardless of the size of your shooting location, much of your important action may be staged in the middle ground. This is the zone where dialogue can unfold, a couple can dance, or a car can pull up to a stop sign. All or most of the physical action is visible within the frame. The audience are likely to receive all of the information within the shot when the main action is staged here. The middle ground is much easier to establish in wider shots such as medium and long shots (Figure 3.22). With the close-up family of shot types, it gets trickier to find the depth to show all three zones, but it is still possible if you plan well.

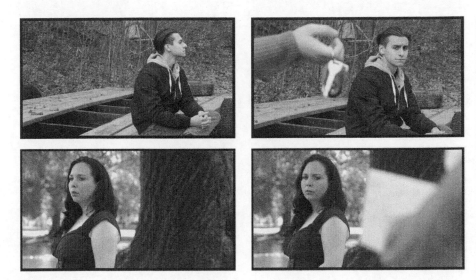

FIGURE 3.22 The subject occupies the middle ground of the image. The entrance of the foreground element later in the shot underscores this and adds to the complexity of the story and enhances the illusion of deeper film space. (Photo credits: A & B – Anthony Martel)

In addition to your subject's distance from the camera, be aware that choices such as lens focal length and depth of field focus placement will also play into your middle-ground delineation. (Keep reading this chapter to learn more on these topics.)

Background

You now understand foreground and middle ground, so it will be easy to guess what the background is: everything behind the MG out to infinity (Figure 3.23). Of course, if you are shooting an interior location, such as a restaurant, then there will be no infinity. The physical space behind the main action being recorded will be the background of your shot. The other patrons eating, the servers walking about, and the wall at the back end of the room all become part of the shot's background. The BG zone can be rather barren, like the dunes of a desert, or rather busy, like the commotion found along a city's avenue. When shooting on location, you may be limited by how much you can control the BG, but you should try to frame your shots so that the background does not overpower the main action in the middle ground. Later, we will discuss how focus and lighting can help to direct the attention of your audience into the various depths of FG, MG, and BG; the OTS shot discussed earlier is a good example of this practice (Figure 3.24).

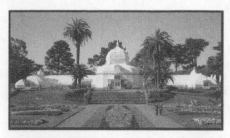
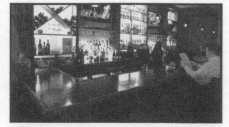
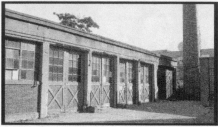
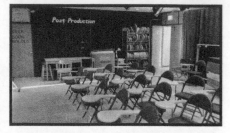

FIGURE 3.23   The background is like the backdrop of a theater stage. It sets the location for exterior and interior scenes.

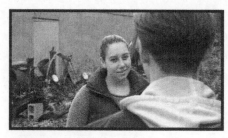
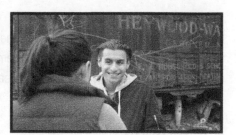

FIGURE 3.24   A traditional OTS shot represents all three "grounds" in the depth of the film space. Objects occupy FG, MG, and BG. (Photo credits: Anthony Martel)

Depth Cues

Overlapping

The combination of foreground, middle-ground, and background elements helps to create the illusion of three dimensions on the 2D film frame through overlapping. The physical objects in your video frame accomplish this just like the layers in your photo-editing or animation software. A tree branch in the foreground will partially obscure the elements of the MG and BG. The main action that takes place in the MG will obscure visual elements found in the BG zone. So, just like in real life, when objects (static or moving) appear to be in front of one another, it allows our brains to establish depth cues (Figure 3.25).

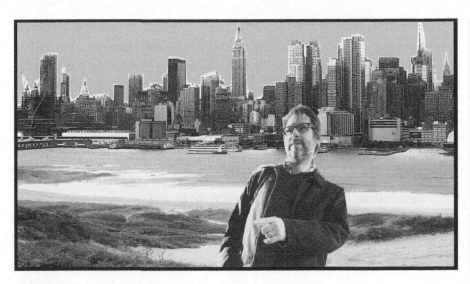

FIGURE 3.25 The layers of this simple motion graphic animation overlap to help to create depth cues.

Object Size

Building on our understanding of diagonal lines, perspective, and vanishing point, we can learn a little bit more about the illusory world of object size relating to depth cues. In Figure 3.26, we see a representation of telephone poles down a train track receding to the horizon line. We know that all of the poles depicted are supposed to be 40 feet tall, yet

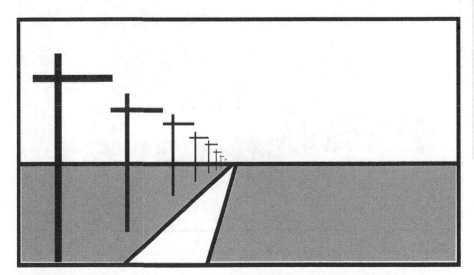

Depth Cues

FIGURE 3.26 The telephone poles are the same height but appear to get shorter as they recede into the distance. Known object size and linear perspective indicate a greater shot depth in this composition.

the pole nearest to the horizon line appears to be a mere fraction of the size of the closest pole in the foreground. A viewer will pick up on this relationship between apparent size and implied distance and assume that the background of the shot goes far away into the horizon. Linear perspective, this visual trick of the eye, is once again at play in our imagery.

The relative size of a known object will trigger depth cues like this in your shots. Large objects, such as a city's skyscrapers, appear in your composition. They seem comparatively small when viewed along with the other objects in your frame. From their real-life experiences, the audience will understand that a skyscraper is not a small object, and for it to be seen as small in the image, it must therefore be far away – somewhere deep in the background of the film space (Figure 3.27). Cartoonists and animators use this technique in their illustrations, as did the Renaissance painters who refined and popularized this artistic illusion for creating depth on a 2D plane.

However, many filmmakers (especially those interested in special visual effects) play with this optical illusion to create a false sense of depth where scale and perspective are tricking the eyes and brains of the audience. Oversized props in the MG can look like normal objects in the FG. Miniaturized models of larger items placed in the FG or MG can have the appearance of "normal"-sized items (Figure 3.28).

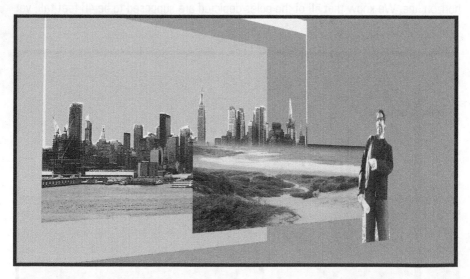

FIGURE 3.27   A city's skyline is significantly larger than a beach path or a man, but its small size in this image indicates that it is far away.

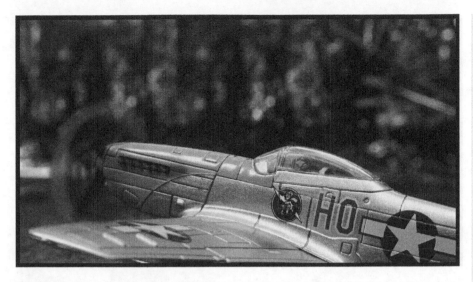

FIGURE 3.28   This airplane: is it real or is it a toy?

Atmosphere

Another depth cue, found especially in wide or long exterior shots, is **atmosphere** (or **atmospherics**). If you have ever looked up a long street in the city or stood atop a hill in the countryside and stared off toward the horizon, then you may have experienced the dissatisfaction of a less than clear view. Perhaps the distant hills or distant buildings seemed blurry or hazy or even totally obscured. This is often the result of what are called atmospherics: the presence of particulates suspended in the air (Figure 3.29). This is most often water vapor, but it may be smoke from a nearby fire, dust, pollen, or even pollutants.

When you stand in this atmosphere, it may not obscure your vision of local objects very much (unless it is thick ground fog), but, when viewed across a greater expanse (as in an XLS), the cumulative effect of the particles in the air causes distant objects to be obscured. If you were to record a shot in such an environment, the viewing audience would immediately understand the depth cue. Fog machines are often employed for just such a purpose on film sets, in addition to the diffusion of light and the creation of mood (Figure 3.30).

Depth Cues

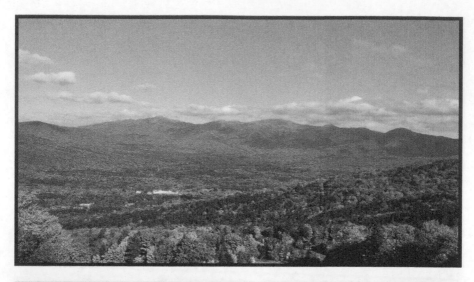

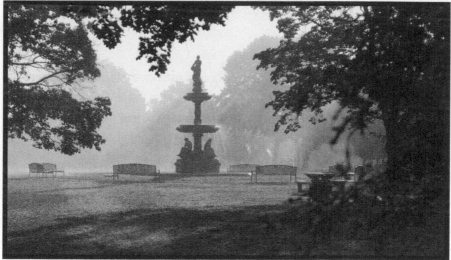

FIGURE 3.29 The atmosphere obscures the background, implying greater distance.

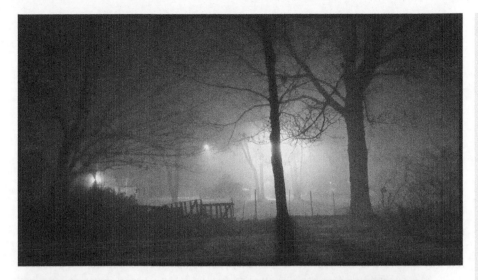

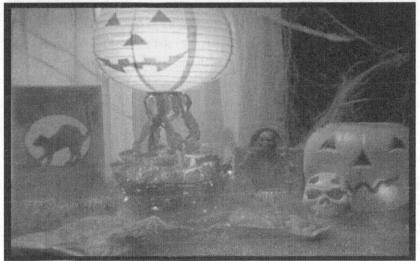

FIGURE 3.30   Manmade "fog" on set helps to create a mood in these environments and catches backlight.

The Camera Lens: The Observer of Your Film World

All of this talk of frames, headroom, lines, and depth cues is great, but there would be no grammar of the shots for us to discuss if there were no lens on the camera to record those shots. So, let us switch gears a bit and focus some attention on an extremely important piece of visual storytelling equipment: the camera lens.

The Camera Lens: The Observer of Your Film World

For all of its complexity, the modern camera lens still performs the same tasks that it has done for a very long time:

- It collects light rays bouncing off the world in front of the camera (the scene you are shooting) from a particular range or **angle of view**.
- It focuses those light rays onto whatever recording medium you are using (a video camera's digital sensor or maybe emulsion film).
- It controls the amount of light that hits the light-sensitive recording medium in your camera.

It can be that simple, yet the job of the lens, the types of lenses, and the quality of lens materials can vary widely.

It is through the lens that your frame is bound, your composition is created, the perspective is set, and the **exposure** is controlled. Depending on the lens that you choose and how you use it, you can achieve very different and stylized looks for your story. Because we do not have the time to delve deeply into the history and current technology of cinema and video camera lenses, we will try to touch on the main points of interest that will help you to make good decisions about your shots and to understand how the choice of lens affects the grammar of those shots.

What Is a Camera Lens?

In its simplest form, a photographic or cinematographic camera lens consists of a few essential parts. A circular glass front element (with a certain diameter and convex curvature) is tasked with gathering the light. A circular glass rear element (which lives closest to the camera body and has a different diameter and convex curvature) is tasked

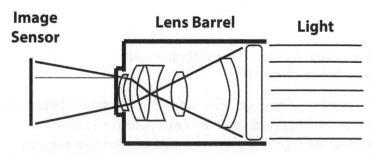

FIGURE 3.31 A cut-away cross-section of a basic photographic lens. Light travels through several glass elements until it is "focused" on the image sensor inside the camera body.

with placing the light rays onto the imager inside the camera. (More complex lenses have more internal glass elements.) An iris or variable aperture is used to control the quantity of light passing through the lens. The glass elements and the iris live inside an otherwise light-tight metal barrel that attaches to the camera body. This lens barrel typically has at least two telescoping sections that allow for the compression and expansion of the barrel's length, causing the front and rear glass elements to get closer or further apart. This enables the light rays to properly focus on the imager inside the camera (Figure 3.31).

Primes v Zooms

Camera lenses for motion picture creation come in two major categories: **primes** and **zooms**. Both types of lens are gauged by their ability to capture light (the **focal length**) and by their ability to pass more or less of that light through (the **f-stop** or **iris**). Filmmakers need to be familiar with both the technical differences and the corresponding aesthetics associated with each characteristic. This is not the place for getting deep into the mathematics and physics of optics and light energy, so we will keep the main concepts rather basic.

- Focal length (FL) is measured in millimeters (mm) and represents the lens' ability to bend the light rays for a greater or lesser angle of view.
- Lenses with lower focal length numbers (e.g., 10mm) have glass elements that bend more light to a greater degree over a shorter focal distance and therefore capture a wider angle of view (you see more of the film space in a larger field of view).
- Lenses with larger focal length numbers (e.g., 300mm) have glass elements that bend less light to a lesser degree over a longer focal distance and therefore capture a narrower but seemingly more magnified angle of view (you see less of the film space, but what you do see is enlarged).
- F-stop is a measurement calculated in fractions of the lens aperture (iris or opening) at a particular focal length and is used to help to gauge exposure. Professional cinematic lenses may have a t-stop (true stop) scale that does the same job.
- Smaller f-stop numbers (e.g., 1.4, 2, 2.8) signify a larger lens opening, allowing more light into the camera and letting you shoot in slightly darker environments.
- Larger f-stop numbers (e.g., 16, 22) signify a smaller lens opening, allowing less light into the camera and letting you shoot in slightly brighter environments. (See Figure 4.3 for more insight into f-stops.)

The Camera Lens: The Observer of Your Film World

The Prime Lens

Historically, prime lenses came first. They are distinguished by the fact that they have only one focal length (e.g., 50mm, 200mm). A filmmaker would have to have several separate prime lenses in his or her "kit" in order to render different magnifications or shot type framings from the same camera position. If you had a camera with only one prime lens and you wished to change the relative size of your subject in your frame, you would have to either move the camera closer to the subject or vice versa. Our initial shot type examples from Chapter One used this technique to generate the images.

Having few glass elements (lenses) built inside, prime lenses tend to be "sharp" and can render a very detailed image when properly focused. The basic construction of the prime lens also allows for it to be "fast" and yield maximum light transmission with lower f-stop numbers (larger apertures). Prime lenses tend to be smaller in size and lighter in weight than zoom lenses.

Prime lenses are used a great deal in professional still photography and high-end motion picture production. They are typically less expensive than the more complex zoom lenses, but you would have to purchase or rent several prime lenses in order to cover your desired range of focal lengths. Most amateur filmmakers cannot consider using primes because their video cameras come with built-in zoom lenses (although DSLR and "prosumer" point-and-shoot type digital cameras have interchangeable prime and zoom lens options).

The Zoom Lens

Most likely, you will be shooting your projects with some format of a digital high-definition video device. Your camera will probably have a built-in lens and that lens will most likely be a zoom lens. The zoom lens is very popular, especially with video camera manufacturers, because the single, built-in lens provides a large range of focal length settings (e.g., 28mm–135mm). You can optically create a variety of shot frames – from a short FL with a wide angle of view to a long FL with a tighter, more magnified field of view – without having to change the camera-to-subject distance.

On your camera's zoom control, the wide end of the lens view is usually marked with a "W" (for "wide") or maybe a "–" (a minus symbol for "less magnified"). The narrow angle of view of the lens setting resulting in greater magnification of the recorded subject is usually marked with a "T" (for "telephoto") or maybe a "+" (a plus symbol for "more magnified"). DSLR and other more professional video cameras can employ interchangeable "cinema" zoom lenses that use a focal length ring on the lens barrel (measured in millimeters or mm) to manually change the magnification of the image and alter the recorded field of view.

Zoom lenses are a complicated construction of many glass elements, telescoping barrels, and sliding rings that all work together to collect light. They can be expensive and often heavy, due to the numerous glass elements needed to achieve the longer focal lengths. Zoom lenses are often not as "fast" as prime lenses. Most of the less expensive ones cannot open to very wide apertures and therefore are not as good to use in low-light conditions. The extra glass elements in zoom lenses may also cause them to not be as "sharp" as prime lenses – particularly around the edges of the image.

Image quality will also suffer greatly if your camera uses a virtual **digital zoom** function rather than an optical zoom. Most smartphone and many low-end video cameras employ a trick, creating a picture that looks like it was taken with a long-focal-length lens setting but, in fact, is digitally generated by merely enlarging an area of representative pixels. This fake zoom factor yields images that are rather blocky, blurry, and of questionable resolution, so it is best not to use them in your higher-quality productions.

Until this point, our discussions of shot types, framing, and composition have all been based on the camera's proximity to the subject. This means that if we had wanted to frame a CU shot, we either moved the camera closer to the talent or moved the talent closer to the camera. This is just like your own eyes. If you want to see something in more detail, you must move closer to it or move it closer to your eyes. The obvious point here is that we do not have zoom capabilities with our human eyes. We have one focal length to our vision, and that is relatively wide (recall the finger-waggling trick from Chapter One). Because we cannot zoom with our own eyes, the zooming shot that moves quickly through a large range of focal lengths can feel very unnatural to the audience. We will further discuss the differences between reframing a dynamic shot with "zooming" or "dollying" in Chapter Six.

Lens Perspective

Having a fixed-focal-length lens in our eyes, we get to see the world from a constant perspective. Camera lenses are manufactured to also have this "normal" field of view (between the extremes of the wide end and narrow end of the zoom range). They appear natural or neutral in their perspective on the subject or scene shown, just as if the scene had been recorded through a pair of human eyes. There is no apparent wide-angle distortion or telephoto compression. Without getting too technical, the "normal" camera lens angle of view depends on the camera-to-subject distance when considering the focal length of the lens, the diameter of the lens, and the size of the format imager (35mm film, HD video, 4K, etc.; see Figure 3.33).

The Camera Lens: The Observer of Your Film World

All of this leads up to one key point, and that is the feeling that your shot perspective conveys to the audience. The normal or neutral field of view captures the shot as if we were there personally observing the action. As soon as you move to the extremes of the zoom range, however, the optical illusions start to creep in.

A wide-angle shot (from the short end of the focal length range with low millimeter numbers) generates an illusion of perspective change between the near and far subjects in the shot. It appears to expand the depth of the shot and optically exaggerates the space between objects, therefore playing up the 3D perspective of the image (Figure 3.32). A wide-angle lens is helpful if you want to make a small film space appear larger or deeper on screen (closet, car interior, airplane bathroom, etc.). It is also good for shooting establishing shots of locations and broad vistas as in an XLS. Due to this illusion of expanded space, any moving object (either toward or away from the camera's wide-angle lens) will appear to move quickly and cover a good deal of film space without much effort. This perspective illusion of quick movement can be used for certain stunt work and for comic purposes.

An image shot with a narrow telephoto angle of view (from the long end of the focal length range with higher millimeter numbers) appears to de-emphasize 3D space. Through magnifying all subjects in the foreground, middle ground, and background equally, an apparent compression of the depth of the film space takes place (Figure 3.34). Objects in the frame have the appearance of being closer together on the screen than they actually are in real life. This illusion of space compression can help you to safely record action sequences or stunt work and is used heavily in the coverage of sporting events when the camera cannot physically be located on the playing field. Be aware that this long lens magnification can make it more difficult to hold moving objects within the tighter frame.

Of course, the more extreme the focal length, the greater the illusion of perspective distortion within the image. This holds especially true for short-focal-length, very wide-angle lenses (sometimes called **fisheye lenses**). You are probably most familiar with this ultra-wide field of view from extreme sports POV action camera footage of surfing, skateboarding, motocross, etc. These ultra-wide lenses create infinite sharp focus, allow for capturing the majority of the action in the unmonitored frame, and help to reduce the appearance of "image shake." These action cams can really warp the depth cues of your shot and exaggerate the 3D space on close subjects (Figure 3.35).

Such extreme fisheye lenses are not typically used to capture most video projects, but a standard wide-angle lens can still cause unwelcome image distortion where objects in the very near foreground appear warped and straight vertical or horizontal lines appear

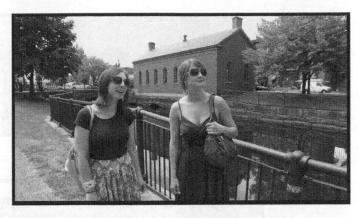

FIGURE 3.32 Subjects seen through a wide-angle lens. Note the apparent distance between the subjects and the background: the illusion of spatial expansion.

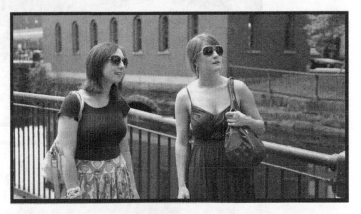

FIGURE 3.33 Subjects seen through a "normal" lens. Note the apparent distance between the subjects and the background.

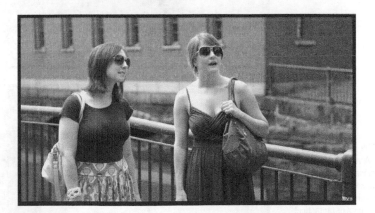

FIGURE 3.34 Subjects seen through a long (or telephoto) lens. Note the apparent distance between the subjects and the greatly magnified background: the illusion of spatial compression.

The Camera Lens: The Observer of Your Film World

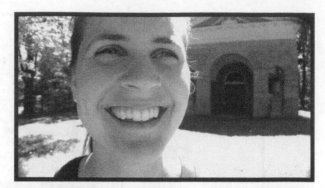

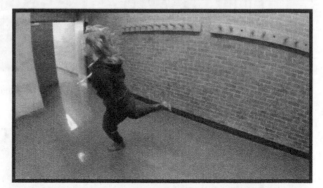

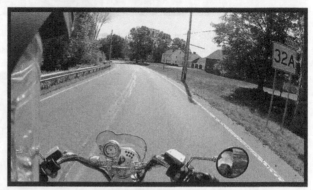

FIGURE 3.35 "Fisheye" lens distortion. A very wide-angle lens very close to your subject can yield this sort of physical distortion within your image. A surreal, comic, or fantastical feeling may be generated by this lens choice. (Photo credit: D – Anthony Martel)

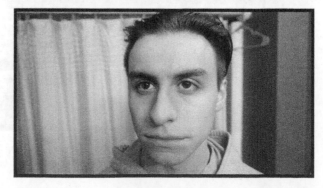

bent or bowed outward. If done for thematic reasons, the grammar of shots like these tells your viewer that there is a warped or distorted view of the film world going on. Something is not quite right. Perhaps it is a nightmare sequence or a fantasy episode, or a character is thinking or behaving in an altered state of some kind. Whatever the creative visual reason, it certainly is not "normal." Much as in still portrait photography, it may be advisable to shoot your subject's close-up shots with a slightly longer-focal-length lens from further away so that you do not exaggerate his or her features (enlarged nose, receding ears, etc.) (Figure 3.36).

When you combine a long lens with subjects further away from the camera, you get a more compressed perspective (Figure 3.34). This compression can imply a "tight" or "flat" life being led by a character, or a place that is constraining or prison-like. The "slice" of background or environment around your subject is also small and confining. When you use a very long lens and you have a subject move from the depth of your shot to a position much closer to the camera, it seems to take a very long time for that subject to cover a very small distance. This illusion is often used to give the impression that this character's movements are futile: he or she just cannot get anywhere, no matter how hard he or she tries. Filmmakers use optical perspective tricks such as these as another tool in their visual toolbox – another part of their cinematic language.

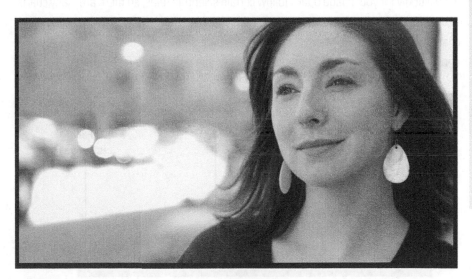

FIGURE 3.36 Using a slightly longer-focal-length lens combined with a greater camera-to-subject distance often leads to pleasing portraiture of subjects in close-up framing. Blurring out the background compels viewers to look at the "in-focus" face.

The Camera Lens: The Observer of Your Film World

Lens Focus: Directing the Viewer's Attention

We now understand that a big part of the look of a shot is established through camera format, proximity to subject, angle, and lens focal length. Creating a composition of subjects that is interesting and appropriate to your story's visual style is a major goal. You will now be staging those visual elements with the rule of thirds and along diagonal and curved lines into the frame's "depth." The foreground, middle-ground, and background zones in your film frame also allow you to unlock an additional tool in your shot construction tool kit: **focus**.

Your eyes can only focus on one thing at a time. As you look from one object to another, your eyes instantly change focus to the new distance of the new object. The illusion of constant focus is achieved, but, in reality, you are only able to focus on one physical plane or distance from your eyes at any one time. Go ahead and try it. Look around you at things at different distances. What is in focus? What is out of focus?

A camera lens behaves in the same way. It can only generate clear, crisp focus at one distance from the camera at one time. This point in space is called the **plane of critical focus**. There is a zone around this distance of critical focus that may also appear to be in acceptable focus (not yet blurry), and this zone is called the depth of field (DOF) (Figure 3.37). Luckily for you, image optics follow certain scientific rules, so there are many charts and tables available to help you to predict this changing depth of field. Referencing these charts will allow you to creatively stage your visual elements into the depth of your set and establish what may be in or out of focus within your frame (see internet and book

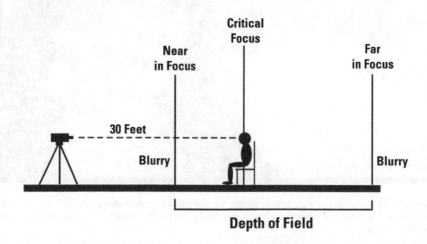

FIGURE 3.37 The plane of critical focus set to the main subject, while the depth of field occupies a distance roughly one-third in front of and two-thirds behind that plane of critical focus.

references for DOF charts in Appendix A). The factors that combine to determine your DOF are discussed in the following few paragraphs.

Depending on the size of your production and crew, setting focus on the lens can be the job of the focus puller, the camera assistant, or the camera operator. Of course, developments in digital camera technologies have been amazing and there are some cameras that use multi-point auto-focus functions that yield fantastic results. Regardless of who or what controls the focus, understanding the uses of focus in showing a story is a key component to creating interesting and effective shot grammar.

Determining what important object within the composition of the frame gets treated to the primary critical focus is often the job of the director and/or the director of photography. As blocking talent and staging the set dressing deep into the shot are now possible, you get to determine where (what distance from the camera) the focus is set and can therefore control what the viewing audience will most likely pay attention to on the screen. Here's another bit of shot grammar for you: what is in focus in your shot is the important thing for the viewer to watch.

Again, the human visual system creates the illusion that all things at all distances are in focus all of the time. We are not accustomed to seeing things blurry (unless we need corrective lenses and choose not to wear them). A camera lens does not know what is or what should be in focus. Only you, the filmmaker, know that. You set the plane of critical focus and the corresponding depth of field according to what you wish to have in proper focus. The audience will want to look at the objects within that zone of most clear and crisp focus. Anything outside the depth of field will appear blurry to the viewer's eye and therefore not be an attractive element to watch.

TABLE 3.1 How to Manually Focus Your Camera's Zoom Lens

1	If your camera is equipped with one, ensure that the viewfinding system diopter is focused and set correctly for your vision prescription.
2	Zoom the lens in onto your subject (face if human) using your longest focal length (highest mm number). This gives you a big "target" to check for proper focus.
3	Set the lens/camera iris setting (exposure aperture) to its widest (lowest f-stop number, largest opening) in order to maximize the amount of light entering the camera.
4	Focus on the subject's face/eyes using the manual focus ring on the lens or the camera controls if so equipped. Moving back and forth "through" the plane of critical focus will help you to determine just exactly where the best point of focus will be.
5	Reframe your zoom lens to your desired focal length and reset your shot composition without touching and/or changing the focus ring or focus controls.
6	Stop down the iris (exposure aperture) to the desired recording f-stop.
7	Record your shot with properly set critical focus.

The Camera Lens: The Observer of Your Film World

As you can see, selecting the focus object is a key component in directing your audience's experience as they watch the elements within the width, height, and depth of your frame. Because the human face and eyes are usually the main objects of interest, you may wish to keep the DOF narrow on the face but blur out the possibly distracting BG (Figure 3.36). This way, the audience pay attention to the subject and not to the unimportant visual elements behind her.

While shooting, check and recheck for proper focus on your subject. Large video monitors on set can help, as can instant playback of video media files that are in question. The keen eyes of the viewer easily notice soft-focus or slightly blurry shots, and unless there is an immediate correction or introduction of some element within the frame that comes into clear focus, the viewer will reject the shot and disassociate from the viewing experience. We are, as viewing creatures of habit, intolerant of things that lack crisp focus. Improper focus remains one critical element of film production that still cannot be "fixed in post," so be extra cautious with how you set it and maintain it throughout your shots.

Pulling Focus or Following Focus

A shallow depth of field allows you to place critical focus on your one subject in your frame; the foreground and background elements will blur out and the audience are left to pay attention to one thing. However, what if you want to have another subject enter the same shot but at a distance that is outside the established depth of field? The new character will be blurry – unless you shift the DOF closer to or away from the camera depending on the distance of this new subject in your shot.

This practice is called **pulling focus** or **racking focus**. If your goal is to keep focus on one moving object within your frame, then you may call it **following focus**. Many less expensive camera lens technologies allow only auto focus, so focus shifts of this nature are harder to achieve. A camera with a manual focus setting or a very advanced multi-point auto-focus function unlocks this creative control for the filmmaker. You can manually move the lens' focus ring in order to actually (optically) shift the focus from one distance to another in the depth of your shot. The current popularity of full-frame DSLR HD video cameras is partly due to this "cinematic" capability of the manually controllable still camera lenses. This shifting of focus within the depth of your shot is yet another technique to help you to direct the viewer's attention around your frame.

As a filmmaker, having the option to pull focus or to follow focus on a particular object requires that certain elements composed in the near and far zones of your shot cannot be in focus. This scenario is typically the result of your conscious manipulation of the depth of field. As you will remember, the DOF is the zone around the plane of critical focus that will appear to be in acceptable focus, and it can grow larger to infinity or shrink smaller to just a few inches or centimeters. As a general rule of thumb, the DOF will be found roughly one-third in front of and two-thirds behind the plane of critical focus (Figure 3.37).

What determines your DOF is a combination of various factors involved in capturing the image. In order to keep it simple, we will just say that the focal length of your lens, the aperture (iris) set on the lens, the size of the format (HD or 4K video sensor or 16mm/ 35mm film), and the distance from the lens to the object of primary or critical focus all work together to determine the overall DOF. The two extremes are shown in Table 3.2.

What this chart tells us is that when you shoot a daylight exterior wide shot of your subject with a short-focal-length (wide-angle) lens, you will generate the largest possible DOF. Most likely, a few feet from the camera out to infinity will be in acceptable focus. Conversely, when you shoot a dimly lit interior XCU with a long-focal-length (telephoto) lens, you will generate the shallowest DOF. Perhaps only a few inches to a few centimeters might be seen in acceptable focus just in front of and just behind the plane of critical focus.

The lesson is that you can face difficulties in controlling (reducing) your DOF in well-lit locations. Lots of light calls for a "stopping-down" of your lens iris (closing to a smaller hole and larger f-stop number) to maintain proper exposure – which expands your depth of field. You can employ tools such as **neutral-density (ND) filters** on the lens to help to lessen the amount of light entering the lens, especially for bright daylight exteriors. ND filters reduce the quantity of light striking the imager without altering the qualities of that light. Some cameras handle this exposure limit digitally inside the camera's processor but still call it an ND adjustment.

A common problem with shooting low-light night-time interiors is a DOF that is too shallow. Your subjects, especially if they are moving, will fall in and out of focus, moving in and out of the very shallow DOF. In order to get exposure, the lens iris has to be wide

TABLE 3.2 Factors that Control the Depth of Field Without Regard to Size of Format

	Large Depth of Field	Small Depth of Field
Focal Length	Short (wide); lower mm number	Long (narrow); higher mm number
Camera-to-Subject Distance	Far; larger distance between	Near; smaller distance between
Lens Aperture	Smaller hole (higher f-stop number)	Larger hole (lower f-stop number)

The Camera Lens: The Observer of Your Film World

open. Adding more light will allow you to use a smaller aperture lens setting and therefore expand the depth of field; more of the important subject can then be in focus (Figures 3.38 and 3.39). If you do not have access to more **illumination**, you may try raising the video camera's digital **"gain"** setting to increase sensitivity, but image quality will most likely degrade and the DOF will not be improved. If so equipped, your camera may also allow

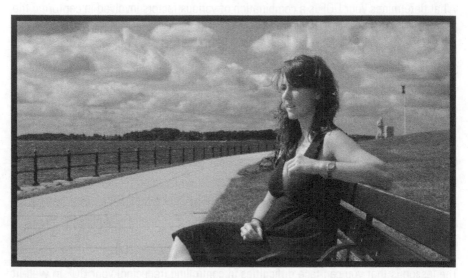

FIGURE 3.38 A large depth of field allows all visual elements in the FG, MG, and BG to appear in rather sharp focus. This can often make it difficult for your viewer to know where to look for the most important visual information.

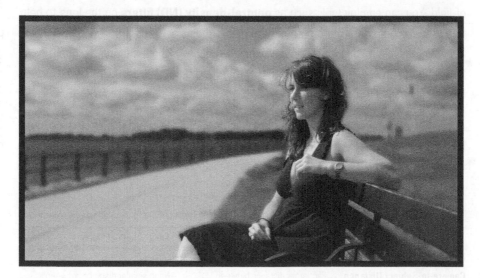

FIGURE 3.39 A shallow depth of field keeps the critical focus on the main subject and blurs the other elements outside the near and far distances of acceptable focus.

for ISO, shutter speed, and/or frame rate changes in order to compensate for exposure/ iris settings and help to further control your depth of field.

Chapter Three – Final Thoughts: Directing the Viewer's Eyes Around Your Frame

The basics of shot grammar began with a visual language consisting of shot types (a method for framing a subject in full or in close-up detail). Our discussion of expanded motion image composition brought the depth of the film space into the conversation. As a 2D medium, video production needs cinematographers and directors to choose angles, frames, staging, and blocking that accentuate the depth of the set or location where action is taking place. Setting the horizon line, incorporating diagonal or curved lines, playing with perspective/foreshortening/vanishing points all work together to help to draw the eyes of the audience deep into the film world.

Lenses, focal length, and setting focus become important considerations for the film-maker. Audiences will search out the object in best focus on the screen. In addition to lines, focus placement is another key tactic that motion imagery creators use to help to draw the viewer's attention around the width and height and into the depth of their shot composition. In the following chapters, you will see how light and movement are also important aspects of image creation and audience guidance.

Related Material Found in Chapter Seven – Working Practices

#8, 10, 12, 13, 17, 18, 30

Chapter Three – Review

1. Elements of your shot composition may be arranged to create the illusion of depth on a 2D image.
2. Keep the horizon line level and steady and place it across your frame for thematic reasons. Raise its height across your frame by tilting your camera lens down slightly. Lower the horizon line in your frame by tilting your camera lens up slightly.

3. Vertical lines indicate solidity, structure, or strength and are good for dividing up the frame into smaller sections.

4. Dutch or canted angle skews horizontal and vertical lines to create imbalance, implying that something is not quite right within the film "world" at that time.

5. Diagonal lines force perspective to a vanishing point at the horizon and create depth. They draw your viewer's eyes into the depth of your shot.

6. Curved lines, natural and soft, help your audience to move their eyes gracefully around and deep into the frame.

7. The depth of the film space: the foreground, the middle ground, and the background are zones where you stage action and that exist at varying distances from the lens (near to far).

8. Overlapping objects are a depth cue that creates layers of objects from the FG, MG, and BG, obscuring or highlighting certain objects in the depth of the shot to showcase their importance.

9. Object size: larger in the frame means nearer, and smaller indicates further.

10. Atmospherics: great distance is implied via water vapor or airborne particulate obscuration.

11. Prime lenses have only one focal length and are often small, "fast," and lightweight.

12. Zoom lenses are single lenses that have the ability to move through a series of wide-angle to telephoto focal lengths and therefore can capture a wide field of view to a narrow field of view of the film space. They are often larger, "slower," and heavier.

13. The fisheye effect is due to an ultra-wide-angle lens whose front element curvature causes near objects to distort bulbously and "bends" horizontal and vertical lines outward toward the edges of the frame.

14. Wide-angle lenses cause an illusion of film space expansion. Objects moving into or coming from the depth of the film frame appear to do so rather quickly.

15. Long-focal-length lenses cause an illusion of film space compression. Objects moving into or coming from the depth of the film frame appear to do so gradually or with very little progress for all of the visible efforts.

16. Creatively shifting focus within your film world's space will direct the audience's eyes around the width and depth of your frame and keep them engaged; pull, rack, or follow focus accordingly. Blurry images are not "artsy," they are physiologically annoying to the human visual system.

17. Only objects within the DOF will appear to be in acceptable focus to the audience. The near distance of the DOF occupies a certain space one-third in front of the plane of critical focus, and extends beyond that point by another two-thirds to the far distance. Several variables help to determine the relatively exact depth of field. Expand, contract, or shift this zone in order to achieve more creative compositions in the depth of your shots and generate energy and visual interest for the viewer.

18. Narrow depth of field is created by combining a long-focal-length lens setting with a large aperture and a close camera-to-subject distance.

19. Expanded depth of field (possibly out to infinity) is created by combining a short-focal-length lens setting with a small aperture and a large camera-to-subject distance.

Chapter Three – Exercises

1. With any camera, go out into the world and record images that have differing horizon lines, strong verticals, diagonals, and curved lines. What physical elements did you use to create each kind of "line?"

2. Compose and record a long shot with a single human subject in the middle ground. Now recompose this shot with some overlapping visual element in the foreground. What object did you choose and where in the frame did you place it? How is the focus? What kind of distances did you have to spread between the camera and the foreground object and the subject in the middle ground?

3. If you have access to a video camera with a zoom lens, place a human subject at least 10 to 15 feet from a stationary camera. Changing only the zoom lens' focal length, frame and record a wide shot of the subject. Then zoom in to a medium shot and record it. Finally, zoom in to a close-up and record it. Next, pick a "middle-ish" focal length on your lens and reshoot the same wide, medium, and close-up shots of your subject, but this time move the camera closer each shot to achieve similar framing and subject magnification as the first set of video clips that you made using the zoom lens only. Compare the results. Edit them together in a simple sequence to watch the paired shots. What differences do you notice? What similarities exist?

Chapter Three – Quiz Yourself

1. What happens when you shoot in outer space? How and where could the horizon line be established?

2. What might it mean for your story if your horizon line is slightly canted or tilted on purpose?

3. What optical illusion (spatial perspective) seems to occur when you shoot with very wide lens focal lengths?

4. True or false: the "f-stop" is the place along the horizon line where two parallel lines appear to converge.

5. The depth of field surrounds what "plane?" In general, how much area of the DOF exists in front of this plane and how much exists behind it?

6. How can you use diagonal lines in your composition to direct the visual attention of your audience?

7. How can you use "planes" of sharp focus and blurry areas in your composition to direct the visual attention of your audience?

8. What three "grounds" exist out in front of your camera and how does "overlapping" play into the illusion of depth within these zones?

9. Your movie involves a dream sequence where the hero runs toward the camera but for all of her efforts she does not seem to gain much ground. Would you use a "short" wide-angle lens or a "long" telephoto lens to achieve this optical illusion of compressed space?

10. Name at least three locations or formations (either natural or manmade) that may contain an S curve suitable for use in a composition where a viewer's eye may be led along it to your subject of interest in the frame. How are S curves different from horizontal, vertical, and diagonal lines in film frame composition terms?

Chapter Four
Lighting Your Shots – Not Just What You See, but How You See It

- Light as Energy
- Color Temperature
- Color Balance of Your Camera
- Natural and Artificial Lighting
- Quantity of Light: Sensitivity and Exposure
- Quality of Light: Hard versus Soft
- Contrast
- Color
- Basic Character Lighting: The Three-Point Lighting Method
- Motivated Lighting: Angle of Incidence
- Set and Location Lighting
- Controlling Light: Basic Tools and Techniques

Unless you are using specialty cameras such as night vision, thermal, or infrared, you will need to illuminate your subjects, sets, and locations. Light allows us and our cameras to "see" and it will allow you, the filmmaker, to show your story to the audience – not merely with basic exposure, but also with creative purpose and intent. The lighting that you design for your video projects and animations can guide your audience's attention around the screen, stress what information to process first, and influence how they feel about what they are seeing – or not seeing, as the case may be. Light is a necessary and powerful tool and a key element in the grammar of your shots.

Light as an Element of Composition

In the previous chapters, we have mentioned how you can lead the eyes of your audience around and into the depth of your shot through frame size, camera angle, creative object placement, and focus control. This chapter briefly explores how light can be used to do the same thing. Values of light and dark can generate a sense of depth in the 2D frame; create feelings of sadness, happiness, fear, etc.; underscore themes about characters; and highlight or obscure the more important subjects in a scene. All of this and more falls within the capabilities of film lighting. It will often be the most powerful creative tool in your filmmaker's toolbox, but that does not mean that it has to be the most complex or the most expensive. Learning about and using light effectively is a lifelong process, so let us move ahead and address some of the basics to help to get us started on our way.

In daily life, our human visual system is programmed to respond to movement, light, and color. It stands to reason that when viewing a motion picture we would respond to these same visual stimuli, plus sharp focus. Knowing this physiological visual response of humans is a great creative tool for filmmakers to use in constructing engaging shot composition. It is very important for you to realize from the outset that well-planned and well-executed lighting can make or break the visual success of a motion picture project.

When you approach your lighting design for a particular project, you should be thinking about an overall look that fits the genre and works well with the messaging, purpose, and story. Can the lighting underscore or work against thematic tones? Does a character or the story require a particular color palette or quality of light? To what types of lighting equipment do you have access, and what techniques might achieve your lighting requirements? Any project can benefit from a solid lighting plan.

Many modern digital video cameras work fairly well with **available light**: light found at a location, either natural or manmade. It is easy for newer filmmakers to just show up, grab a camera, tell the talent what to do, and record their shots – without ever really giving any thought to the lighting. The camera (in auto settings) got a good exposure so is that not good enough? Well, no, not really. Any motion media producer, especially one who is new to the field, should be conscious of his or her use of lighting. Music videos, commercials, and narrative fiction films allow for greater experimentation, but documentary and non-fiction programming require solid attention to the use of light as well.

The art and craft of film and video lighting is a huge topic that is covered well by many qualified training manuals and film production textbooks (see internet and book references on film lighting in Appendix A). We do not have the luxury of addressing all of the scientific, technical, and aesthetic aspects of light and film lighting here, but we will hit on some of the more important terms and practices involved with the discipline.

Light as Energy

No matter what generates it, emits it, or reflects it, light is energy: energy waves of electromagnetic radiation that happen to live in a zone of frequencies known as the **visible spectrum**.

Light itself is invisible, but the surface materials of objects can reflect light in such a way that the human visual system sees it as white, black, or combinations of colors or **hues** from violet, through blue, green, yellow, and orange, to red.

When **white light** (all color wavelengths combined equally) hits an object, and that object's surface reflects all wavelengths equally, you see that object as white.

If an object absorbs all light energy wavelengths, then the object is seen as black. It reflects no significant light energy for you to detect.

When an object absorbs all colors but reflects only one wavelength, you see that object as being that one reflected color. So a yellow object appears yellow because its surface is absorbing all light wavelengths except those from the yellow area of the spectrum.

Not all light sources emit pure white light in a balanced spectrum, but luckily we have ways of measuring the color of light.

As with many forms of energy, light can dissipate across distances. A lighting fixture close to your scene or subject can deliver its light energy more efficiently and at an appropriate level for its intensity (often measured in lumens, lux, or footcandles). As you move that same fixture further from your scene or subject, the effective output remains the same, but the light energy that reaches your subject across this greater distance will be diminished. Be aware of this "drop-off" when you place your lights and/or your subject in your shooting environment. The more powerful the lighting fixture and the more focusable the beam intensity, the greater chance you have of projecting that light source across a larger distance. If you wish to learn more about the mathematical formula surrounding the measurement and calculation of light drop-off, then check out the **inverse square law**.

Light as Energy

Color Temperature

Color temperature, along the scale of **degrees Kelvin**, helps us to understand what color the invisible light is. It is measured in thousands of degrees (roughly 1000–20,000 degrees Kelvin). Without going into all of the science behind it, you should just understand that there are two main colors of concern along the Kelvin scale for film and video shooting: amber/orange and blue. The numbers associated most commonly with these color temperatures are 3200 and 5600 degrees Kelvin, respectively. Film lights (with lamps or light bulbs that have tungsten filaments manufactured specifically for use in motion picture production) generally emit light that is at 3200 degrees Kelvin. Noontime sunlight is roughly around 5600 degrees Kelvin. The lower the number of degrees Kelvin (0–4000-ish), the more red/amber/orange the light will appear. It is often described as "warm" light. The higher the number of degrees Kelvin (4000–10,000 and above), the bluer, or "cooler," the light will appear (Figure 4.1).

The terms "warm" and "cool," used above, do not refer to the actual temperature of anything. Taken from painting's long tradition of color theory, these terms describe the perceived psychological and emotional value given to those color groups by humans who experience them. Reddish/amber can conjure "warm" or "stimulating" feelings associated with firelight, candles, sunlight, natural brown leathers, etc. The "cooler" blue values tend to be seen as "calming" and are associated with overcast skies, moonlight, ice fields, and even morgues, etc. Audiences have grown to accept (and to some degree

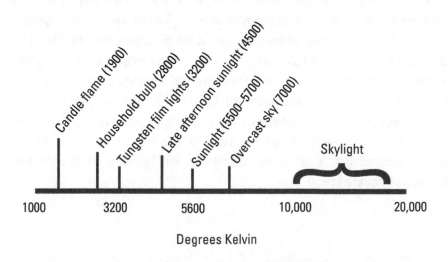

FIGURE 4.1 The Kelvin scale showing various examples of color temperatures of common light sources.

even expect) these color values in film scenes involving such elements. We will discuss more creative uses of color in film production later in this chapter.

Color Balance of Your Camera

These values of degrees Kelvin are extremely important to motion picture production whether you are using digital video or emulsion film. Each, as a light-sensitive medium, is balanced by the manufacturer to see either 3200-degree light as "white" or 5600-degree light as "white." For emulsion films, the balance toward 3200 is referred to as **tungsten balanced**, and the film that seeks 5600 is called **daylight balanced**. The digital light sensors in most video cameras and smartphones (either **charge-coupled devices (CCDs)** or **complementary metal oxide semiconductor (CMOSs)**) are also calibrated to record tungsten (3200) or daylight (5600). Older video cameras often have a setting for both, but modern cameras can usually calibrate across the entire range of color temperatures – either set manually by the camera operator or automatically by the camera's internal processor.

The human visual system (the eyes with their rods and cones, and the primary visual cortex in the brain) does not allow us to see one unchanging field of colors when we look at the world around us. Our brains actually adapt to the mismatched or overpowering color wavelengths that we perceive in a given environment and will, relatively quickly, neutralize or balance out the colors in the picture that we create in our mind. We eventually even out the tones to make it appear "normal."

In a similar fashion, most digital video cameras do a fair job with auto white balance (AWB). The processor examines the light energy and makes its best guess (using algorithms and such) at what color casts need to be removed from the "color neutral" elements of the image being recorded – meaning the white, black, and gray areas. The remaining color scale shifts accordingly and things kind of fall into place. Some cameras (and even smartphone photography apps) allow you to "white balance" or "neutralize" the light entering the camera. This can be accomplished by placing a white card under the light sources that you are using, zooming the lens in on this white card until it fills the frame, properly setting the exposure, and then setting the "white balance" (usually a button found on the camera body or under the menu settings). Whatever the color temperature of the light that you are using, it will now be seen as color neutral by the camera: whites will now appear white, blues will be blue, reds will be red, etc.

Color Temperature

Natural and Artificial Light

Our world is illuminated by two types of light sources: natural and artificial. Motion media producers need to understand both and find ways to use each alone or both mixed together in their lighting schemes. **Natural light** sources include the sun, the moon, flames, and organisms or substances capable of bioluminescence, and each can have different Kelvin temperatures. However, there are manmade film lighting fixtures (**HMIs** and new **LEDs**) that also emit light waves around the region of 5500–6000 degrees Kelvin. These lights can be used to augment or replace natural sunlight/daylight. The daylight calibration derives its name from its chief supplier, daylight, and it may fall under the category of natural light. When shooting daylight exteriors, an easy way to add to your light levels is to bounce or reflect the free and available light onto your film set or subjects (more on this technique later).

Any kind of light source generated by a manmade device can be called an **artificial light**. Examples could include neon lights, a household incandescent or CFL bulb, overhead fluorescent lighting, a computer or TV LCD screen, LEDs, street lights, car headlamps, a flashlight, etc. Because artificial lights produce light of a wide range of color temperatures, filmmakers try to use special lighting fixtures and lamps that have a known or programmable color output, or they use all the same kind of lamp in multiple fixtures so that there is at least some consistent color output on the scene. Tungsten lighting was the traditional film light for much of the latter half of the 20th century, and is so called because tungsten is the chief element in the metallic filament inside the light bulb (or lamp) that glows "white" hot when electricity is run through it. Many people also refer to this kind of light as film or quartz lighting and, when new, these bulbs emit 3200-degree Kelvin waves.

Correcting or Mixing Colors on Set

You must be careful which light sources you use with which color temperature-balanced film or video. If you give daylight energy waves to a tungsten-balanced medium (film or video sensors expecting 3200 degrees Kelvin), it will record an image with a bluish tint. If you give tungsten light to a daylight-balanced medium (film or video sensors expecting 5600 degrees Kelvin), it will record an image with a reddish tint (Figure 4.2). Generally, you should match the color temperature of your light source with the color temperature sensitivity of your film or video medium.

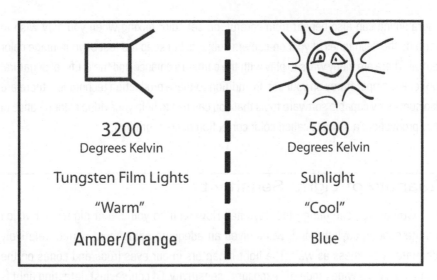

3200
Degrees Kelvin

Tungsten Film Lights

"Warm"

Amber/Orange

5600
Degrees Kelvin

Sunlight

"Cool"

Blue

FIGURE 4.2   The two main color temperatures for video and film.

Traditional compensation for color imbalance on film sets is achieved with a wide range of colored gelatin sheets that are placed on the lighting fixtures to alter or correct the color output of the raw lamp. The two most common **gels** used are **Color Temperature Orange** (**CTO**) and **Color Temperature Blue** (**CTB**). These, and other gel sheets available, typically come in various gradations of strength (such as 1/8, 1/4, 1/2, and full) and may be combined in various ways so that the lighting fixtures match your camera's balance and other light sources in use on set.

Advancements in lighting technology (particularly fluorescent and LCD fixtures) have made this process a bit easier. The LED film **luminaire** can be "dialed in" to emit both a variable intensity and a variable color temperature through the 3200 to 5600 range. An additional perk in using LED lights is that they have a very low power consumption rate and a very low heat output, and, being typically a flat-panel form factor, take up less room around the set or location. The traditional tungsten bulb in artificial film lighting units requires a large amount of power, generates large amounts of heat, and, depending on the size of the lamp's wattage, can live inside a rather large and heavy metal housing.

It is possible to mix natural and artificial lighting and color temperatures for creative or dramatic purposes. Often, you will see a night-time interior scene with warm household lights juxtaposed with cooler "blue-ish moonlight" coming in the windows. This kind of color treatment in fiction filmmaking is an additional tool that can help you to show your story and emotionally manipulate your audience. Non-fiction or documentary

Color Temperature

programming can also benefit from careful, on-set color mixing when you may wish to warm up the flesh tones of your on-camera subjects but keep the rest of your image color neutral. There are many ways to play with the camera's balance and the artificial or natural light color temperatures on your set. In addition to these production techniques, there are also some very capable software tools that you can use to help your video color balance in post-production: a process called color correction or color grading.

Quantity of Light: Sensitivity

How well do you see during the daytime? How well do you see at night? Our vision is quite good in daylight, and, when given an adequate adjustment period, relatively adequate in darkness as well. The light receptors in our eyes (rods and cones on the retina) do have a wide range of "exposure" sensitivity. Of course, just detecting light is one thing but forming a good image is another. We have a particular minimum threshold for reacting to light energy – a bias toward needing more light to see properly in both **luminance** (brightness) and **chrominance** (color) values. The majority of emulsion films and video sensors are modeled after our own vision capabilities: they are also biased toward needing a fair amount of light to create a quality image. Remember that light is energy; when you have less light, you have less energy to cause a reaction on the imaging device.

Unlike our eyes, most light-sensitive material is manufactured to have one "recommended" or "best-performance" light sensitivity rating or "speed." We say "recommended" because although the technology is calibrated to this rating for best results, you are free to creatively deviate from this suggested value. It is most often represented by a number calculated by the International Organization for Standardization in an ISO rating), or it is noted in the form of an exposure index (EI) or perhaps even an ASA or ANSI rating. These light sensitivity ratings are a scale of numbers. Lower values (50, 64, 100, etc.) indicate that a large amount of light will be needed for proper imaging, while higher values (400, 800, 1600, etc.) indicate that less light is required to react and form an image. Many digital video sensors are built to a moderate/high sensitivity of 320. DSLRs and other more "processor-based" imagers can dial in a very wide variety of ratings that you get to choose in the menu settings. Be cautious when selecting higher ISO settings (1600, 3200, etc.) because the video quality will typically degrade: blocky, pixelated/grainy, with poor color rendering and milky contrast levels.

Quantity of Light: Exposure

With this sensitivity rating in mind, you can provide your camera's light-sensitive medium (CCD, CMOS, film) with the manufacturer's recommended quantity of light and yield a good image. This is known as achieving "proper" exposure. You have exposed the imager to the "right" amount of light. We've gone quotation mark happy in this section because so much of this practice is subjective – relative to the technology's abilities and your story's creative visual needs. Traditionally, a "proper" exposure represents an image with a wide-ranging tonal or **gray scale** (dark areas to bright areas: see Figure 4.9) and a faithful depiction of color or hue values. However, what is appropriate for the look of one project may be totally inappropriate for the visual mood or tone of another.

Keeping things simple, the basic exposure for your camera's sensitivity settings is affected by several factors:

- *Quantity of light on your scene*: Are you using very bright, direct sunlight, many large film lights, or just a single candle flame? The amount of light that you place on your actors, set, and location helps to determine how faithfully your image is created in the camera. Typically, more light is better than less light because it is easier to reduce the amount of light entering your camera but it can be difficult to add to it.

- *Camera aperture*: How much light do you let through your camera lens? The iris (often related to the f-stop scale) controls the quantity of light entering the camera to expose the image sensor. "Opened up" (larger aperture) lets in more light, while "stopped down" (smaller aperture) lets in less light (Figure 4.3).

- *Shutter speed/exposure time per frame*: Some cameras are set to 1/30th of a second for each frame, others are 1/50th or 1/60th, and still others have a variable electronic shutter speed to control the "length of time" that the sensor is exposed to the light, down to 1000ths of a second. Higher shutter speeds create more crisp, "frozen-in-time" renderings of the image in motion, but require more light on the scene to do so. Lower shutter speeds require less light for exposure, but usually result in motion blur of moving objects within the frame.

Given the quantity of light on your scene, most video cameras can automatically adjust for proper exposure. Certain models have manual settings where you get to control your iris, shutter, etc. Either way, you most likely have a **light meter** built into the video camera. When calibrated to your medium's light sensitivity rating, this internal meter is used to help to measure the quantity of light reflecting off your scene and recommends the

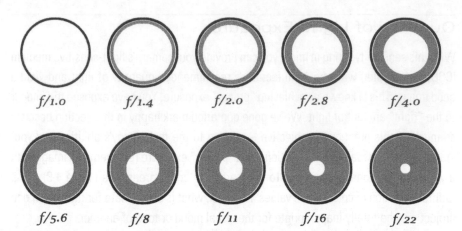

FIGURE 4.3 The iris scale, or aperture settings of a lens. Note that the larger openings seem to have lower numbers, but, in fact, all f/stop numbers are fractions under "1/" so 1/2 is indeed larger than 1/16.

appropriate iris setting given the shutter speed (automatic or continuously compensating exposure). With manual options, you have greater creative control over how the lit scene gets recorded by the camera.

If you recall, neutral-density (ND) filters (either lens adapters that you affix to the front of the camera lens or some selectable option built into camera electronics) will help you to reduce the amount of light hitting your sensor. These useful filters reduce the quantity of light but do not alter the quality of light, which can certainly come in handy while controlling exposure and your depth of field. Gain control is also present on many older cameras, allowing you to increase the amount of electronic processing that the video signal receives. Although it may appear to help to make a darker scene brighter, it typically comes at the cost of image quality.

If you provide too much light to your camera, you can **overexpose** the image. This is done by flooding your filming environment with large quantities of light energy, by opening up to the largest iris setting, or by cranking up your ISO setting. You shift the gray scale up to show only middle gray and white and there will be no black values (deep shadows, etc.) in the recorded frame. The resulting image will be too bright and have "blown-out" highlights (Figure 4.4). Of course, your story may call for such a visual treatment of a scene.

Filmmakers have used overexposure to indicate being in Heaven, a flashback or dream sequence, a POV from a character who has been drugged, a hot desert scene, etc. Overexposure is also used a great deal in music videos. Be aware that most video cameras do not react well to large amounts of light and will not record image details in those bright areas of your frame. If your video image has serious overexposure (burn-out in the highlights), then it will stay that way forever because there is no fix for this lack of image data in post-production color correction.

If you do not provide enough light to your image sensor, you can **underexpose** the image. This is done by shooting in a very dark environment, by stopping down your iris too much, or by severely lowering your ISO setting. It will be, overall, too dark. The gray scale shifts down to mostly dark and only up to mid-gray without having any bright or white areas in the image at all (Figure 4.4). Details in the dark areas of the frame cannot be recorded and color values suffer as well.

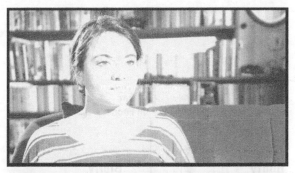

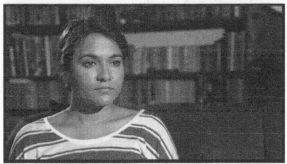

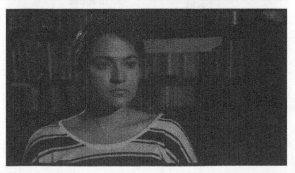

FIGURE 4.4 The range of exposures. A – Overexposure blows out highlight regions of the image;. B – Averaged exposure should represent all portions of the gray scale: C – Underexposure loses details in the shadow regions. "Proper" exposure is whatever the story calls for. Creatively speaking, you may wish to severely under- or overexpose a few shots in your film due to story requirements, but most shots should be in a moderate range of exposure.

Quantity of Light: Exposure

You may decide that a certain scene for your story could benefit from being underexposed, but be aware that video cameras will often produce "video noise" (like film grain) when you do not provide enough energy to make the imager react properly. The image can look muddy with speckled, muted colors popping around the dark areas. It may be better to provide plenty of light to the subjects that you do wish to see and stop down the iris. The brighter things that you care about will be exposed well and the darker areas can reveal more detail but retain a truer representation of "black values."

Achieving basic exposure of the visual elements within your frame is just the beginning. Achieving creative control over how much light you put on your film set, where you place it, and what quality of light you use is your real goal. As you have seen, light affects many other creative choices.

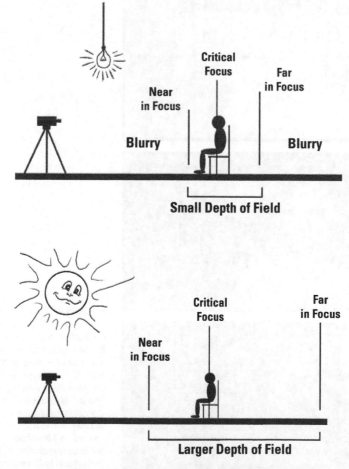

FIGURE 4.5 The amount of light on your scene can directly affect the depth of field focus range.

One easy lesson to remember about the quantity of light and exposure is that the more illumination you have available on set, the larger your depth of field (DOF) can be (think daytime exterior). You would have to close down your camera's iris to block out more of the available bright light, which, in turn, increases your DOF. The less light you have on your scene, the more shallow your depth of field will be when you open up your iris. So purposefully limiting the light used for your scene's exposure can not only illuminate certain areas as needed, but can also help you to creatively alter what is in or out of focus in your shot (Figure 4.5).

Quality of Light: Hard versus Soft

Beyond the color temperature and the quantity of light, most filmmakers are also concerned with the quality of the light: not how good or how bad the lighting looks, although that is extremely important, but how hard or how soft the beams of light are that illuminate the subjects and the set or location. Let's explore what we mean by the terms "hard" and "soft" light.

Hard Light

If you have ever stood outside on a cloudless day, you no doubt noticed how distinct your shadow was. A hard-edged shadow is the primary giveaway that you are using a **hard light** source. The sun, as a **point-source** light, sends its light waves to Earth and, for the most part, they are parallel to one another. They create a single, deep shadow with well-defined edges (Figure 4.6).

These parallel light waves are very **directional**. As they leave their source and encounter some physical object, they will illuminate the nearest surface brightly, get blocked by that object, and cause a hard-edged shadow on the background. This does not mean that hard lights (with parallel rays) are brighter (have more energy or intensity) than softer lights; they are just more focused. Hard light can cause objects in your frame to "pop" off the screen or stand out from other objects. Because it is so directional and therefore more controllable, you can pinpoint your light beam to strike very precise areas of your set. When placed at the side or back of your film set, hard lights can create rims, halos, or "kicks" of light around people or on surfaces.

Hard light, depending on its application, can also create scary, harsh, or mysterious environments (think film noir, horror, etc.). It is often less pleasing on the human face and can cause harsh eye socket shadows (top light), highlight skin imperfections (think the

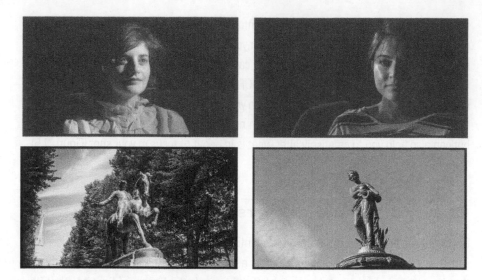

FIGURE 4.6   Examples of hard light. (Photo credit: C – Brennan Marlow)

surface of the moon), and, from the front, flatten features, etc. That is not to say that hard light is not or should not be used to illuminate the human subject – it is and it can be; just be aware of what it does and how you can use it most effectively in lighting shots from your story. As you will see later, the **angle of incidence** for a hard light source can have great influence over how "well" it illuminates your subject or location.

The biggest and most readily available hard light source is our sun (on a cloudless day). It is free to use, so take advantage of it during your production as much as possible; just be aware of a few factors. Consider the sun's direction (angle from up in the sky) and where it puts the shadows. What is the actual exposure/iris setting and your resulting depth of field? How long will it take to shoot your scene coverage versus how much time is left in usable sunlight? Remember that motion media production on location can take a significant amount of time and the sun will be constantly changing position. Depending on your latitude and the season of the year, you may have the best luck shooting during midday hours with the angle of the sun (and its apparent color temperature) not changing as much or as quickly as it does during early morning and late afternoon. Just watch out for harsh shadows under eyebrows and noses. Did you look at the weather forecast? Is there impending cloud cover that can change your lighting look? There are apps to help you with these important details.

In addition to the sun, artificial hard light sources can include fixtures known as open-face units, enclosed Fresnel units, HMIs, and newer LED spots.

Soft Light

Soft light is very diffused light. If you were to go outside on a very cloudy, overcast day (with no direct sunlight visible), you would not easily see your shadow at all or, if you did, it would be very faint and not hard-edged. The hard, parallel rays of sunlight hit the clouds in the atmosphere and then get all jumbled up and diverted into many different directions and bounce around our atmosphere. This diffused light of multi-directional energy waves comes at objects from many sides and therefore it illuminates more evenly all around – not hard and directional from one side but soft and diffused from all angles.

Almost any light source can be made into a soft light by diffusing it or bouncing it off bright or white walls or ceilings (Figure 4.7). Soft light sources tend to be more flattering to the human face because they cause little in the way of deep shadows. The light seems to wrap around the curves, bumps, and contours of the facial structures (brows, nose, cheekbones, etc.), smoothing out the surfaces. For interior scenes, soft light may feel more natural because most lighting fixtures in reality (in homes, offices, stores, etc.) emit non-parallel rays. Because of this, soft lighting can imply a sense of warmth, friendliness, or romance when used in motion pictures (Figure 4.8).

Soft film lighting fixtures include fluorescent lights, anything with a frosted lamp, and any light housing that diffuses the light energy either by passing it through a diffusing material or by bouncing it off curved, internal surfaces. Actual hard lighting fixtures can be softened by bouncing their directional beams off a white but marginally textured surface or by passing the beam through a diffusion gel sheet or white silk flag before it falls on the subject (Figure 4.7).

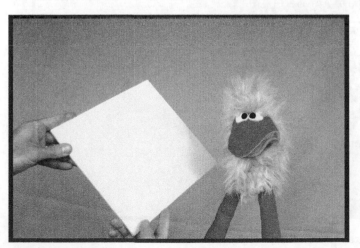

FIGURE 4.7
Reflecting or bouncing light off bright or white matte-finish surfaces (like bounce cards, painted walls, or acoustic tiled ceilings) will diffuse the light rays and soften the light falling on your subject. This is also an easy way to get usable fill light from your key source.

Quality of Light: Hard versus Soft

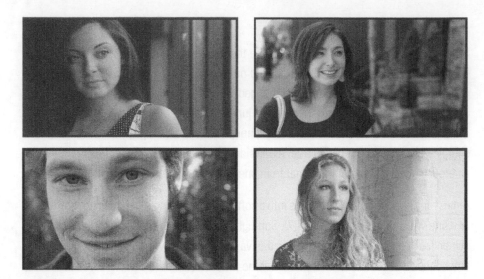

FIGURE 4.8 Examples of soft light. Notice the lack of deep, hard-edged shadows on the talent's face and neck. Soft light is often considered more natural, pleasing, and forgiving. (Photo credits: C – Darby Andersson; D – QiHui Zhang)

Contrast

The relative differences between light areas and dark areas within your frame are referred to as the image's **contrast**. Most often, the image creator's goal is to have a well-balanced contrast within the frame where there are bright regions, dark regions, and a good representation of "grayscale" tones between them (Figure 4.9). An image with good contrast is said to have "snap." A **high-contrast** image is one that contains both areas that are

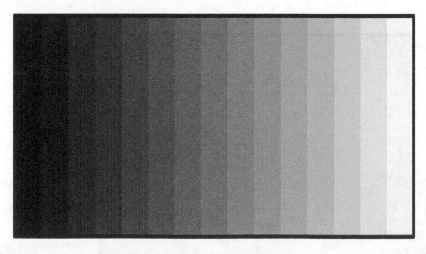

FIGURE 4.9 The gray scale from black, through mid-gray, up to white.

very bright and areas that are very dark, but it lacks a strong component of middle-gray values between the two extremes. High-contrast images can be described as "moody" or "dramatic." A **low-contrast** image contains more even lighting levels across the whole frame such that the delineation between light and dark regions is not well defined. Mostly shades of middle gray, the low-contrast image can look flat and bland.

If you've been using image filters on Instagram or Snapchat, then you've already been playing with image contrast controls to post-process the look of your pictures. Most people gravitate toward preferring mid- to high-contrast pictures and not low-contrast or washed-out images. Low-contrast or washed-out imagery (especially when combined with a muted, less saturated color palette) is often called retro, old school, or vintage because its faded appearance reminds us of old pictures from the 20th century. Use it in your narrative film during a flashback to olden times or maybe during a dream sequence.

Low-Key Lighting

High-contrast, snappy, or "punchy" lighting schemes can make for more dramatic or suspenseful imagery, but they also yield more depth to your frame. The interplay of light and areas of deep shadow across the foreground, middle ground, and background of your shots helps to create a layering effect within the set's deep physical space. The irregularity of objects in the frame, including the human face and body, gains a relief or modeling

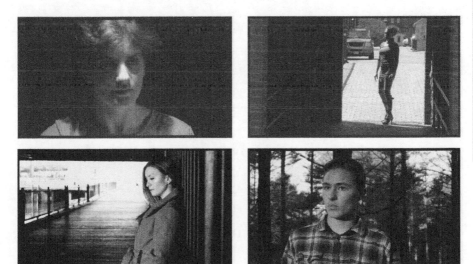

FIGURE 4.10 Examples of low-key lighting schemes showing strong areas of darkness and brightness. (Photo credits: C – Andrew Conley; D – Darby Andersson)

from these pockets of light and dark. This helps them to achieve a 3D appearance in the 2D film frame. A lighting design such as this is often called **low-key lighting**. Hard, directional beams of light (from one or several directions) striking precise locations or objects in your scene can help to create this visual style (Figure 4.10).

High-Key Lighting

Low-contrast, flat, or even lighting schemes can make images seem more open, friendlier, or "brighter," but they also yield a flatter, less visually separated frame. Often, the point of low-contrast or **high-key lighting** is to provide overall even illumination so that all elements of the frame are visible to the viewer. Talk show, news broadcast, and situation comedy sets are often lit in a low-contrast fashion. This way, the multiple cameras that record the events can all receive proper exposure without the need to continually adjust lighting levels on the set. What you gain in even visibility, you lose in dramatic flavor. Additionally, the 2D frame, including all objects in it, will appear flatter and, in the opinion of many, less visually interesting (Figure 4.11).

It is certainly possible to combine the use of both low-key and high-key lighting schemes across your video project. Just as you may mix hard and soft lighting treatments in your motion picture for thematic reasons, scenes with strong **chiaroscuro** can juxtapose well with evenly lit environments or situations. The moods of the story (and the reactions of the

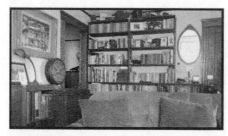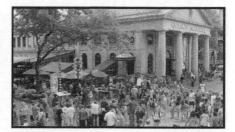
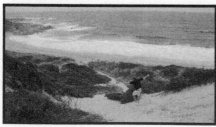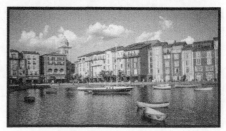

FIGURE 4.11 Examples of high-key lighting schemes: more evenly lit overall. (Photo credits: C – Darby Andersson; D – Brennan Marlow)

audience) change with the differences in lighting. Non-fiction and documentary projects can also benefit from the use of low- or high-key lighting set-ups. A documentary about volunteers who help to save a community center might call for the talking-head interviews to be recorded with high-key soft lighting and a shallow depth of field accentuating the happy faces of the subjects. Meanwhile, a non-fiction program about the victims of a violent poltergeist haunting may call for shadowy, low-key hard lighting.

Color

Color is another great creative tool for a filmmaker. Your visual plan for your motion picture project should include color considerations from the outset, as there are many color choices to be made during production and post-production. This is especially true if you are creating an animation, and you have to be aware of every color of every character, object, and background element.

Historically speaking, black-and-white (B&W) still photography and cinematography came first. For several decades, the emulsion film technologies could only reproduce B&W or gray-scale imagery, even though they were formulated to react to the different wavelengths of energy from the different colors of light. The original video formats for television were also only capable of B&W pictures. Filmmakers initially experimented with hand painting each frame of celluloid or ink tinting entire strips of film in order to achieve a color effect. Advancements in color processes for both film and video were very expensive and often reserved just for musicals, adventure stories, or grand entertainments. It is popularly understood that viewers of the day felt B&W movies were more realistic and color films were fantastical – an ironic twist, considering that we see reality in color with our eyes every day and B&W visual treatments are a visually creative fiction.

Today, the quality or look of your recorded color imagery is related to many factors. The type of camera that you are using (image sensor color sampling, compression processing, bit depth, etc.), the quality and quantity of light energy that you use for exposure, and the actual colors of the wardrobe, set dressing, exterior environment, etc. all play a role. We will not dig into the numerous technologies and processing algorithms here, but instead we will touch on some of the basic characteristics of color and how you might use color more consciously in your motion media projects.

As we know from our discussion on light energy and color temperature, the colors of light have particular wavelengths. These energy wavelengths are interpreted as electronic voltages in both video cameras and on computer editing systems and show as particular hues. Color **saturation** is directly related to how much light energy you have on your scene and the "color reflectance" values of the object being recorded. If you have very little energy on the scene, you will generate low color voltages and the colors will render as muted or de-saturated. If you have a larger amount of light energy, the voltages are higher and the colors will be more saturated.

Saturated colors (deeper, more vivid) in combination with a higher contrast level will make the image "snappy" and more vibrant. Children's programming, cartoons, commercials, music videos, and musical theatrical films can all use highly saturated color palettes. They generally make the audience feel happy, bright, energized, etc. Low-contrast, low-energy images can appear more de-saturated, muted, or grayish. Images with this look lack that visual "snap" and can seem somber, dull, low energy, or "vintage" to the audience.

Colors can be used as symbols or identifiers as well. Countries have colorful flags, sports teams have colorful jerseys, and film environments can have colors associated with them as well. The "soulless" financial executive sits in his modern, high-rise office awash in a muted, steely blue-gray. A small-town hero is shown around lush green lawns, brown natural woods, and tanned leathers. The nuclear bunker is a jaundiced yellow-green. The princess' rooms are decorated with deep reds and warm golden hues. The color palettes of these places not only help to orient the viewer as to where physically within the film world they are, but also help them to feel a certain way toward the people or events seen in those environments. Additional subtextual information is being conveyed to the audience through these color choices (see color theory references in Appendix A).

Similar color treatments can be done for a character's wardrobe. The angel on Earth, whom no one knows to be an angel, always wears a white suit. The possessed little girl in your horror film always has a red ribbon in her hair. You could also purposefully withhold a particular color from a character throughout the story until there is a dramatic change in personality or world-view – only then allowing that character to be clad in or photographed near that previously absent color. Be aware that darker hues can absorb more light and may be harder to "read" (be seen) on screen. Lighter hues reflect more light and are typically easier to record faithfully in your image. Traditional art color theory also holds that cool colors (blue, green, etc.) appear to recede from the scene in the image, while warm values (red, orange, pink, etc.) appear to advance out toward the viewer. This may or may not have much effect in motion video, but give it a try and see what happens.

Beyond the basics of accepted color treatments (blue for moonlight and cooler temperature locations, such as a meat freezer or the Arctic Circle, or amber for warm, safe places, such as inside a family home at night or a candle-lit dinner for two), a filmmaker can use colors to underscore a story's themes or represent subtextual aspects of a character.

The important thing to remember is that you should always be conscious of the colors in your frame, whether you are using them creatively or not. To actually see color examples of some of the concepts mentioned here, please visit the companion website for *Grammar of the Shot*.

Basic Character Lighting: The Three-Point Lighting Method

How you use hard light and soft light to gain selective exposure on the talent and on the set is a fun part of creative lighting for composition. There are innumerable ways for you to place light on your subjects, and hopefully, over your career as a filmmaker, you will have the opportunity to experiment with many of them. Starting off on solid ground is useful, however, so we are going to explore the most basic standard in subject illumination: the **three-point lighting method**.

The three points actually refer to three distinct jobs that lighting fixtures perform when put into particular placements around the film set. Rather than describing the lights' properties, these terms describe their purposes.

- KEY – The **key light** is the one light source around which you build your lighting scheme. It provides the main illumination to your film set or location. You "key" your other lights (quantity and quality) off this main source. The key light may live anywhere around your subject, but is traditionally placed 45 degrees (horizontally and vertically) off the axis of the camera's lens and above the height of the talent's head.
- FILL – The **fill light** is a light source used to help to control contrast. The light energy that is used "fills in" the shadows often created by the brighter key light. The traditional physical placement of the fill light is on the opposite side of the subject from the key light, roughly 45 degrees (horizontally) off the lens axis.
- BACK – The **back light** is the light that defines an edge, or halo effect, around the backside of the subject. Because it lives behind the subject (the opposite side of the film set from the camera's lens) and provides a light "rim" to the outline of the subject, the back light serves to separate objects from the background and enhance the illusion of depth within the film frame.

The quantity of light from these three light sources must be enough to achieve exposure on the scene. Clearly, the key light will provide the most illumination. The fill light will contribute varying degrees of additional illumination, depending on how low or how high

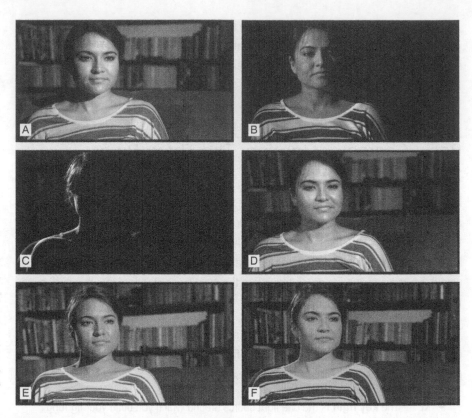

FIGURE 4.12　The evolution of the three-point lighting method in several combinations. A – key only; B – fill only; C – back only; D – key + fill; E – key + back; F – key + fill + back.

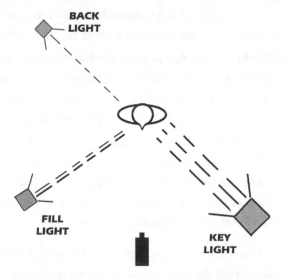

FIGURE 4.13　An overhead schematic of a three-point lighting fixture placement in relation to the subject and the camera.

a contrast difference you would like to have (how much or how little shadow). The back light need only apply enough glow to the edge of the subject to "read" or be recorded by the medium (Figures 4.12 and 4.13).

It should be mentioned that the three-point method for illuminating a subject is a solid, tried-and-true approach, but it is not the only way to achieve appropriate lighting. In fact, it might be preferable to begin your lighting set-up by only placing one lighting fixture. If that single source can achieve the desired look and provide the appropriate exposure levels, then you are done and you may record that shot. If that one source does not fulfill all of the needs, then add a second, third, fourth, or sixtieth (big budget) lighting fixture until you have created the overall look that you desire. Setting lighting fixtures and tweaking their results can take a tremendous amount of time, especially if you are new to using these devices. A key light plus a **bounce board** for fill may generate the same look using less electricity, saving time and therefore also saving the production company money. You will rarely have enough time or enough money for your projects, so help to save on both by being as efficient as possible with your lighting set-ups.

Contrast Ratio or Lighting Ratio

The lighting contrast specific to the human subject is a relationship known as the **contrast ratio** or the ratio of the key + fill side of the face to the fill side of the face only (often shown as key+fill:fill). The quantity of light can be measured with a handheld light meter,

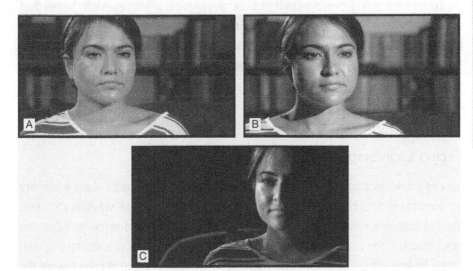

FIGURE 4.14   A – 1:1 lighting ratio; B – "average" lighting ratio; C – high lighting ratio.

but you really should develop your "eye" to gauge the relative amounts of light on each side of the face: is there more or less shadow present? Even light levels on each side of the face would be a 1:1 lighting ratio and would create a high-key scene of even and flat lighting. Differing quantities of light on each side may yield a higher contrast ratio, such as 4:1 or 8:1, and would create a low-key scene with more deep shadow regions on one side of the face (Figure 4.14).

Motivated Lighting: Angle of Incidence

In fictional narrative cinematography, the lighting you see is generally **motivated**, meaning that it is supposed to be generated by some source within the "reality" of the film world you are watching. A desk lamp, a computer screen, a lantern, and even the sun itself are all examples of objects that can motivate light on a film set. This does not mean that these "sources" actually contribute to the illumination of your scene (although they can). It is the job of the film lighting fixtures (tungsten lamps or LEDs, etc.) to add light to your frame and make it look as though the motivating sources are actually providing the exposure. The camera's sensor gets the light energy that it needs to create the desired image and the illusion of a knowable and relatable reality will be conjured in the minds of the audience.

Where you place your film lights around your set is partially dictated by the location of these motivating light sources within the film world. The point of origin for a beam of light determines its angle of incidence. If the light is supposed to be coming from a lighting fixture in the ceiling, then the film light must have an angle of incidence from higher than the subject's head – from above, or **top lighting**. If someone stands next to a campfire, then the film light fire effect must have a lower angle of incidence and come from below the level of the subject's head. To help to sell the illusion of this film world reality, your film lighting fixtures must be placed around your set or location such that they cast their illumination from the same or similar direction as the motivating source.

Front Lighting

Just as you know that the camera can be placed around the subject along imaginary horizontal or vertical circles, lighting fixtures can be placed in similar ways; in this case, think of them more as hemispheres above the subject's waist and below it. When the lamp head is in the upper hemisphere and near the recording camera's neutral angle on action (or lens axis), it is called **front lighting**. If the subject's face is open toward the camera, this lighting tends to flatten out the features by evenly illuminating all surfaces.

This technique is used in fashion portraiture of women because it diminishes the presence of the nose while fully informing the details of the eyes and mouth. The loss of shadow across the face and body can also lessen the perceived dramatic impression for the audience and reduce the illusion of 3D in your composition (Figure 4.15).

Depending on the height of the lamp head in this scenario, you may also cause a shadow on any visible surface behind the subject who is front-lit. Upper-hemisphere lamp heads with a higher angle of incidence force the shadows down along the floor. Any lights at or

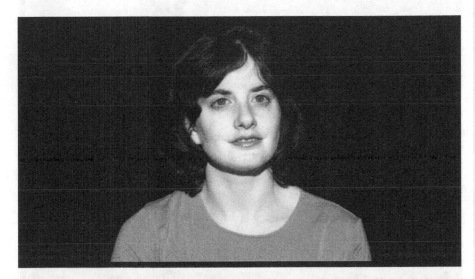

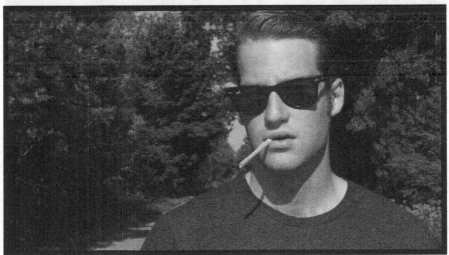

Motivated Lighting: Angle of Incidence

FIGURE 4.15 Examples of even, flat front lighting. Notice how it renders a smoothing-out of the bony features of the face. (Photo credit: B – Darby Andersson)

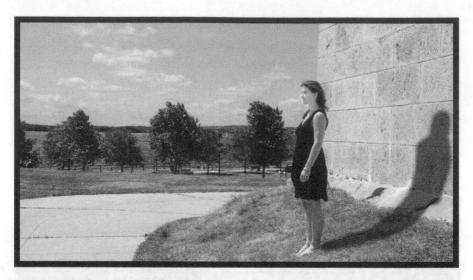

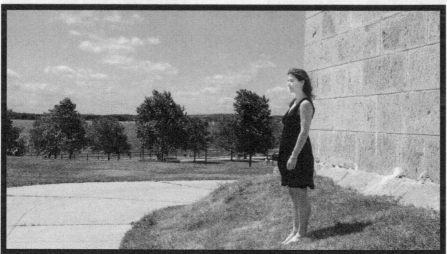

FIGURE 4.16 A lamp height (angle of incidence) may create a subject's shadow that is visible to the camera's lens. If possible, place film lights so that they cast unwanted shadows outside your frame's field of view, either off the side of the set or down to the floor.

below the talent's physical height will throw shadows across and up the set, which can be visible to the camera lens and are often neither visually pleasing nor part of your visual plan. In general, shadows of actors are not welcome on film sets (fiction or non-fiction programming), unless you place them there on purpose because they fulfill a creative or thematic purpose in the story.

Side Lighting

If we continue our way around the imaginary circle and place a lamp head 90 degrees away from the camera, it is called **side lighting**. This holds especially true if the light source is at the same height as the talent's head. Examples might be a bedside lamp, a window, light coming through a doorway from another room, sunrise, and sunset. Hard side lighting can generate a half-bright, half-dark face split along the bridge of the nose (Figure 4.17). Without any fill light, this lighting style makes a bold statement and can conjure feelings of mystery, half-truths, or a split personality. The higher you raise the film lighting fixture, the more it will resemble traditional upper-hemisphere lighting from above, but without a fill light that sense of mystery may still remain.

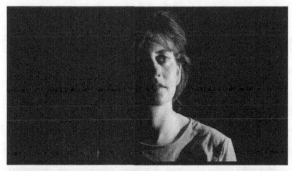

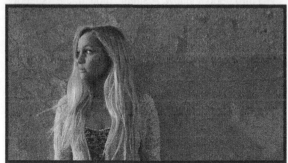

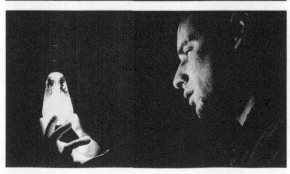

Motivated Lighting: Angle of Incidence

FIGURE 4.17 Examples of hard side lighting. (Photo credits: B – Darby Andersson; C – Andrew Conley)

Lighting from Behind

When the light is behind the subject, opposite the circle from the camera lens, it is often called a back light. As discussed earlier under three-point lighting, the back light helps to separate the subject from the background. Traditionally, it has a higher angle of incidence. If the lamp head is placed between 90 degrees and 180 degrees away from the camera's position, it may be called a **kicker light,** or a **rim light**, highlighting the edges of the hair, the shoulders, and sometimes the jaw bone of the subject. A hard light source may work best for this "hot-kick" lighting glint, as softer back lights tend to yield a more even or dulled-down halo effect with less punch. Backlighting is also used to illuminate water vapor from a fog machine, falling rain, and wet pavement or shiny polished floor coverings like marble, hardwood, and high-gloss vinyl (Figure 4.18).

Lighting from Other Places

Most light sources in the real world, and subsequently in the film world, come from above and slightly away – somewhere in the upper hemisphere. Many lights in our public and private spaces come from above and sometimes from directly overhead. This light that comes from directly above (top lighting) is not always replicated exactly in film lighting. Whether hard or soft, top lighting causes the brow ridges on most faces to block the light from the eye sockets, putting the eyes into deep shadow. A small "moustache" shadow

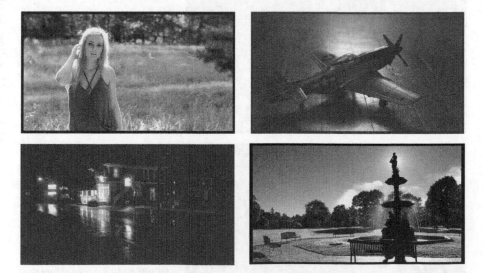

FIGURE 4.18 Backlighting can rim a subject and add highlights to the ground or set dressing. Water, rain, or fog should be backlit for higher visibility in the image. (Photo credit: A – Mike Neilan)

will also be cast on the upper lip by the nose. By keeping the eyes of the character in deep shadow, you take away one very important visual means for the audience to relate to the character. If they can't see the eyes, they probably cannot trust this person (Figure 4.19).

Conversely, if you light from below, you are creating a rather unnatural lighting effect, as very few lights actually exist below the level of our heads in daily life. **Under lighting**, as this is called, causes the structure of the human face to take on a scary or ghoulish appearance and therefore is often used in horror films (Figure 4.20).

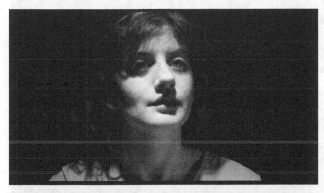

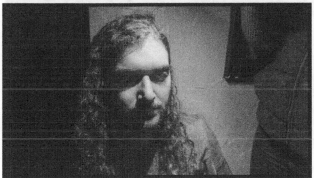

Motivated Lighting: Angle of Incidence

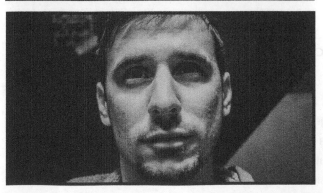

FIGURE 4.19 Top lighting can obscure the subject's eyes. (Photo credits: B – Zach Benard; C – Andrew Conley)

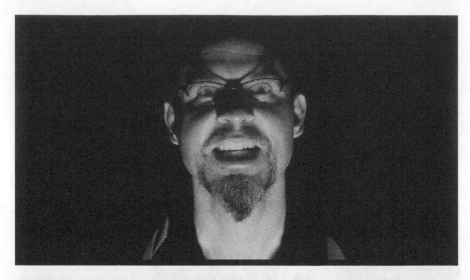

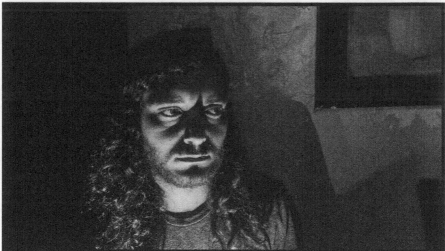

FIGURE 4.20 Under lighting can turn good people into scary people. (Photo credit: B – Zach Benard)

Set and Location Lighting

Placing light on your set or location (on the walls, furnishings, floor, trees, cars, etc.) is often just as important as lighting the faces of your subjects. Certainly, you need to add light to your set for general exposure, but placing light on specific areas of the set or location can add to the ambience of the scene, and change its tone or mood. When shooting dark environments or night scenes, placing lights in the deep background can also help to create an illusion of 3D space by drawing your viewer's eyes into the "depth" of the shot. They can also "rim" a subject and help to further separate him or her from the darker background, etc.

If you have a lighter background on your film set and only illuminate that background and not your subject in the middle ground, you will create what is called the **silhouette effect** (Figure 4.21). Exposing your camera for the well-lit background, and leaving your talent's face in darkness (with no fill light), you form the silhouette. The camera is manipulated to see the bright background as "normal" and it shifts the exposure range on the dark

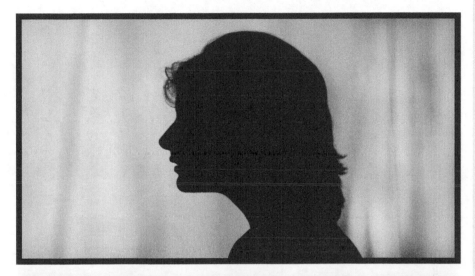

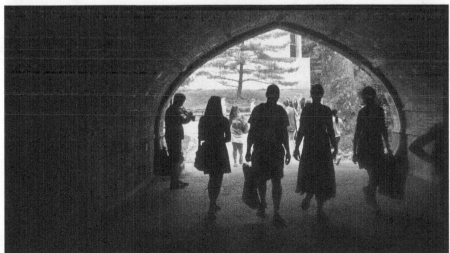

FIGURE 4.21 Whether you are protecting the innocent or creating an air of mystery, the silhouette keeps the subject in constant shadow while the background remains visible. (Photo credit: B – Nicole Girard)

face down into the underexposed values of blackness. Use this for a sense of mystery or intrigue, or to protect the identity of an informant.

Any working lighting fixture that is part of your set dressing or diegetic lighting design (and emits light and adds to exposure levels) is called a **practical**. Its job is to appear within the frame and provide light to the scene. Most often, practical lamps are not bright enough to generate good exposure levels on their own, so they are usually accent lights that provide points of visual interest around the set or act as motivators for other (off-screen) larger

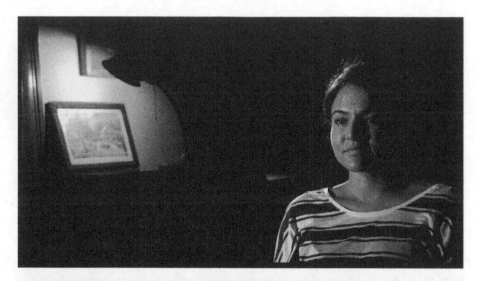

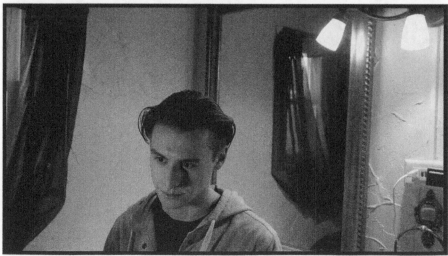

FIGURE 4.22 Examples of practicals. This functional lighting source on set actually helps to give the image exposure but is usually augmented by an off-screen film light. (Photo credit: B – Anthony Martel)

film lights that raise exposure levels on the set (Figure 4.22). These augmenting film lights would need to be of matching light quality, color, and angle. Practical lights can also be a good source of motivation for creative color usage, as in "warm" amber firelight, "cool" blue refrigerator interior light, deep red neon light, etc.

If you are making a **period piece** from the days before electricity, or your story involves a power outage, then you may use light sources such as lanterns, candles, firelight, flashlights, automobile headlamps, smartphones, or any light that is battery or solar powered or runs off a back-up generator. Most recent digital video cameras can get a decent exposure with lower-light conditions. If you cannot or choose not to augment the practical source with film light illumination, then it helps if you shoot most of your shots in medium to close-up framing with minimal camera-to-subject distances. Light energy "falls off" in its intensity over distance, so a faint light source will just look more faint from further away. Keep it close to faces and to the camera for best results in exposure.

Almost any other light-emitting or light-reflecting source can be used as a practical in almost any other film story situation. The important thing to remember is that effective output (intensity of light) may not actually be enough for exposure, so additional film lights will be needed to add levels but maintain the illusion that the light is coming from the practical fixtures. You should also be aware that the color temperatures of these practical lights can vary widely and some color balancing may be necessary. You may use colored gels on your lights, change the color temperature of your LEDs, alter your camera's white balance, or try a combination of all or some of these solutions.

Lighting film set locations can also be wrought with logistical challenges. Does the location have an accessible and reliable supply of electricity? A gasoline-powered generator may be needed to run your film lighting fixtures, so beware of fuel supplies, air quality, and audio contamination on set. Are the **alternating current** (**AC**) power outlets in another room or on another level of the building? A healthy supply of electrical extension cords (stingers) should be brought along. Do you have access to the electrical breaker panel? If not, keep the telephone number of the property manager or maintenance person handy in case drawing too much power on one circuit trips a breaker (Figure 4.23). Know your shoot day's sunrise, arc, and sunset times and locations. Remember that traditional tungsten or "quartz" lighting fixtures can get very hot, causing safety issues for heat-detecting fire alarms, lighting technicians' hands, and the comfort of the talent on set who must perform under these very warm lights. Knowledge of electricity, long-sleeved shirts, and thick, leather gloves are good things to have for anyone handling film lights. Safety first – always!

Set and Location Lighting

Watts / Volts = Amps
3300 / 120 = 27.5
Okay for 30 Amp Circuit

FIGURE 4.23 A very useful formula to help to reduce lighting headaches on set. Ohm's Law will help you to calculate the maximum electrical current draw on a circuit at your location's breaker panel.

Controlling Light: Basic Tools and Techniques

A film lighting fixture is rather like a big bucket of light. Set it up, plug it in, point it to where you want the light to go, and turn it on. If your goal were to just get exposure levels on your subject, then you'd be done with your lighting. Fortunately for all of us, there is more to the process of good film lighting – or at least there should be.

Sculpting with your lights – applying their energy where and how you want – is often the best approach to creating great-looking images. There are many tools and techniques to help you to do this (far more than could be listed in this book). **Grip equipment** will be your best friend to help to control your lights on set. You'll become familiar with such things as C stands, solid flags, nets, silks, and the ever-popular cucoloris (or cookie). If you do not have access to grip equipment, then there are things that you can do just with the film lights that you might have.

Most hard lighting fixtures have "barn doors" (metal blades) that close over the output hole and knock down the amount of light coming out of the unit. These doors can also help to sculpt the light. Hard lights also typically have a knob for "flood"/"spot" that spreads the beam out over a larger area or focuses it into a small "hot" spot. Hard lights, in general, being more directional, are easier to control, cut, block off, etc. Hard lights can also become sources of soft light by using diffusion gels, bounce boards, **bounce cards**, or **shiny reflectors**.

Soft light, being less directional, is not as easy to control. You will need larger "blockers" to keep the diffuse soft light off certain areas of your film set. It is always wise to also have a good supply of spring-loaded, wooden clothes pins – sometimes referred to on set as "bullets" or "C-47s." (For more on lighting control, see resource references in Appendix A.)

Chapter Four – Final Thoughts: Learning to Light . . . and Lighting to Learn

This chapter has covered just some of the basic concepts in the art, science, and craft of film lighting. It is hoped that as you develop your overall skills with shot composition, you will expand your abilities in the use of creative lighting techniques as well. You cannot have one without the other. As you will grow to understand more and more, everything in filmmaking is related to everything else. Light relates to lens optics, aperture, CMOS sensitivity, exposure, ratios, color, emotional audience reaction, thematic/character interpretation, etc. Let us just say that you should always be conscious of how you are lighting your shots regardless of the type of motion media project that you are producing. Your lighting and compositional choices need to serve your story and not fight against it or leave it wanting or incomplete. What you choose to reveal to the audience (through the use of controlled lighting) or hide from them (through the use of carefully placed shadows) will yield more or less information, more or less understanding, and more or less enjoyment of your project.

Related Material Found in Chapter Seven – Working Practices

#1, 5, 10, 19, 20, 29, 34, 36, 38

Chapter Four – Review

1. Lighting is one of the most powerful and creative tools available to the filmmaker.

2. Light is energy: energy waves of electromagnetic radiation that happen to live in a zone of frequencies known as the visible spectrum.

3. The color temperature of light is measured in degrees on the Kelvin scale. Interior film lighting is approximately 3200 degrees Kelvin and noontime sunlight is roughly 5600 degrees Kelvin.

4. A camera set for tungsten light color balance will see daylight as bluish. A camera set for daylight balance will see tungsten film lights as amberish.

5. Most manufacturers build their video cameras to have a particular exposure index or ISO rating for sensitivity to light levels (e.g., EI 320). Some cameras can have a wide range of ISO settings (e.g., 100–6400). Lower ISO/EI numbers mean

that more light is needed for the imager to react. Higher ISO/EI numbers mean that less light is needed for an acceptable exposure on the image.

6. Image exposure is affected by the amount of light on the subject, the lens aperture, the sensitivity rating of the recording medium, and the shutter speed or time of exposure.

7. Neutral-density filters reduce the quantity of light hitting the camera's imager, but they do not alter the quality of light (color, etc.). They are often used in very bright, sunlit exteriors.

8. Hard light comes from sources with very directional, parallel beams of light, such as the sun on a cloudless day.

9. Soft light comes from sources with very diffused or scattered beams of light, such as the sun on a cloudy day.

10. Contrast refers to the amount of very dark, mid-gray, and very bright areas in your image. High contrast is mostly black and white with very little gray. Low contrast is mostly gray tones with very little pure black or pure white in the image.

11. Color refers to a particular hue or a palette of hues (ROYGBIV), and to the associated saturation or intensity of that color wavelength.

12. Choosing a particular color palette for your film will help to show your story on a thematic level.

13. The traditional three-point lighting scheme for video is: key, fill, and back. Each light does a job and can be placed in many regions around your subject.

14. The placement of a lighting fixture (or light source) and the placement of the subject in relation to that lighting fixture dictate the light's angle of incidence: high angle for top lighting and low angle for under lighting. The standard key light is 45 degrees above the subject's head and about 45 degrees off the axis from the camera lens. In reality, you may place the key light wherever you wish provided it suits the look of your scene.

15. Practical lights are light sources on the film set (such as a desk lamp, computer monitor, etc.) that actually emit light and add to the overall exposure and look of the images. Practicals also provide motivation for the extra, off-screen film lighting fixtures used for both exposure levels and to achieve the intended lighting design.

16. The formula watts/volts = amps will help you to calculate safe loads on electrical circuits.

17. Grip equipment (C stands, flags, nets, silks, bounce boards, etc.) helps you to control the quantity and quality of light used on your film set.

Chapter Four – Exercises

1. Take two series of photographs with any digital still camera.

   - Series 1 – Find any interior space that has a window to the outside. Photograph this interior space from an angle where you do *not* see out of the window – in the morning, in the mid-afternoon, and at dusk.

   - Series 2 – Record images of any exterior space in the morning, in the mid-afternoon, and at dusk.

   Compare the quantity and quality of light from each location at the three different times of day. What do you notice?

2. Acquire at least three or four different subjects (a mix of male/female, younger/older, etc. would be good). It would be best to perform all of the following during one session. If you have access to film lights of some kind, set up a standard three-point lighting scheme and make it look as good as possible on the first subject. Record some video of that set-up. Then, without changing anything about the lights or camera, sit your next subject in the same place and record some video of that person. Do this process for all subjects. Watch your video and note what worked and what didn't for each subject. Think about what is causing these differences. Return your camera to the same position if you moved it for image review, sit your second subject again, and tweak the lights to improve the look. Do the same process for each remaining subject: sitting, tweaking, and recording an improved look. Take note of what was different about each subject and what you had to do to the lights in order to get the best look. To challenge yourself, put a broad-brimmed hat or a pair of glasses on one of your subjects. How does that costuming change alter your lighting approach?

3. Set up an MCU on a subject in a room where you can control the lighting. With your camera in place and your subject seated, darken the room. Have an assistant hold a desk lamp or powerful flashlight and move it slowly around your subject from different heights (above/below) and angles (front/back/side). Review the recorded video results and take note of how the light from different angles of incidence interacted with your subject's facial structures (nose, eyes, brow, chin), hair, and clothing.

4. Use whatever video camera you can access and record clips of a friend or family member under both hard and soft lighting conditions. Try several locations and different times of day. Review the results. Where did you find soft light sources?

Where did you find hard light sources? Did the time of day or season of the year make any difference in the quality of the light you used?

Chapter Four – Quiz Yourself

1. What is the color temperature (Kelvin scale) for most manufactured tungsten film light bulbs?
2. If you are shooting under direct sunlight, typically what color temperature would you need to set on your video camera so that it balanced to your exposure light?
3. What do the terms "white balance" or "neutral balance" refer to?
4. What factors can affect the exposure of your recorded image?
5. How does light quantity affect your recorded image's depth of field?
6. What could you do with a hard light source in order to make it appear as soft light on your subject?
7. What do you call a functional lighting fixture on a film set that is part of the set dressing or art direction but also contributes light to the set and subject, helping both the exposure and the look of the scene?
8. True or false: a "low-contrast" image will have both very dark areas and very bright areas but not many grayscale tonal values in the middle range of exposure.
9. True or false: a light meter measures the distance from a lighting fixture to the floor underneath it, determining its angle of incidence to the subject.
10. Name three key differences between LED and traditional tungsten lamped film lights in terms of qualities, attributes, and physical construction.

Chapter Five
Will It Cut? Shooting for Editing

- The Chronology of Production
- Continuity and Performance
- Continuity and Screen Direction
- The 180-Degree Rule
- Jumping the Line
- The 30-Degree Rule
- Reciprocating Imagery
- Eye-Line Matching

It is important to remember that the planning and recording of your shots is only one part of the visual storytelling process. No matter what type of motion media project you need to create, the scripting stage is the basis for the content: the story. The careful filmmaker will generate shot lists and storyboards from the script: think of these as the "paper edit" formed during pre-production. He or she will have a vision of what the final project *should* look like, and these visions become the actual picture and sound files when the cameras roll and the action is performed during the production phase. It is during post-production (during the edit) that the story can actually be told – as completely as possible given the production materials that were provided.

There is a certain degree of "psychic" ability required of the filmmaker to predict the needs of the editing team. When using the master scene technique for fiction films or other means of capturing events or actions for documentary or non-fiction programming, the filmmaker must shoot the appropriate coverage of the material and deliver a variety of shots that will best show the story. This is called shooting with editing in mind. What will the editor need to cut to at this point? What would the audience like to see next? How can this information be shown at its best? Which shot framing will engage and inform the viewer? Which shot is new, exciting, cool, or absolutely necessary? Etc., etc., etc.

By recording a variety of shot types (coverage of the scene, event, interview, B-roll, etc.), you provide the editor with more choices. The editor can then decide at what point the viewing audience will desire fresh information and how much or how little information to show. A scene or a section of a show is created when the editor assembles together all of the important and usable information found in the shots that you provided. If the planning went well, and the shot lists were followed, then the editor should have enough valid material to work with and the audience should be able to understand what is going on in the story. To learn more about the editing process, feel free to review the contents of our companion book, *Grammar of the Edit.*

The Chronology of Production

In the narrative film production process, principal photography can span days, weeks, or even months, but the resulting images recorded during this time, when edited together, will need to appear as though they were all captured at the exact same time with fluid movement, matching actions, and seamless continuity.

Depending on the availability of locations and people, the quality of the weather, etc., the shooting schedule for a project can be erratic. You may shoot the wide shot of a scene

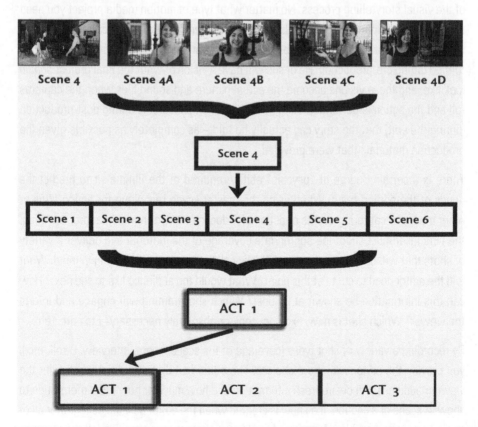

FIGURE 5.1   The evolution of a motion picture's building blocks: shot > scene > act > motion picture.

on a Monday, but you may not get to the close-up of a supporting actor until the following Thursday. The look of everything (camera positioning, eye-line, costuming, lighting, performed actions, etc.) will have to match to be useful to the editor. This also holds true for coverage of exterior and interior shots for the same scene recorded on different days – or even whole scenes shot at different times that must follow one another in the movie.

The individual shots that you create on set are just parts of a greater whole. They are pieces of a bigger visual puzzle. In the end, they will have to work with one another, intercut with one another, and show an entire visual story when they cut together. Based on the chronological events of the script, the shots (usually recorded out of sequential order) are assembled to make a scene, the scenes can become sequences that cut together to make an **act**, and the acts cut together to make an entire motion picture (Figure 5.1). Maintaining consistency in your visual elements is very important and we have a few ways to help you to stay aware of the potential glitches.

Matching Your Shots in a Scene

When using a single camera to shoot master scene coverage of scripted dialogue between multiple characters, you will most likely need to run through the action several times. Start with the wide shot, run through one character's shots into the close-ups, then turn it around and shoot the other character through to close-ups. Recording each pass from a different angle and with a different shot type in your camera set-up will help to ensure that the editor has the right material to assemble a complete, meaningful, and visually interesting scene. The performances of your actors and the framings of your shots all have to maintain some consistency throughout these repeated runs of the same dialogue and actions. The coverage has to match and flow to generate a seamless viewing experience for the audience once edited together.

Continuity of Performance

Having the actors repeat the same actions and dialogue from shot to shot requires that you pay attention to **continuity**. Continuity of performance is the consistent repetition of movement, action, and dialogue by the actor from one camera set-up to the next. If you plan a wide shot and a two-shot and then an MS, an OTS MCU, and a clean single CU for each actor, you will have eight camera set-ups for one simple dialogue scene. That becomes a lot of repetition of dialogue delivery, expressions, body actions, etc. for each actor – and then multiply that by the number of takes that you have to do in order to get all of those variables the way that you want them. Yikes!

This gets tricky to follow even when you are paying attention. Recording fewer takes can save time and money and keep your talent fresh. Continuity of performance is often overruled by the quality of performance when an editor assembles the visual material from a scene. A way around some of these performance issues is to use the **long-take** style of filmmaking. All of the dialogue and action of a scene unfolds in one long master shot, but you shoot no coverage angles of details. There is no need for a cut because there is nothing to cut away to. This style is more like recorded live theater.

Most films and television programs do, however, rely on differing shot coverage to visually construct a scene – and continuity will need your attention. Some filmmakers have adopted the multi-camera technique where several cameras are running on set simultaneously as the actors perform. Each camera records a different shot type and covers the actions of the scene with different framing. Editors may like this style of shooting coverage because there is always a matching action to cut to. Unfortunately, not all productions can afford that many cameras and that many crew members.

Continuity is not just making sure an actor moves his or her hand the same way in each take of each shot. Continuity, on a cinematic language level, involves a much wider range of planning and attention to detail as well.

Continuity of Screen Direction

As we know, the camera occupies the fourth wall, allowing the audience a privileged view of locations and actions within the film space. It invites them to observe the actions and events that happen inside this other world. As a result, filmmakers have a responsibility to the audience to present a knowable world that conforms to some consistent, and familiar, attributes of the physical world, such as up, down, left, right, near, far, etc.

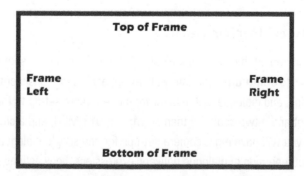

FIGURE 5.2 The motion picture frame has four edges and corresponding areas of interest: frame left, frame right, top of frame, and bottom of frame.

This prevents the audience from getting spatially confused while watching the motion picture. The horizon line mentioned in Chapter Three is a stabilizing device, but there are other ways that you can keep your audience grounded.

The frame itself is a useful tool. The top, bottom, left, and right edges of the frame act as references of direction for the audience. The character looks off frame left; the car exits frame right (Figure 5.2). The viewer associates the edges of the frame with the directional attention of a character or the movement of subjects in the film space. It should be clear, then, that **screen direction** – the left/right or up/down movement of a subject – must be maintained from one shot to the next. Figures 5.3–5.6 should help to illustrate this concept of continuity of screen direction.

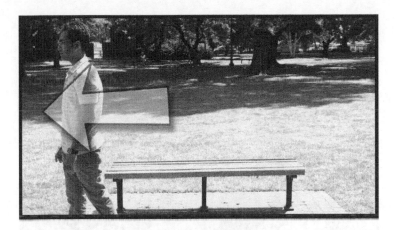

FIGURE 5.3   The action shows a person walking toward and exiting frame left.

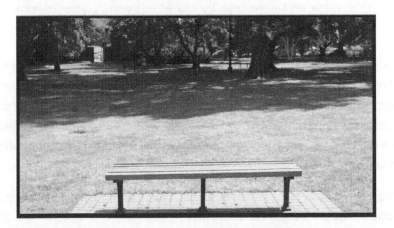

FIGURE 5.4   Holding on an empty frame for a bit just after the person has exited.

Matching Your Shots in a Scene

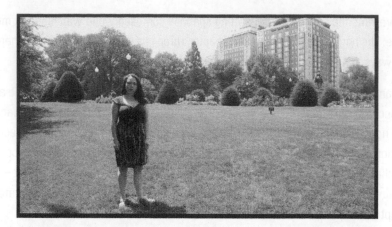

FIGURE 5.5 Cut to a new shot of a new location, but the subject has not arrived just yet.

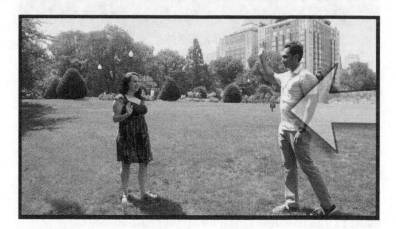

FIGURE 5.6 The new shot plays and the same person continues his walk, but this time he is entering the shot from frame right. The action follows a continuity of screen direction across the film space and across the cut.

The audience member viewing the edit of these recorded actions on the screen assumes that there is a larger "film world" just beyond the four edges of the frame. Because this film space exists in its own version of reality, the rules of physical movement (the concept of directional space) should be followed as in reality. (Please keep in mind that cartoons, science fiction/fantasy, and even video game cinematics can take their liberties with this guideline.)

If a person moves away to the left, he or she must keep moving away to the left until we see some change in his or her movement happen on screen. That is, if, during a shot, a person walks out of frame left, and we don't see him or her turn toward a new direction, then we could assume a continuation of movement in that established direction – which is to the left. Logic dictates that if that character is still moving to the left when the new shot cuts onto the screen, then he or she should enter this new shot from frame right. The continuity of screen direction for movement within the film space has been maintained across the cut.

The Line: The Basis for Screen Direction

Not all screen direction is based on large, physical movements. A good deal of important narrative information and spatial relationship data can be discerned by the viewing audience just through their observation of the directions of **attention**. This concept plays a major role in engaging the audience and keeping them actively involved in the images and in the story. Fortunately for filmmakers, humans are "programmed" to watch other humans – for all sorts of cues. One major reason for this is to draw our attention to other things in our shared environment, such as a source of danger. Have you ever been walking down the street when someone near you, someone you don't even know, quickly looks over at something? What do you do? If you're like most people, you look over to see what the other person is looking at. Maybe it's a safety mechanism or maybe it is just curiosity, but we are very good at picking up on connections between people, objects, and patterns in general.

Most often, each subject within the film space pays attention to some other subject or object within the same film space. The couple look at one another (Figure 5.7); the pool

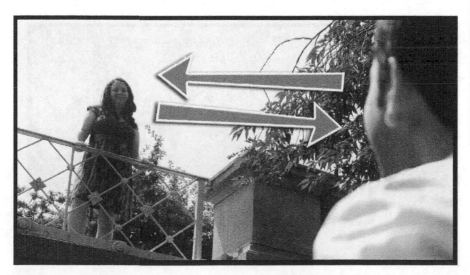

FIGURE 5.7 The young woman and man look at one another. A line is created.

player aligns her shot (Figure 5.8); the hungry woman eyes the juicy apple (Figure 5.9). The audience are keen on observing these attentions (what some film folks call the gaze). They use these connections between people and people, people and objects, etc. to establish **lines of direction**, which are also called **sight lines** or eye-lines. Good filmmakers know that the audience want to follow these lines of attention, so they use this phenomenon to compose shots, help to establish narrative meaning, and reinforce spatial relationships within the film world.

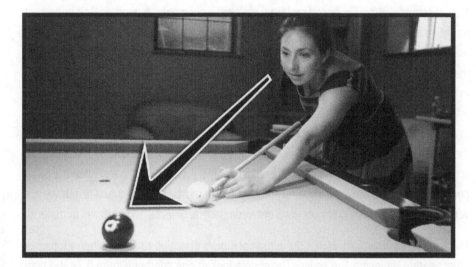

FIGURE 5.8   The player aligns her pool shot. A line is created.

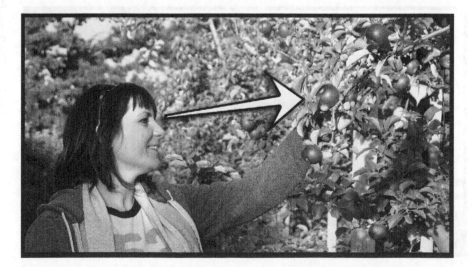

FIGURE 5.9   The hungry woman spies the best apple. A line is created.

The Imaginary Line: The 180-Degree Rule

The lines of attention need to be understood, established, and respected by the production team. As the audience rely upon these lines to receive and maintain spatial cues, it is very important that they remain consistent throughout the editing of a scene. To help to maintain lines of attention and screen direction from shot, to shot there is a popular filmmaker's concept known by several names: the **180-degree line**, **imaginary line**, **action line**, or **axis of action**. As some of the names imply, it is an imaginary line drawn through the shooting location, roughly where all of the main action occurs, and it is established by tracing the sight line of the subject within the shot.

This concept's other name, the **180-degree rule**, will surely help to clarify how this all works the way that it does and why it is considered important. The horizontal camera angle circling around your stationary subject (which we looked at in Chapter Two) brings us again to imagine that your subjects are at the center of a large circle. For your first shot, a wide two-shot, the camera is once again positioned at the outer ring of the circle, facing in toward the center where your action is occurring. Now superimpose in your mind the action line cutting across the diameter of the circle from frame left to frame right (Figure 5.10).

Once you have established this first action line, it stays in place for as long as these characters maintain this same attention between each other. Of course, to shoot the coverage of your subjects, you will have to move the camera around the film space, but

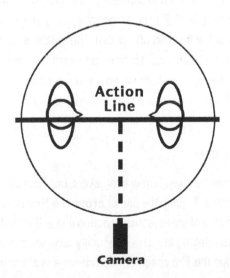

FIGURE 5.10   Bird's-eye view of the action line.

The Line: The Basis for Screen Direction

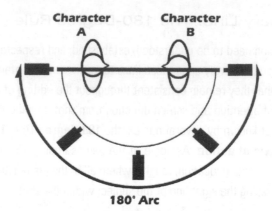

FIGURE 5.11   Keep your camera set-ups within the 180-degree arc on the near side of the established action line.

now you will have to respect this initial axis of action. The line has cut an arc out of the imaginary circle that is 180 degrees around from side to side. Your camera must now operate within that 180-degree arc when you set up for your new camera angles and coverage shots (Figure 5.11).

In our example, the first wide shot establishes frame left and frame right and also establishes the line of attention through the film space. Character A is talking with Character B. A is sitting frame left and his sight line is traveling from frame left to frame right. B is sitting frame right (receiving A's attention) and is looking back at A (sending a sight line from frame right to frame left). When you compose your shot for a CU single of A, you will need to maintain screen direction and continuity. A is still frame left with his attention pointing frame right (even though B is no longer physically visible within the frame, the audience have an idea of her location off screen). The matching coverage of B in her CU would necessitate a similar treatment. B is framed toward the right, looking over to frame left (toward the area of film space where we now know A exists). The series of shots and overhead diagrams in Figure 5.12 should help to clarify this practice.

Jumping the Line

Jumping the line happens a lot with new filmmakers, but most do not notice it until they get into the editing process. To jump the line or **cross the line** means that you place the camera on the opposite side of the established action line and record coverage shots from the wrong side of the 180-degree arc. This effectively reverses the established directions of left and right and flips the film space on the unaware viewers when they watch the shots edited together.

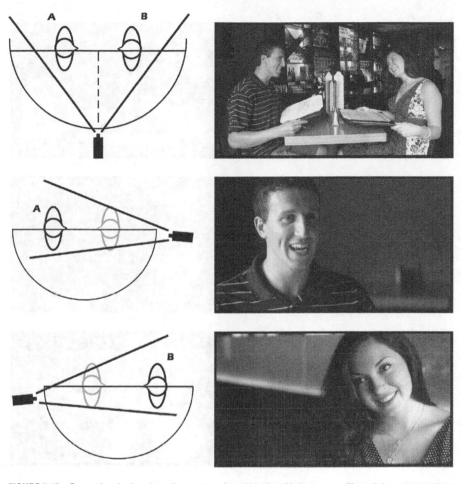

FIGURE 5.12   Respecting the imaginary line and staying within the 180-degree arc will result in correct continuity of screen direction across the coverage shots for this dialogue scene.

In the series of shots shown in Figure 5.13, the first two are repeated from our example given earlier, but the third shot is taken, by mistake, from the far side of the arc. The result is a nice CU of Character B, but the real mistake is not apparent until the three shots are edited together. B's screen direction and line of attention are reversed and therefore the cuts make no sense. It now appears that both A and B are sitting frame left looking off frame right, rather than looking back and forth at one another across the table as was established in the earlier, wide two-shot.

Crossing the line is acceptable under certain circumstances that involve moving talent and camera, but these are explored in more detail in Chapter Seven. For now, just think of how you would have to cover a couple slow dancing cheek-to-cheek on a dance floor.

The Line: The Basis for Screen Direction

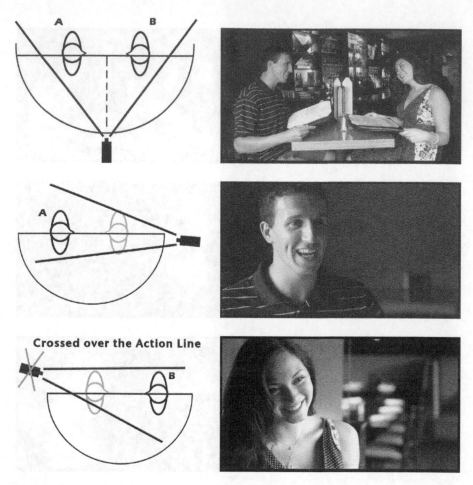

FIGURE 5.13 Only when the shots are edited together do you see the incorrect screen direction of Character B's attention in the close-up. The camera has jumped the axis of action and both subjects are now incorrectly looking frame left to frame right.

You would have one face on one side of a head and the other face on the opposite side, with the axis of action cutting through each. In order to see the faces in coverage, you would have to cross the line to set up your tighter shots or perhaps **choreograph** the actors' dance steps to turn heads toward camera just at the right moments of dialogue delivery and facial reactions.

As you may have picked up by now, there are very few absolutes when it comes to the guidelines and "rules" presented in this book. If you have creative reasons to execute a certain shot or group of shots in a certain way, then do it, even if it flies in the face of convention. Just make sure that your shot choices show your story best when edited.

The 30-Degree Rule

Grounded in the execution of the 180-degree rule is another important guideline called the **30-degree rule**. Simply put, when you are seeking various angles on action for a variety of shot coverage within your 180-degree arc, you should ideally move the camera at least 30 degrees around the semi-circle before you begin to frame up a new shot of the same subject. A focal length change would also be necessary (Figure 5.14).

The angle of view or perspective on the same subjects is then considered "different enough" when the camera is moved away from the previous set-up by at least 30 degrees (Figure 5.15). Each shot or view of the action is supposed to show new information to the audience. It makes sense that you would not wish to create two separate coverage shots with very similar framing. No one expects you to have a protractor on set measuring the 30 degrees — just get a good feeling about eyeballing it!

Following the 30-degree rule can help to avoid what is known as a **jump cut**. A jump cut occurs when you edit together two shots of the same subject that have very similar framing and composition. The similarity in subject placement in each shot causes a visual "jump" for the viewer in either space or time, or both, when they are juxtaposed at the edit point (Figure 5.16).

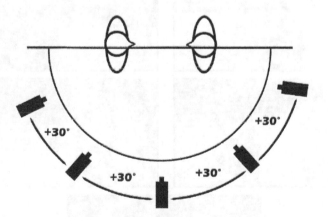

FIGURE 5.14 A 180-degree arc from the action line broken down into 30-degree slices (not to scale).

The Line: The Basis for Screen Direction

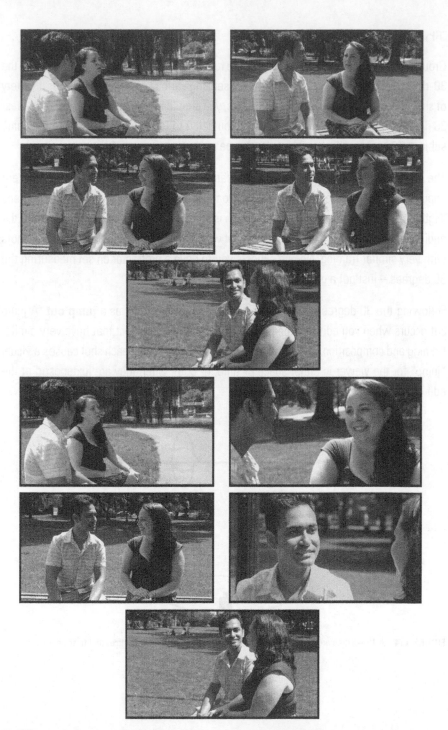

FIGURE 5.15 The same subjects as seen through the camera at five 30-degree slices around the 180-degree arc. The first set has no focal length changes and may not cut that well together. The second set incorporates angle and FL changes. This maintains the action line and achieves a new framing and angle on action appropriate for the edit.

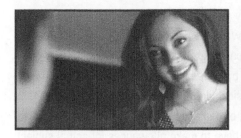
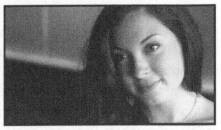

FIGURE 5.16 Taken from within 30 degrees of one another, these shots (even with different subject sizes), when cut together, cause a visual jump on screen due to their very similar but not exactly matching compositions.

Reciprocating Imagery

Our recent example of shots cutting from a wider two-shot to two singles in a medium close-up serves well to illustrate our next point. Whenever you shoot one type of shot to cover one character in a scene, you should create a correspondingly similar composition for the other character in the scene. This is called **matching shots**, **reciprocating imagery**, or the answering shot (Figure 5.17).

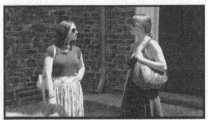

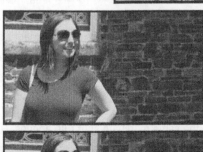
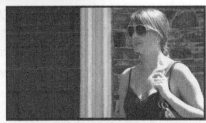

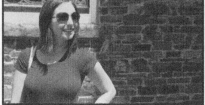
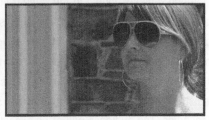

FIGURE 5.17 Shooting matching shots for medium close-up coverage is best. Providing an editor with an MCU of one character but only a CU of the other may cause issues during the edit because the shot types do not match.

The Line: The Basis for Screen Direction

Tradition holds that an editor might normally assemble a scene from the outside in. The action will start off with wider shots to show environment and character placement. As the action progresses, the coverage moves on to tighter and closer shots. This will show more intimate detail or enhance the drama by the end of the scene. A filmmaker, wishing to structure his or her scene in this classical film fashion, would have to ensure that each new camera set-up with new framing of each actor would match for subject size and subject placement. Of course, you may have to make allowances for actual subject size, hairstyle, hat, or other accessories that may require slightly different framing. Your main goal in most cases will be to provide the editor with equal numbers of shot types and matching compositions for each character. When the time comes to edit the scene, the editor can progress through shot types as needed – from the outside in or in whatever order of shots the scene or the visual style of the project calls for.

The same can be said for the camera angle itself. Generally speaking, when you cover two separate characters with single shots from the same scene, you should take care to match the camera height, camera angle (tilted up or down or neutral), the lens focal length, and especially the quality and quantity of lighting. The overall horizontal camera angle on action is tied in with the 180-degree rule, so the associated geometry really helps to keep everything organized. Of course, because you must take your storytelling needs into account, not every aspect may match exactly.

If you record Character A from several angles around your established 180-degree arc during this cycle of coverage for the scene, then you should reset the camera around your arc, tweak the lighting as needed, and shoot Character B from the corresponding angles for his or her cycle of coverage. Provided you keep the same camera height and lens focal length and focus, you should be able to easily generate the reciprocating images or answering shots of Character B that will match the framing of Character A's shots (Figures 5.18 and 5.19). A camera log or notebook will help to maintain all of this meta-data for reference. There are apps available to help with this, too.

When two subjects appear in the same frame, the same matching shot rule applies. For example, the over-the-shoulder shot allows the audience to keep track of the physical placement of each character in the scene. Lines of attention and screen direction are still required to maintain spatial relations. When you establish a frame that favors Character A's face, you include a portion of the backside of Character B's head and shoulder. For consistency in editing purposes, the reverse shot, favoring Character B's face, should also be recorded. The audience will often expect that reverse shot to be matching in subject size, subject composition, camera height, angle on action, etc., unless you are providing

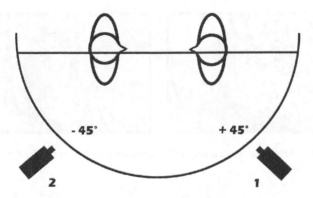

FIGURE 5.18   Camera Set-Up 1 records an MS of Character A from 45 degrees on the arc. Camera Set-Up 2 records an MS of Character B from −45 degrees on the opposite side of the same arc. Use the same lens height and focal length to achieve matching shots.

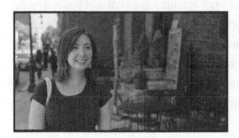 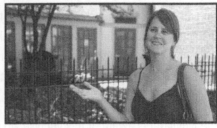

FIGURE 5.19   The resulting matching MS shots of Characters A and B from +45 and −45 degrees around the arc.

purposefully altered framing for storytelling reasons. When cutting from one OTS shot to another, any differences in these image factors will be very apparent and the mismatch will cause your audience, perhaps just on a subconscious level, to have an unfavorable reaction to the scene (Figures 5.20 and 5.21).

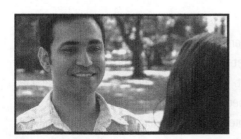 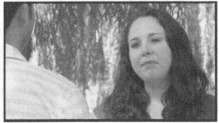

FIGURE 5.20   Height differences between the actors require a tweak in the over-the-shoulder shots for Characters A and B. Framing, subject size, and angle are roughly matching.

The Line: The Basis for Screen Direction

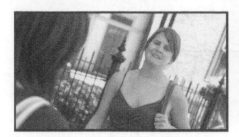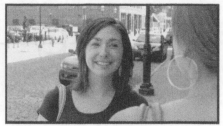

FIGURE 5.21 Mismatching over-the-shoulder shots for Characters A and B. Note how framing, subject size, and angle are not consistent.

Eye-Line Match

Another important consideration associated with shooting for editing is the concept of **eye-line match**. This takes the line of attention or sight line from one shot and ties it directly with an object in a new shot after a transition or cut. Eye-line match usually involves a character isolated within a frame (perhaps illustrated most easily with an MS or an MCU shot) when his or her attention is directed somewhere outside the four edges of that frame. The audience trace an imaginary line from the character's eyes to the edge of the frame where he or she is looking. The audience want to see what the character is looking at.

The filmmaker is aware of this impulse "to see," and may choose to show the audience what the character is looking at. The next shot would then be that object of interest revealed to the audience. And it's not just revealed in some arbitrary composition. It should be shot from a similar direction, angle, and height that closely match what the perspective would be from the vantage point of the character observing the object in the previous shot. This does not have to be a direct, subjective POV shot, but it does have to maintain and respect the eye-line established with the observing character so that the audience feel adequately informed that they, too, are seeing the same object as the character in the film.

Eye-line match is a "set-up-and-pay-off" scenario. The first shot sets up an expectation and then the second shot fulfills that expectation. The important thing is to frame the second shot from a corresponding vantage point. The illusion of connectivity to the character and the "realities" of continuity are maintained in the minds of the audience (Figure 5.22). Please note that it is also commonly accepted in narrative filmmaking to establish the "set-up" shot (the character looking off screen at some unknown object), but to then *not* cut to the "pay-off" shot revealing the eye-line-matched object of desire. Denying your audience that information is an easy way to develop suspense in the storyline. When will we know what was so shocking, upsetting, or funny to the character?

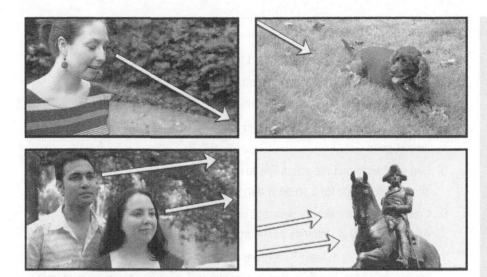

FIGURE 5.22   The first shot sets up the subject and the eye-line of interest. The second shot, presented from a correspondingly subjective viewpoint, reveals the object of interest.

Chapter Five – Final Thoughts: Be Kind to Your Editor

Almost all motion media projects will be edited in some way, shape, or form, which means that the people involved in the production phase are responsible for anticipating the needs of the editor. This chapter has provided some of the basic approaches to composing and recording traditional coverage such that the resulting motion imagery will cut together well enough. The 180-degree rule, continuity of screen direction, action, and performance, eye-line matching, and reciprocating imagery are all guidelines to follow when the project requires smooth and seamless editing flow. Giving your editor mismatched visual materials could end up giving him or her a big headache. Be kind to your editor and record shots that you have thought through and envisioned editing together well.

Related Material Found in Chapter Seven – Working Practices

#2, 3, 4, 7, 9, 15, 17, 21, 23, 24, 25, 26, 27, 28, 29, 33, 34, 35, 36, 38, 39

Chapter Five – Review

1. The shots you create must be edited together, so plan for that process.

2. Watch for continuity of action in performance.

3. Maintain continuity of screen direction from one shot to another.

4. Let the subject's line of attention connect objects for the audience, even across an edit point.

5. Use sight lines and the action line to maintain proper screen direction while shooting coverage for a scene within the 180-degree shooting arc.

6. Crossing the line (taking a coverage shot from the opposite side of the established arc) will change a character's line of attention – in a bad way.

7. Move the camera at least 30 degrees (or more) around your shooting arc and change your focal length so that no two shots of coverage seem to come from the same horizontal angle on action during the same scene.

8. Jump cuts happen any time that an editor is forced to juxtapose two shots whose visual content is either nearly the same or very similar in its composition. The audience feel as though time has "jumped" forward but space has remained very much the same.

9. Match your coverage shots for framing, angle, focal length, and lighting when shooting a multi-character scene, unless you have a creative motivation to do otherwise.

10. An eye-line match across a cut keeps your audience informed and grounded. A character looks at something off screen, and then the next coverage shot edited together would typically reveal that object of interest. Expectations are set up in one shot and paid off in the next.

Chapter Five – Exercises

1. Plan and shoot coverage of a simple two-person traditional dialogue scene. What helped you to maintain screen directions? What would happen if you added a third or fourth character to this same scene?

2. Create a scenario where two characters occupy one film space, but at opposite sides and with one sitting and one standing. They talk about and look at an object just off screen. Record the MCU of the object that both characters are looking at from different locations within the same environment. How are you going to address the eye-lines and angles on the object of interest?

3. Record a subject entering and leaving the frame at five unique locations. Did you manage to keep screen direction consistent in all five shots? If you changed the subject's screen direction from shot to shot, how did you handle that?

Chapter Five – Quiz Yourself

1. In filmmaking, what is the "fourth wall?"

2. What are "attention lines" and "sight lines," and how do they work into shooting coverage?

3. How does "jumping the line" mess with coverage shots when they are edited together?

4. You are going to move your camera around your 180-degree shooting arc to get more coverage of a subject. How many degrees around that arc will you have to move the camera until you get a frame that looks dissimilar enough from the previous set-up so that a jump cut will not be created in the edit when these two shots are cut together?

5. Why is it important to have matching answering shots in your two-person dialogue coverage? What shot attributes should be reciprocated to get the shots to match?

6. What factors should you consider when you are shooting an insert shot of an object of desire? Think of this shot as the reveal of what a subject in the preceding shot is looking at.

7. What is the "axis of action," and with what common film "rule" is it associated?

8. True or false: directors and actors can achieve perfectly matching continuity of action in each performance for each take in each camera angle and shot type.

9. True or false: continuity of screen direction within the film space only matters for human subjects and not things like cars, airplanes, horses, or animated fish.

10. You only record an OTS MCU for Character A, and an OTS MLS for Character B as coverage for a simple dialogue scene between these two characters. What issues might exist for an editor when he or she tries to cut back and forth between these two OTS shots of mismatched framing?

Chapter Six
Dynamic Shots: Subjects and Camera in Motion

- The Illusion of Movement on a Screen
- Slow Motion and Fast Motion
- Subjects in Motion: Talent Blocking
- Handheld Camera
- Pans and Tilts
- Dolly Moves and More

We have been talking about basic guidelines for creating motion media imagery, but we have not really discussed the motion part yet. Presenting the illusion of moving objects on a screen has been the main attraction of movies and television since they were first introduced. Beyond still photography and live theater, motion imagery (film, video, 3D computer animations, etc.) has been able to successfully engage audiences and show them virtually any information or entertainment that can be imagined.

In this chapter, we will explore the basic approaches to handling subject and camera movement during motion picture production. These concepts and practices can also be replicated and engaged during the manufacture of imagery for any animated programming as well. Let us start with a quick review of how we even perceive the illusion of motion on a screen when we watch a movie.

The Illusion of Movement on a Screen

Motion pictures or movies are so called because, unlike still photographs, their image content appears to move when presented on a viewing screen to the audience. This ingenious and relatively straightforward process evolved out of existing still photography technologies just over 100 years ago. Rather than taking a single exposure (or a single frame of an image) in a fraction of a second like still cameras, a motion picture camera is able to record many exposures (or discrete individual frames of imagery) during that same second of time. During the silent film era, that image capture rate, on average, was around 18 **frames per second** (18fps). This number is generally around the number of individual image frames that, when flashed in front of our eyes, at that same rate, will be interpreted by our visual systems as having continuous movement. For various reasons, the sound film era (also known as talkies) settled on 24fps to represent "normal" motion – for both image capture and projection rate.

A flipbook that you might draw or animations that you create in software operate on the same principle. A certain number of discrete images must be shown in rapid succession and for precise durations for our eyes and brains to be tricked into seeing fluid movement on the playback screen. Analog video systems developed for broadcast television during the 20th century settled on 30 interlaced frames in the USA and 25 interlaced frames in Europe. The refresh rates of the phosphors inside the cathode ray tube (CRT) were dependent upon the rates of the electrical alternating current that powered the television set (60Hz in USA and 50Hz in Europe). Digital technologies are now allowing for greater experimentation in capture and playback frame rates. The histories, sciences, and technologies related to film and video are rather complex, and go well beyond the scope of this book.

Presentation Speed: Slow Motion and Fast Motion

When it comes to the presentation speeds of "normal" motion, you now understand that playback for high-end, theatrically released digital video and emulsion film projection has traditionally been 24 frames per second (fps). Most broadcast television and other video devices have been 30 frames per second (25fps in Europe). Technologies surrounding image capture are changing all of the time, but one basic rule still applies: changing the capture frame rate of your medium while preserving the standard presentation frame rate of that medium will create a change in the perceived speed of objects in motion.

Slow Motion (Overcranking)

The term **overcranking** originated way back in the days of hand-cranked emulsion film cameras. The camera operator regulated the speed of the film transport system by turning a handle or crank that controlled both the time of exposure and the frame rate per second. People today still use this term. Capturing images at a higher frame rate than "normal" (24/30fps) will yield the appearance of objects moving slower than normal when displayed at the normal frame rate speed. Basically, the movement of an object (athlete, racehorse, bursting water balloon, etc.) is broken down into many more representative "slices" or frozen frames by increasing the frame rate/shutter speed of the camera. The more frames you can capture in one second, the slower the object will appear to move.

When you have many more frames of motion to display but you show them at the normal rate of delivery, each shot (not frame) plays on screen for more time than the original action took to complete. The audience will therefore see movements in slow motion.

Scientific films and sports playback have used slow-motion imagery for motion analysis for many decades. Fictional narrative and animation films have also used slow-motion cinematography to great effect. Watching events play out in slow motion can be a very dramatic, moving, powerful, and, sometimes, comedic viewing experience for the audience.

If you want to achieve slow-motion effects with a digital video camera, it must be able to process frame rates above 30fps. 60, 120, and 240fps (or above) are becoming more common in camera devices (even smartphones), but all of these rates require video-editing software to play back all of the extra frames at the normal speed to achieve that slow-motion look. Keep in mind that these cameras, typically, must also compromise on the image's recorded resolution (potentially lessening quality), and the higher the frame rate, the more light you will need to gain proper exposure of the video.

Fast Motion (Undercranking)

Capturing images at a slower than "normal" frame rate (24/30fps) will yield the appearance of objects moving faster than normal when displayed at the normal frame rate speed. This method is used to create time-lapse motion images, such as speeding traffic flow, sunrise or sunset, or cloud movements across the sky. It condenses events that take a long time to unfold and displays them at a much faster rate for the audience to watch.

Fast motion is often associated with the silent comedy movies of the early 1900s. It is used in educational films, scientific visual studies, industry promotional videos, and fictional narrative and music videos – just about any motion image project that seeks to condense actions across time. Time-lapse videos are really just a series of single still frames taken across longer intervals and edited together to show incredibly fast motion of events.

Subjects in Motion: Blocking Talent

The human visual system responds well to brightness, color, and movement. The movement of subjects within a static frame is a great way to give your shots visual energy. The term "staging" is often used to describe the physical placement of objects on the film set and within the borders of the recorded frame. The term "blocking" is often used to describe the physical movement of subjects on the film set and within the recorded frame. Creating interesting blocking can engage the audience's eyes and keep them involved with the imagery and in the story. We like to watch things move around on screen. So, talent blocking across the screen (left to right or vice versa) helps to reinforce direction. Talent blocking deep into the set or location adds to the illusion of a 3D film space and draws the audience's attention into the depth of the frame (Figure 6.1).

Static shots and stationary subjects, when arranged in compelling compositions, can have a visual energy and power all of their own, and can serve as contrast to moving shots when edited in sequence. It depends on the type of motion picture project that you are creating. Talent movement, when blocked creatively, will also add dynamic physical energy to your shots. In some schools of film theory, even the direction of movement can have meaning within the narrative. As an example, in an American frontier story, characters on a long journey to the territories may always have a screen right to screen left movement, perhaps implying that the right is East and the left is West: "civilization" is ever marching westward – toward frame left. Maybe a character is always moving from the foreground of a shot into the background: perhaps this means that he or she is running away or is too mysterious to be captured up close within the frame for very long.

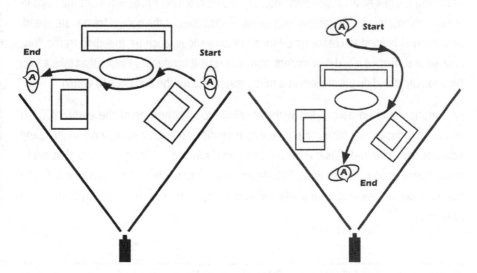

FIGURE 6.1   Talent blocking may be across the frame, deep into the frame, or both.

Camera in Motion

If having your subject move within a static frame puts energy into your shot, then imagine what will happen once you start moving the camera while recording your images. Because the camera is the proxy for your audience, a moving camera will really take them on a ride. Gauging just the right kind and amount of movement is one of your creative and technical decisions. Does a slowly moving camera match the energy of the scene? Does a quickly moving and shaky handheld camera match the tone of a scene depicting a chess match? Does it have to? In order to figure this out, it would be helpful if we explore the various ways in which the camera can move.

Handheld

Perhaps the best place to begin a discussion of camera movement is with the most basic yet most challenging approach: going **handheld**. You may find it convenient to hold a smaller camera in your hands, but just because it is convenient does not mean that it is appropriate and it certainly does not mean that it is easy to do well.

The first factor involved is a technical one: the camera that you are using to shoot your project. Modern digital video technologies have allowed cameras to be quite small and quite capable; they can weigh a few ounces to just a few pounds. If you are working on an emulsion film motion picture, the nature of the medium requires much heavier and much more substantial camera equipment, often weighing in at 20 to 40 pounds or more. This is not necessarily conducive to handheld shooting, although there are specially designed cameras and support (like a Steadicam™ or a Glidecam™) for just such a purpose.

The smaller, more lightweight handheld camera is simultaneously a blessing and a curse. It allows for easy movement, but that often leads to too much movement. Having and using a tripod is always encouraged, especially if you are new to shooting motion pictures. Remember that everything you do with your shots should have a purpose. Shooting handheld should not happen because you lack the appropriate camera support, but rather because you know that your story will benefit from the kinetic energy that a well-controlled handheld camera can bring to motion imagery.

Due to the spontaneous and uncontrolled nature of the shooting environments, documentary and news recording will often use a handheld shooting style. When replicating similar real-life events – a riot, armed conflict, natural disaster, etc. – fictional narrative filmmakers will also employ a handheld camera to lend that feeling of reality to the experience on screen. Amateur videos are mostly shot handheld and, for similar reasons, filmmakers will use this style to mimic "amateur" content in their professional films. Handheld camera is also used when shooting action sequences, or any scene with quickly rising drama, to lend them a visually frenetic style. This can enhance feelings of tension and suspense in the audience. Reality TV programming (and spoofs of reality shows) also employ handheld – again relying on the audience assuming that handheld camera coverage means real and immediate events unfolding (unscripted) right before their eyes. Music videos use a fair amount of handheld camera coverage, as do video camera POV "found footage" horror movies.

Perhaps it would be best to compile a brief list of advantages and disadvantages for the handheld camera option.

Advantages of handheld:

- It is easy to readjust framing on the fly.
- It creates a sense of personal immediacy within the scene (subjective POV).
- It allows the operator to move freely around the set or location.
- It infuses shots with a lot of energy from motion.
- When it's wanted, it can easily make the audience think of documentary/news/ amateur video.

Disadvantages of handheld:

- It easily becomes too wildly shaky or causes swaying on the horizon line.
- It is difficult to manage focus with a narrow DOF.
- Handheld camera shots are difficult to cut with static camera shots.
- It is subjective, which may be inappropriate for the neutral "voice" of the motion picture.
- It generally limits focal length usage to wider angles of view because the more environment visible within the frame, the more "stable" the image will appear.

During your pre-production phase, when you are planning the look of the motion media project, you should really think long and hard about why shooting handheld (for all or some of the imagery) is appropriate. Regardless of your choice, you would be wise to always have a tripod available just in case.

Pan and Tilt

Pan and **tilt** refer to the horizontal and vertical repositioning of the camera lens. A pan (or panoramic shot) requires the camera lens to rotate or swivel either left or right across a horizontal arc. The camera pivots in place around its y-axis, and more of the surrounding environment is revealed. As an example, you are producing a public safety video and want to demonstrate an incorrect way to cross a city street. As the talent walks across the street without stopping and looking both ways, the camera operator pans to the right to follow the movement of the subject – only stopping the panning swivel once the subject has reached the far side of the street (Figure 6.2).

A tilt requires the camera to pivot on its x-axis. The camera lens will either swivel up or down during the recording of the shot. As an example, a young man is climbing a short

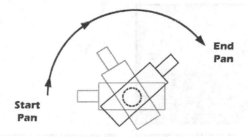

End Pan

Start Pan

Bird's-Eye View

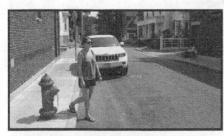
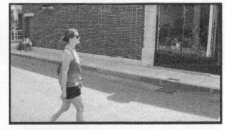
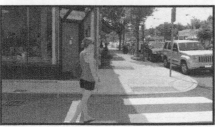
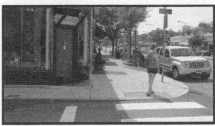

FIGURE 6.2   Overhead of the camera panning horizontally during a shot. The camera pans right to follow the subject's actions.

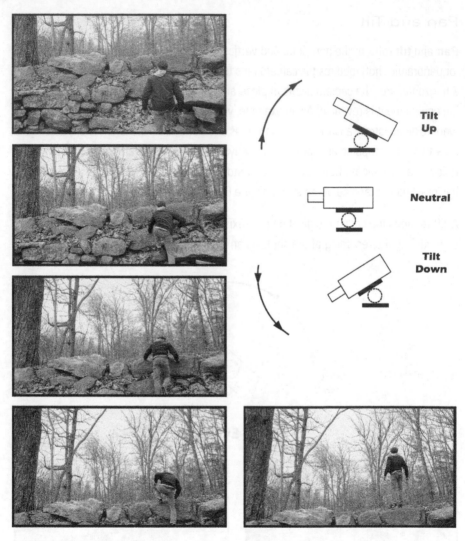

FIGURE 6.3   Profile view of the camera either tilting up or tilting down from the neutral position. Sample images from a tilt-up shot. (Photo credits: Anthony Martel)

stone wall. As he ascends the stones up to a new elevation, the camera operator, remaining at ground level, tilts up to follow his motion, maintaining proper headroom (Figure 6.3). Both the pan and the tilt replicate the movements that you make with your own head to follow action or look off in a new direction. Twist your neck left or right to pan your eyes left or right, and up or down to tilt your eyes upward or downward.

There is also a moving shot that combines a pan with a tilt. The camera lens is simultaneously panned across the film space and tilted up or, conversely, the camera is tilted down while panning across at the same time. Either way, this results in a diagonal motion through the film space in front of the camera. An example could be two people walking through a sculpture park. As they pause (frame right) to look up at a tall sculpture (currently out of the frame left), the camera sweeps up and across the location to the left to end the shot on the sculpture itself. An upward diagonal **tilt–pan** has been executed to cover both the people and the taller work of art (Figure 6.4). This is similar to the eye-line match across the cut discussed in Chapter Five, but here both pieces of information are presented inside one unedited shot. The "set-up/pay-off" scenario is contained in the moving camera's coverage of the talent and the object of interest in this one, unbroken tilt–pan shot.

The smooth, continuous action of a pan or a tilt is actually an unnatural experience for the human visual system. Our eyes and brains do not make smooth pans or tilts while viewing our surroundings. Instead, the eye travels along the horizontal or vertical path, locking onto points of interest, registering with the brain, and then darting along quickly to the next point of interest. It becomes a very rapid series of starts, stops, starts, stops, with the resulting illusion that we have panned along the city street or tilted our eyes up the building or mountainside.

A motion picture camera lens cannot be as selective, so everything that it "sees" throughout the duration of the pan or tilt gets equal treatment. The smooth execution of a pan or tilt and the speed of that execution directly affect how the audience receive the

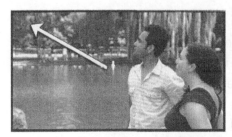
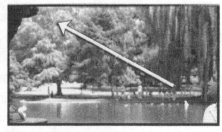
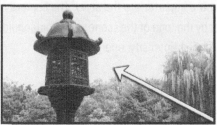

FIGURE 6.4 These are frame grabs from one continuous tilt–pan up and across this location. One shot provides the audience with the visual information of the subject's eye-line match through this tilt–pan movement.

information within the movement of the shot. Be aware, however, that certain camera shutter speeds and frame rates may cause a strobing or stuttering effect in the imagery when you pan or tilt the camera at particular rates – especially if bold vertical or horizontal objects occupy the environment where the movement is being recorded.

To help the audience to accept the camera's panning or tilting movement, it is often good to motivate the move. In our examples so far, we have provided these motivations. The audience would like to see what happens to the woman as she crosses the street or the man as he climbs up the wall. The subjects' movements motivate the panning and tilting of the camera to follow their actions until they are completed. Then we have the two characters who stop and stare up at the interesting sculpture. The power and attention of their eye-lines (from frame right across to upper frame left) motivate the diagonal camera tilt–pan up to reveal the taller work of art. All of the important narrative information is delivered in one continuous moving shot. The camera fulfills audience expectations by showing the object of the characters' interest without having to cut to a new shot.

Recall that the audience often place themselves in the position of your camera. When the camera moves, it takes on a sort of intelligence, following action or seeking information as a proxy for the engaged viewer. Motivating your camera moves (pans and tilts especially) helps to keep the flow going and feeds the inquisitive nature of the viewing audience. The movement of a subject or object provides a reason for the camera to pan or tilt along with it.

There are times, however, when you have no visible motivating action for the camera to follow on a pan or a tilt. Perhaps you wish to shoot a long, slow pan of displayed photographs depicting several generations of a family, or maybe there are many different pairs of shoes in the front hallway of a home that you would like to record. There is no motivating movement of these subjects, but the camera takes on a "mind of its own." It becomes a disembodied narrator or an independent and conscious observer showing the audience things that are important to the story. The camera can pan or tilt slowly or quickly. The pacing is set by the tone of the scene: slow for languid, emotional, or mysterious moments, or quick for high-intensity, energetic scenes.

Shooting the Pan and the Tilt

Traditionally, there has been a preferred method of accomplishing a good pan or tilt shot. When you first start out operating a camera on pans and tilts, they should have three components: the **start frame**, the **camera movement**, and the **end frame**. A pan or tilt composed of all three elements can be edited into your scene more easily than if you had just movement alone.

The Start Frame

Almost every pan or tilt shot should begin with a static camera position. Your starting frame of the shot should be well composed: it could stand alone as a good still image. It is from this start frame that the subject that motivates the pan or tilt begins its action. Keep the camera still, let the action begin, and then begin the camera's panning or tilting. We do not discuss editing much in this book, but a quick word to the wise: cutting on movement, either into a shot already in motion or out of a shot once in motion, is a visually complicated thing to do and often poses an editorial challenge. Your editor will thank you when you begin your pan or tilt shot with several seconds of a static start frame.

The Camera Movement

Once the subject's motion has begun, your camera movement also begins. The camera's motion should ideally be smooth and steady and actually "lead" the movement of the subject. By this, we mean that proper headroom, look room, and pictorial composition should be maintained throughout the life of the pan or tilt action (Figures 6.2 and 6.3). Any individual frame extracted from the shot during the camera movement phase should be able to stand on its own as a well-composed still image. Because the camera is leading the subject's progress, the camera should naturally reach the end of its horizontal or vertical arc prior to the subject completing its movement.

The End Frame

As the camera has already come to a rest before the subject completes the movement, the end frame has been reached successfully. This end frame should, once again, be a well-composed static shot that can complete the pan or tilt action in a visually compelling fashion. You should linger on this end frame, recording several seconds of it while there is no camera movement. The editor now has a steady, locked-off frame to cut out from at the end of your pan or tilt, if the edited story calls for it.

As you become a more experienced filmmaker, you will be in a better place to experiment with a moving camera on pan and tilt shots without static frames at the **head** (beginning) and **tail** (end), especially if they cover a series of very fast action shots. The easiest visual test to see if static start and end frames are required for a panning or tilting camera move is to record it twice: once with and once without. In your editing software, create two versions of your sequence of shots. One version will use the video clip with static start and end frames while the other version will have just motion. Most often, the static start and end frames will help during the editing process – but either way, you should decide for yourself.

Equipment Used to Move the Camera

Pan and tilt shots require no equipment to be accomplished successfully. They can be done with a handheld camera. As previously mentioned, one of the problems inherent in using a handheld camera is the lack of consistently steady control over the movements. No matter how stable you try to keep your hands and arms, video cameras, especially the smaller, lightweight ones, pick up on each step, bump, and even breath. And no matter what you think may be a cool or popular style of crazy camera movement, nothing can take the place of smooth, steady shots that engage the audience rather than alienating them. It is almost always advisable to use some sort of camera support that will not only steady the camera, but also allow it to achieve more well-controlled, precise movements and help to maintain proper focus. The following section discusses some of these devices.

Tripods

As already seen, the camera should usually have a companion piece of support equipment to keep it stable and level when you need it. The **tripod** is the ideal tool for this job. Tripods, also commonly referred to as **supports**, **legs**, or **sticks**, come in different sizes and weights, depending on the camera that needs to be supported, but they all have three legs. The three-leg design allows for solid balance and leveling on most surfaces. You attach the camera to what is called the **tripod head**. On most models, the tripod head is designed to allow pan and tilt movements, so it is often called a **pan and tilt head**.

Attached to the head is a stick that allows you, through the use of torque, to execute rather smooth pan and tilt movements. If the pan and tilt locks are loosened, the tripod head may be swiveled on the horizontal and vertical axes by pushing or pulling this arm in the opposite direction of the desired movement of the lens. This stick is called the **pan handle** and is most often positioned between the camera operator's body and the back of the tripod head itself. Many tripod heads control their axis movements through either plate friction or fluid pressure. The tighter the settings, the greater the resistance, the slower the movement; the looser the settings, the lesser the resistance, the faster the movement. Advanced tripod heads for professional motion picture work are called

geared heads and use two wheels that spin interlocking gears to pivot the camera through pans and tilts; there is no pan handle per se.

A level, locked-off tripod allows you to record extremely stable static shots. Many models of tripod have a built-in "bubble" level on the head, but you can also align any vertical objects (trees, walls, etc.) or the horizon line to the edges of your frame to achieve a useable "level." A tripod with the pan lock loosened allows for very smooth and level horizontal pans. A tripod with the pan lock engaged and the tilt lock loosened allows for very accurate tilting movements up and down without any drifting to the left or right. You would have to have both pan and tilt locks disengaged to maneuver the tripod head to execute a smooth and stable diagonal tilt–pan.

Tripods generally sit directly on the floor or the ground, and have either spiked or rubber-tipped feet or both. A device called a **spreader**, which attaches to all three legs from the center, keeps them from spreading too far apart and dropping the camera too low to the ground. Many people place a **sandbag** on the spreader for extra weight and stability.

Be aware that a tripod with its telescoping legs fully extended may become too top-heavy and unstable when a larger camera rig is placed atop it. The center of gravity is too high for the narrow distribution of weight on the "circumference" of the three small and narrowly triangulated feet. If you are using a long and heavy zoom lens on your camera, be sure to level the head and lock the tilt knob between shots so the extra front weight does not pull the head downward and force the tripod to fall. Any time that a camera is mounted to a tripod on set, there should always be someone next to it to safeguard it from accidentally toppling over – especially on windy exterior locations or hectic and cramped interiors. Lastly, as a reminder, when you are setting up your shot on a tripod, your height does not automatically dictate that the camera/lens should be at that same height.

Dollies

The original motion picture cameras had a hand-cranked film transport mechanism, which meant that one hand (often the right) of the camera operator was constantly engaged in turning the crank motor during the actual recording of the shot. The camera was mounted on a tripod and the entire apparatus did not move during the shooting. The desire for camera movement quickly led to experiments where the camera and tripod were attached to a four-wheeled cart. The operator would stand on a platform, cranking the camera, and other crew members (now called **grips**) would push or pull the entire apparatus around the film set or location. This, in essence, evolved into the modern-day film **dolly**.

At their roots, all dollies are wheeled platforms. Some have three wheels, some have four wheels, and some have many small ball-bearing wheels like those on a skateboard. Many dollies have thick rubber or air-filled wheels that allow them to be pushed or pulled around relatively flat surfaces like a gymnasium floor or along the tiled hallway of a school building. Other dollies have grooved, hard rubber wheels that fit on and roll along tracks laid on the ground. These tracks are like small railroad tracks and come in straight or curved sections, and you can assemble different lengths to create a path for the dolly to follow (Figure 6.5).

Each of these different dolly types has a different way of mounting the camera. Some simple ones are just flat beds that let the tripod and the operator sit on top. Others have a built-in pedestal that can be raised (ped up) or lowered (ped down) via hydraulics. Still others have a **boom arm** that sits atop the pedestal and the camera and a tripod head (without the legs) are mounted to the end of the boom, allowing for wheeled movement and camera height and angle changes all at the same time. In a pinch, a hospital wheelchair, a skateboard, a wheeled office chair, or a blanket being pulled over a polished floor can act as an impromptu dolly as well. Currently, **sliders** (or mini-dollies) are very popular with moving small form-factor DSLR HD video cameras across short three- or four-foot distances.

The basic job of a dolly is to smoothly transport the camera across short distances. You can follow, lead, or move alongside a subject and record its movements across the film space. Slow movements can be less noticeable to the audience, but they can be more difficult to accomplish on set. Fast dolly movements help to instill a dynamic energy or sense of urgency in the shot. Just as the pan and tilt have three components, so should most dolly moves: the static start frame, the camera dolly movement, and finally the static end frame.

Always use extra caution when performing dolly moves or whenever the camera and camera operator are in motion. Personal safety is always more important than getting a good shot.

Let us take a look at the two major movements of direction that can be accomplished with a dolly.

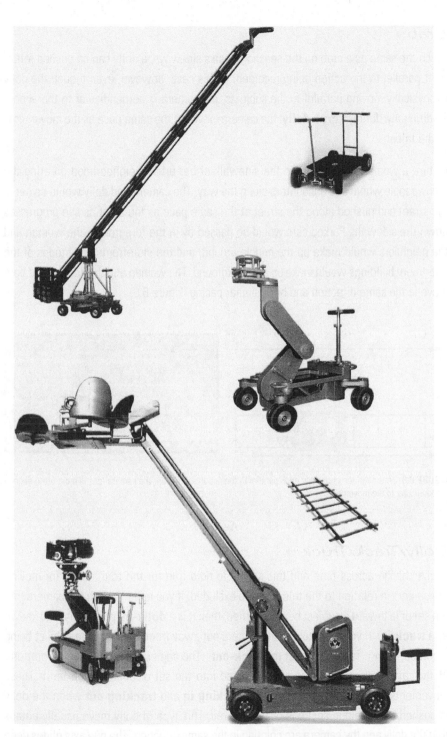

FIGURE 6.5 Various styles of camera dollies and booms. (Photos courtesy of Chapman-Leonard, Inc., J. L. Fischer, Inc., Matthews Studio Equipment).

Crab

Much the same as a crab on the seashore walks sideways, a dolly can be pushed left or right parallel to the action being recorded. In this case, however, even though the dolly is physically moving parallel to the subjects, the camera is perpendicular to the action. Traditionally, during a **crab dolly**, the camera moves at the same pace as the movements of the talent.

Picture a woman walking down the sidewalk of her urban neighborhood greeting the many people whom she encounters along the way. The camera and dolly would be set in the street and pushed along the street at the same pace as the actor as she progresses down the sidewalk. Parked cars would be passed by in the foreground, the woman and the neighbors would make up the middle ground, and the storefronts and stoops of the apartment buildings would make up the background. The woman and the dolly would both move in the same direction and have similar pacing (Figure 6.6).

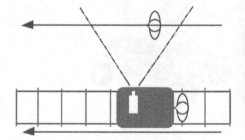 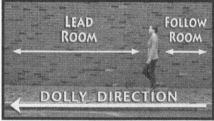

FIGURE 6.6   Although the crab dolly rides parallel to the action's direction, the camera lens is most often aligned perpendicular to the movement.

Dolly/Track/Truck

Terms change across time and this seems to hold true for the terms used for moving the camera in relation to the talent – crab excluded. If you need to push the camera into the set or in toward a subject being recorded, then it is a **dolly-in** (previously also known as a **truck-in**). If you need to pull the camera out away from the set or the subject being recorded, then it is a **dolly-out** (or **truck-out**). The camera is on a wheeled platform (dolly, cart, truck, etc.) and is either pushed into the set or pulled out from it. These movements may also be referred to as **tracking in** and **tracking out** when the dolly is pushed/pulled along sections of track or rail. This type of dolly move usually entails that the dolly and the camera are pointing in the same direction. The one axis glides deep into the set or out of the set in a straight line (Figure 6.7).

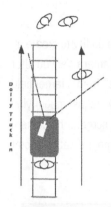

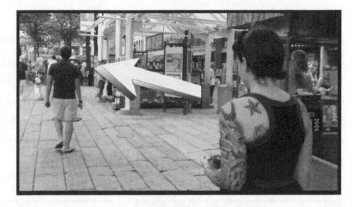

FIGURE 6.7 Overhead showing a dolly move into the set along the tracks. The movement of the subject motivates the move in.

Tracking has grown into a more encompassing term where it now seems to refer to any shot that follows, leads, or moves alongside (like a crab) the movements of a subject without requiring the use of actual tracks or rail and a dolly. Small, handheld cameras, self-balancing gimbals, etc. allow for movement such as a camera chasing after a character running down the street. A subject may face toward and walk at the camera, and the camera can "walk backward" or lead the talent. A camera may follow along with a moving character (perhaps in a state of confusion) and run circles around the wandering actor, seeing the action from all directions and enhancing, visually, the thematic nature of the story at this point. Nowadays, tracking often just means to stay with the moving subject no matter where she or he goes or how she or he goes there.

When a dolly-in is done very slowly, a barely noticeable change in shot type/framing is achieved. A long shot becomes a medium shot and a medium shot ends as a close-up. This is a way to alter framing or shot type without having to perform a change in focal length or have the editor add a cut to the scene. You basically alter the framing and composition of the shot over space and time during the recording of the shot. Unlike a zoom, which alters magnification but not perspective on objects, this movement appears much more natural to the audience as the moving camera lens acts like our own visual system and maintains proper spatial perspective on the changing field of view. When done slowly enough, the dolly movement is barely apparent to the consciousness of the viewer: things just change somehow but no one "sees" how. Some refer to this extremely slow dolly movement as a "creep."

Zoom

As you saw in Chapter Three, the zoom lens (or varifocal lens) has the ability to create an image that appears to "zoom" through the space directly in front of camera. As you alter the focal length during a shot, say from wide to telephoto, you "move" from a larger field of view to a much smaller segment inside that environment. You really are just magnifying that distant object within that space so that it appears larger on the screen; the camera did not have to move closer to it. It is this consistent and uniform magnification factor that distinguishes a zoom-in move from a dolly-in move.

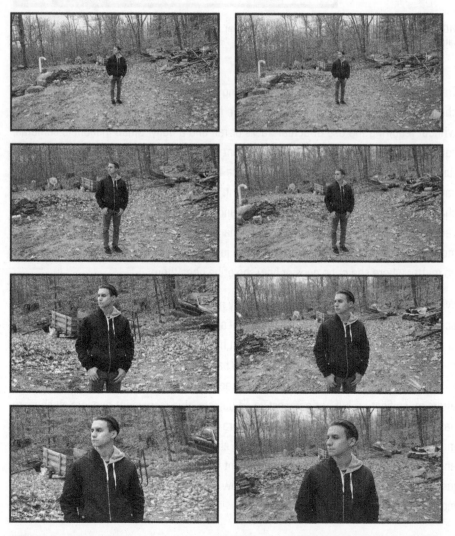

FIGURE 6.8 Column 1 – frame grabs from a zoom-in shot; Column 2 – frame grabs from a dolly-in shot. Note the differences in magnification and perspective on the visible backgrounds. (Photo credits: Anthony Martel)

The foreground and background elements enlarge on the screen at the same rate during a zoom. There is no perspective shift on the subject or visible surroundings because the camera is not moving in relation to the objects being recorded. A dolly-in produces a different optical effect because the camera is physically altering its proximity to the subject (without changing focal length) in order to achieve the same-sized object in the frame. Perspective is altered, as the foreground/middle-ground subject gets larger in the frame at a faster rate than the background elements.

You can certainly combine several of these movements discussed so far in order to create a more complex shot that is sometimes called a **developing shot**. You could have the talent move through the set as the camera dollies along the ground to follow the action and have the camera boom up the pedestal to alter the lens height during the shot. A focal length change could also be introduced during a developing shot. The movement of the dolly and the possible pan or tilt can help to disguise the zoom factor as the focal length change occurs. These types of developing shots can be very difficult to execute, but they can show a lot of story action in one shot and be very visually interesting to the audience.

This has not really been mentioned in this discussion on movements, but it should be made apparent once more that focus is going to be a major concern of any filmmaker engaged in these sorts of movement shots. Camera-to-subject distances will change where focus falls on the set and it is the job of the camera assistant and camera operator to keep these consistent throughout the duration of the shot. This can become quite difficult and requires a great deal of preparation and organization on the part of both the talent and the crew.

It is often best to run through the action for several rehearsals so that the talent, camera operator, camera assistant, and dolly grip all understand what the timing of the shot is going to be like. The crew will use a measuring tape for camera-to-talent distances and set marks on the lens or follow focus wheel. These complex developing shots that involve talent movement, camera movement, focus changes, and possible focal length changes can eat up a lot of time on set, so be careful with your scheduling on that shoot day. Of course, if your digital video camera has a very advanced, multi-point auto-focus function, then you can try to use that to maintain focus across this complex or developing shot, but there is something to be said for knowing how to do it "old school."

Equipment Used to Move the Camera

Steadicam™ and Other Camera Stabilization Devices

For the most part, dollies are limited in the direction of their movements (left, right, in, out, and sometimes around). Handheld camera work can be liberating but you constantly run the risks of bad framing, bad focus, and too much shaky movement (unless your story calls for such a visual treatment). Luckily, a device called the Steadicam™ was invented in the 1970s that allows a camera to be mounted to a spring arm that mounts onto a body harness that is worn by a walking camera operator. This clever device makes it possible for a camera to achieve dolly-like smoothness as it is maneuvered on foot – in essence handheld but with stabilization. An assistant controls focal length, focus, and (sometimes) iris remotely, but composition and movement are controlled by the operator wearing the harness vest. Because the camera is freed from having to follow dolly tracks, the Steadicam™ allows for rather long and intricate tracking shots where the talent moves into and out of sets or locations, up or down stairways, and over rough terrain.

In the film industry marketplace, many similar devices are available. They vary in complexity, size, and expense, but all balance a handheld camera for smooth moving shots. Motorized gimbals and other mechanical camera stabilization platforms are being used more and more in amateur motion media production and the results can be quite spectacular. Just make sure that the visual style is appropriate for the story that you are trying to show. Using a cool, new "toy" is fun, but may not be necessary given your visual language choices.

Cranes and Booms

Sometimes, your motion picture project calls for a grand, sweeping shot of an exterior location. A camera at ground level, regardless of how wide your lens is, just cannot encompass as broad a section of your film space as you would like to see. This is where the use of a **crane** comes in. Just as large cranes allow construction equipment to work up high, cranes employed for film use allow the camera to work up high. There are many different types and sizes of cranes, but the general idea is to lift the camera (and sometimes the camera operator as well) up in the air over the set or location to achieve a very high-angle view down on the action.

Many crane-like devices called **jib arms** and boom arms also have the ability to move the camera from ground level up to a higher elevation during the actual recording of the shot – straight up or in an arc over the location. This movement, although not natural, is fluid and graceful and can add visual power to a scene. Crane shots will help to you show a lot of information from a high angle or even a direct overhead bird's-eye view. You will often see crane or jib shots used as establishing shots to open a scene, or as summation shots to close a scene. Drone cinematography is sometimes now used in place of these larger, heavier, and more labor-intensive pieces of camera support equipment.

Chapter Six – Final Thoughts: Movies Should Move

Still photographs do a great job of capturing and preserving images for commercial advertising, art, news, documentation, identification, personal/family events, and fun times with friends, etc. Moving images, when done correctly, can do all of that as well as display motion and be accompanied by sound. It makes sense, then, that visual storytellers might gravitate toward motion media production in order to express their story or creative vision. Understanding how movements of subjects on the screen can engage the audience is a critical step in planning and executing dynamic shots. Adding camera movement into the mix will really capitalize on the medium's key strength. Learning to be judicious with your static and moving shots will help you to generate the most viscerally and emotionally engaging viewing experience for your audience.

Related Material Found in Chapter Seven – Working Practices

#3, 4, 5, 6, 7, 8, 9, 10, 11, 18, 21, 22, 23, 24, 28, 29, 30, 31, 32, 33, 35

Chapter Six – Review

1. Blocking is the plan of movement for your talent around the set.
2. Slow motion results from the use of more frames per second than "normal" for image capture, but "normal" playback speed for display. Fast motion results from the use of fewer frames per second than "normal" for image capture, but "normal" playback speed for display.
3. A handheld camera should serve a narrative purpose. Beware of shaky cam syndrome and questionable focus. Handheld is often associated with newsgathering and documentary, although a tripod is used there, too, as much as is practical.

4. Horizontal pans and vertical tilts should ideally begin with a static start frame, move smoothly through the camera motion, and finish on a well-composed static end frame.

5. A tripod is the best way to secure smooth, level, stable shots that will cut together.

6. A wheeled dolly or a smaller slider, whether on tracks or just the floor, helps to achieve smooth gliding camera shots in either crab mode or trucking mode.

7. A crab dolly moves the camera parallel to the direction of motion, but the camera's lens is aligned perpendicular to the action that it is covering.

8. A dolly-in and zoom-in achieve similar but different results. The dolly physically moves the camera through space, altering its view of objects due to changes in proximity. A perspective shift occurs between the subject and the visible background, widening the apparent distance between them. A zooming camera does not typically move, but instead uses optics to magnify all features within the visible frame equally. The subject and the background magnify at the same rate and appear to compress together.

9. The Steadicam™, gimbal, or other camera stabilization device combines the best qualities of smooth dolly work with the ease of movement of handheld photography.

10. Cranes, booms, and jib arms help you to get sweeping upward or downward moves that add large areas of information and a sense of grandeur and elevation to your shots.

Chapter Six – Exercises

1. Practice panning and tilting with a handheld camera. Did you create a motivation for the camera movement?

2. Shoot pan and/or tilt shots as part of a scene but do not have static frames at the beginning or end of the move. Edit the scene. Do the pans/tilts work without the static frames? Why or why not?

3. Explore the differences between dollies and zooms. If you do not have a dolly, improvise one out of a rolling chair or skateboard and record a short dolly-in shot of a seated subject that starts wide and ends on a close-up. Recreate the same shot but do not move the camera; zoom in to optically go from the wide shot to the CU. Review the two shots and note any differences and similarities in the imagery. Were there focus issues?

4. Practice recording a crab profile shot (either dolly or handheld) of a person walking slowly, and then once again walking quickly. Was it easy to keep pace with the moving talent? Were you able to maintain lead room, headroom, and focus? (Remember that it is safest to have a spotter, guide, or assistant walk next to you while you are operating a handheld camera like this, making sure you do not fall or bump into things. Safety first, always.)

Chapter Six – Quiz Yourself

1. True or false: "blocking" refers to the focal length settings involved in a long zoom shot.
2. What type of image creation is the term "overcranking" associated with? What is the basic concept behind it?
3. List three advantages and three disadvantages to handheld camera operation.
4. What are the three main components of performing a pan or tilt shot?
5. How is tracking in on a dolly different from zooming in during a shot?
6. Why does a tripod not have two legs or four legs?
7. What does a Steadicam™ (or similar image-stabilizing gimbal rig) offer that a traditional handheld camera cannot?
8. Often, when someone records handheld video, he or she holds the camera up to his or her chest or head height. When might this lens height/angle not be appropriate while recording images for a motion media piece?
9. True or false: a dolly grip is a rubberized pad placed under the back right wheel to prevent the dolly from rolling between takes.
10. Why might someone place a sandbag at the center of a tripod spreader?

Chapter Seven
Working Practices

We have come a long way with our understanding of the grammar of the shot. We should all be more familiar with shot types and the guidelines covering framing and composition. We have also seen how lens choices, focus, lighting, and camera movement help to show your stories with richer visual meaning. And we know that all of our hard work recording the shots during production pays off when we carefully anticipate the editor's needs and deliver the appropriate picture (and sound) elements.

The grammar that you are learning and putting into practice is a well-established and proven set of principles that will help your audience to understand your visual intentions. In filmmaking, as with any discipline or craft, there are many different ways of approaching the material. Finding solutions to the challenges that confront you is part of the learning process and part of the fun. Although not an exhaustive list by any means, the content of this chapter is designed to help to bolster your understanding of cinematic language. It offers tips, tricks, and suggestions (both general and specific) that may enhance your work habits and lead to a stronger and more effective visual presentation – and may also prevent some headaches down the road.

1. Storyboards and Shot Lists

Whether you are producing a short film, a music video, a 30-second commercial, or even an animation, you would benefit from creating storyboards, overheads, and shot lists before the first day of production begins. Storyboards are small drawings that map out what the framing and composition will be for each shot that you want to record. The pictures act as templates for the eventual real set-ups you make, like a comic-book version of the motion picture. Storyboards also allow you to see how the various shots necessary to cover the action will roughly edit together once you enter the post-production phase. The drawings help to get everybody involved in the creation of the actual images on the same "visual page." Animatics (animated storyboards) have become popular as a modern pre-production tool because laptop and tablet usage on set has increased. Of course, older technologies such as a pencil and paper still come in quite handy.

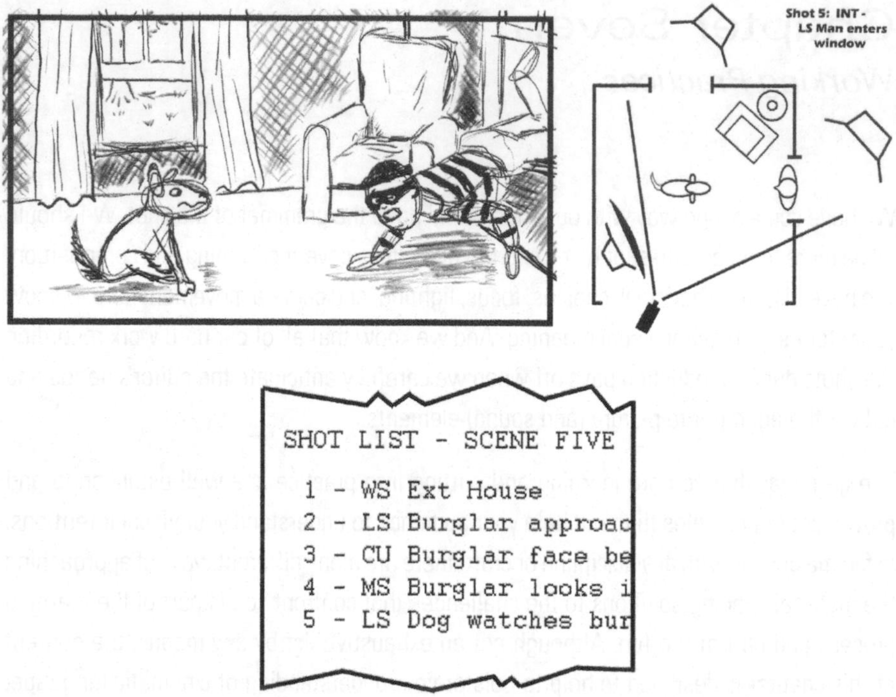

Shot 5: INT -
LS Man enters
window

SHOT LIST - SCENE FIVE

1 - WS Ext House
2 - LS Burglar approac
3 - CU Burglar face be
4 - MS Burglar looks i
5 - LS Dog watches bur

FIGURE 7.1 An example of a storyboard, an overhead schematic, and a shot list.

Overheads can be simple "bird's-eye view" diagrams that map out where on the set you will place the camera, talent, lighting fixtures, etc. They help to get the crew ready to place the right things in the right places when you get to location or arrive on set. Staging and blocking decisions can be sketched out this way also. Finally, shot lists are a way to account for all of the various shots that you will need to record to get the coverage for a scene. The list is often labeled per scene number with separate letters representing each unique camera angle on action (i.e., Scene 1B, Scene 7C). Creating storyboards and shot lists will usually be accomplished before the physical shooting actually begins, during the period referred to as pre-production (Figure 7.1).

2. Slate the Head of Your Shots

Organization is a key factor in successful filmmaking. Even a small project can produce a large amount of video and audio files regardless of the type of motion media production that you are working on. Keeping track of these media assets through post-production is a big deal. It is very beneficial to identify each take of each shot that you record, and using a slate is a long-standing practice that can help with this process (Figure 7.2).

These devices were once made of actual slate way back when and a camera assistant would write important information on them with chalk. Today, they are more like a "white board" and you can use dry-erase markers to pen down the pertinent information. When you record the slate at the beginning of the shot, it identifies what the title of the project is, the scene/shot/take being recorded, the director, the director of photography, and the date of production. Being able to see this information on the screen at the head of each shot helps the editor to organize the material during post-production, because it is common to rename the media file clips in order to better understand the content of each shot.

Beyond the written information, the slate board also helps with the syncing process. Syncing or synchronization is required on emulsion film or video productions that employ **dual-system recording**. The film or video camera captures the picture information and a separate digital audio recorder captures the sound files. Although the video camera may also capture sound data, its quality is typically inferior to that produced by the dedicated audio device unless professional-level **XLR** audio input jacks are present on the camera body and a top-quality microphone and cable are used.

The picture and sound files are synchronized (or married together) during post-production with the aid of the slate board's clapsticks. When a clapper/loader **voice slates** the start

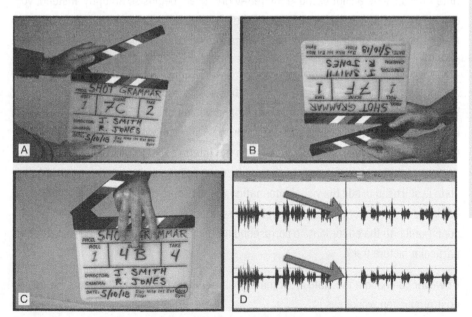

2. Slate the Head of Your Shots

FIGURE 7.2   A slate is used primarily during motion media production when two separate devices record picture and sound information. A – a traditional head slate; B – a tail slate; C – an MOS head slate (where audio is not recorded); D – an audio waveform "spike" showing where slate sticks clap together.

of a take, she or he also physically closes the striped sticks on the slate board, which makes a loud "clack." She or he has marked the take. The picture file for that take has only one frame where the sticks are shown frozen at the moment of closing. The audio file for that take has only one "frame" where the sound of those sticks closing is heard. These two matching frames are paired together and the picture and sound files will then play in sync during the editing process. On high-end film productions, **timecode** syncing makes this process a bit easier. In several editing software apps, the computer can analyze the sound wave data and marry the picture and audio files for you automatically.

When shooting video projects without a separate digital audio recorder, your camera captures both picture and sound information. The captured files on your editing system are already married together on the basis of their timecode; there is no need to sync them. It is still a useful practice to "head slate" the shot on video because the visual and auditory shot identification will make shot organization that much easier for the post-production team. If you do not have the physical slate to write on and record, then you should at least voice slate the head of the shot before "Action" is called so that everyone will still know what the shot is (stating project, scene, shot, take, and date).

There are occasions, especially found in documentary shooting, where you do not have time to head slate a shot because the real-world event begins so abruptly. Instead, you can perform what is called a **tail slate**, where you identify the shot after the event has transpired but before you cut the camera's recording. The physical slate is held upside down for the tail slate (Figure 7.2B).

Sometimes, you will be shooting material that has no usable audio associated with it. When you are recording with emulsion film and you do not "roll" audio for a take, it is called filming "MOS." No sync sound is recorded. This acronym has several possible origins in film history (you can look them up on the internet), but the meaning is the same: do not look for an audio file during post-production because one was never recorded. The slate is still used to add the visual information to the picture track, but the clapper/loader holds his or her fingers inside the clapsticks so that they cannot possibly close – visual confirmation to the editor that no corresponding audio file should be looked for with this particular picture track.

However you handle the slate, your main goal is to help to identify the shots for easier post-production workflows.

3. Help the Boom Operator to Place the Microphone

Unfortunately, for new and experienced motion media producers alike, it is all too easy during the hectic pace of production to forget about certain important factors. It is understandable that when so many people are attending to picture quality and performance that, sometimes, audio may get overlooked. Audio is often a key ingredient in creating a successful project and it would be in everyone's best interest to ensure that the audio department gets as much help on set as everyone else.

A good practice to get into is having the camera operator communicate directly with the boom microphone operator. The camera operator is responsible for verifying proper framing, focus, exposure, etc. while the camera is rolling and recording any kind of performance. The boom operator is responsible for maneuvering the potentially large and cumbersome microphone (and blimp or windsock housing) into position over the heads of the performers to capture the cleanest, clearest, and loudest audio. There are times, however, when the boom may drop down into the top of the recorded frame during a take, or the camera may be reframed to a higher or wider setting, causing the boom microphone to suddenly appear at the edge of the recorded image.

While setting up the shot, it would be best for these two important crew members to develop a communication strategy that will help to set the edge of the frame. Whether

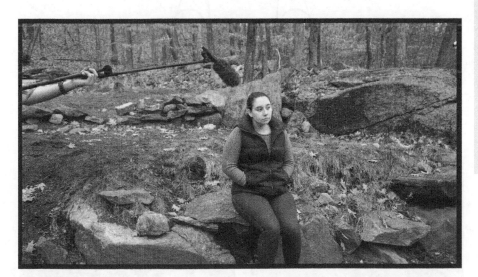

FIGURE 7.3 A boom mic inadvertently entering the frame can ruin an otherwise good take. Camera and boom operators need to work together to help to establish the limits of the active picture frame being recorded so such accidents can be minimized. (Photo credit: Zach Benard)

the boom must come from above, the side, or below the subjects, a boom line must be determined. A quick, verbal, way to establish a safe boom proximity is to drop it down into frame and have the camera operator say something like, "Back, back, back, back, WOOF!" when the boom operator has backed the microphone sufficiently away from the edge of the active picture frame. Any cue may work, so develop your own phrase that is fun and clear to be heard across a potentially noisy set. If you would both prefer a hand signal method, drop the microphone in and find a way to stop when needed with some secret gesture developed between the camera and audio department members.

4. Use of Two or More Cameras

Outside of television studios, where the use of multiple cameras is the norm, most other motion media production will be done with one main camera covering the action. As advancements in digital video camera technologies have increased and their form-factor and expense have decreased, it has become more popular to cover the action from a scene with more than one camera. At least twice as much coverage can be recorded at the same time and, as an added benefit during post-production, you are guaranteeing sync and continuity of action for the subjects being captured.

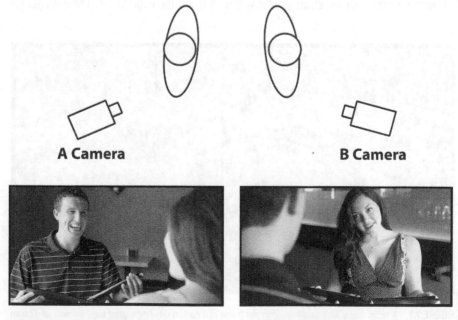

FIGURE 7.4 Filmmakers may choose to capture more material by employing multiple cameras of matching specifications to record simultaneous actions.

Traditionally, film crews use multiple cameras when stunts are performed or large, one-time events are recorded. Today, a simple two-person dialogue or a host of a video (who subjectively addresses the audience via the main camera's lens) may be recorded with more than one camera. Perhaps a filmmaker decides to cover a dialogue with matching OTS shots for each character. Maybe the producer of the host-driven show wants a straight-on MLS and an oblique and canted MCU of the host to make it seem more dynamic when edited together. Although it seems that this technique may save time, it can actually be a challenge for lighting, clean audio coverage, and good blocking and framing – so be aware if pursuing this method of image capture.

It will be helpful to label each camera (perhaps figuratively and literally) with a naming scheme: typically, the primary camera is the "A" camera, then the second is the "B" camera, etc. If employing a dual-system style of recording technologies, remember that one "clap" slate should be used to sync all camera angles' footage during post-production. For this to work, all cameras must be able to "see" and record the head slate closing after the voice slate by the clapper or camera assistant. Of course, these cameras would ideally generate media files that match in video resolution, frame rate, shutter speed, and compression encoding. A test of imagery from these multiple cameras (if they do not exactly match), from production down to edited footage, is strongly encouraged prior to actually shooting the important video for real.

---

5. Be Aware of Reflections

The artificial world conceived and constructed by humankind is often a flat and shiny place. Whether you are recording video near a large plate glass window, a polished marble wall, the glossy paint finish on a car door, or a brass table lamp, the likelihood is high that you will see a reflection of someone or something in the captured image. Film lights hidden off screen provide light levels for exposure, but they can also cause small or large reflections off the surface of shiny objects on set or location. These surfaces may also reflect the camera or crew members, especially if there is a dolly move or similar changes in crew placement behind the lens. The natural world (fields, forests, deserts, beaches) is made of roughly textured and amorphously shaped objects and undulating planes so, beyond the sun's reflection off relatively smooth bodies of water, it is unlikely that a film crew will generate any unwanted reflections on natural exterior sets or locations.

These visual annoyances are caused by the angle of incidence of the light source and the angle of reflection from the shiny surface of the recorded object. Light comes from the source, strikes the surface at a particular angle, and has much of its energy bounce off at the same but opposite angle — typically, straight into the camera lens where it gets recorded as a flare or a light "hit." The basic fix for this issue is to alter either the angle of the light source, the angle of the shiny object being recorded, or the angle of the camera lens pointing at the subjects to be recorded. Dulling spray may also be used to turn the shiny surface into a matte surface and help to reduce the glare or reflection. Sometimes, the solution may be in a combination of several of these actions.

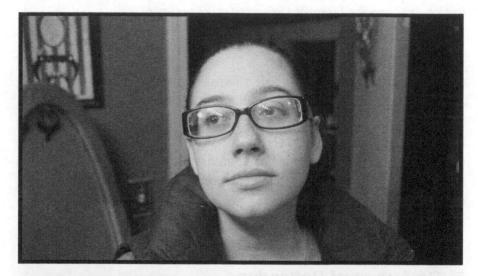

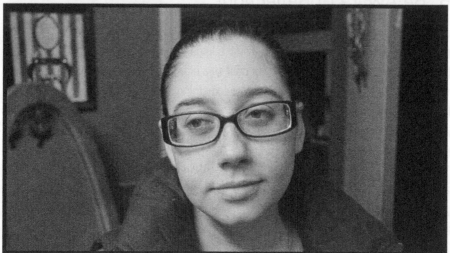

FIGURE 7.5 Unwanted reflections and lighting glares can be caused by the glossy surfaces found on your set or location. Minimize these annoyances by altering the angles of incidence on lighting fixtures or the angle of reflection from the subject or camera lens. (Photo credits: Zach Benard and Anthony Martel)

Of particular concern can be subjects who wear glasses. A video's host, a news reporter, or a character in a short film may need to wear corrective lenses or sunglasses/goggles for safety reasons, etc. Larger, softer lighting sources (such as a 4x4 silk, or a large **soft-box**) can cause larger glare or washout of glasses on faces. Smaller, harder point-source lighting fixtures typically create a smaller "dot" of reflection. Regardless of the cause, minute changes in angles of incidence and reflection can usually alleviate much (but not always all) of the glare or reflection. Using a polarizing filter (to offset the reflected light angle) on the camera lens may rectify an overall soft source glare, like that caused by a cloudy, daytime sky. If the problem is found to be reflections of the moving camera and crew members, then draping the camera in black duvetyne fabric and having the crew wear all-black clothing may reduce such reflections in the recorded image.

6. Communicating with the Talent

Communication is the name of the game. Your motion picture project may be trying to convey a message or information, or evoke a thought or feeling in the audience: communication is happening. Crew members must share their production plans and make the project happen efficiently: communication is happening. During production on set, the on-camera talent needs to be guided toward delivering the best performance: communication is happening. All too often with novice motion media producers, this last need for communication is overlooked.

Trained actors as well as amateurs need help in understanding the limitations of the framing of the shot: how much room do they have to look in/around, move, gesticulate, etc. before they encounter the edges of the frame? Interview subjects need to be advised where to look near the camera and that they should not fidget in their seat. Band members need to know what action to perform during a shot from a music video, etc. So many technical and logistical things are happening on a set that it becomes all too easy for novice filmmakers to forget about the talent, or assume that they "get it." Preparing lights, camera, and sound for a take only counts if the talent is on the same page. When everyone understands what the shot is about, it has that much more of a chance of being successfully done.

When you do communicate with the talent, try to keep the interaction brief, clear, and professional; after all, they are trying to do their job, too. Above all, you should use language that makes sense to them. Remember that as you sit behind the camera facing the talent, they are facing you and your worlds' directions are mirrored. What is to their right will be to your left and vice versa. In order to keep things simple, provide stage

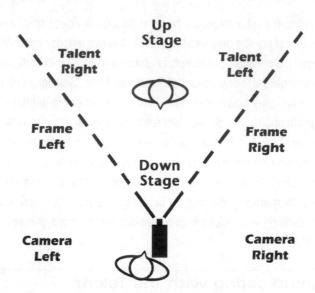

FIGURE 7.6 The camera's frame left and frame right are rarely stage left and stage right for the talent. Speak to subjects in terms of their orientation on set and directions will be easier to follow.

directions that fit with the *talent's* alignment to the set or location. Some people actually use theater stage directions on a set. If the talent are not familiar with that terminology and you need them to slide over to your frame left a bit more, say something like "Please slide to your right by an inch or two." This method makes it immediately clear in their mind in what direction they are to move and by how much (Figure 7.6).

7. Safe Action/Safe Title Areas

Technologies are changing rapidly. The traditional 4:3 "tube"-based television set of the 20th century has all but gone away, HD and UltraHD are on our smartphones and in our homes, and digital cinema 4K and 8K projections are in our movie theaters. The older 4:3 TV, as a receiver and display monitor for picture information, did a valiant job, but it suffered from a peculiarity known as **domestic cutoff**. The TV set actually cut off or did not display the outer edges of the original video or filmed image at the top, bottom, left, and right sides of the screen. This area of lost picture information was roughly 10% in from the edge of the source material. Content creators knew that this cutoff would eventually happen, so they framed their shots within what is called the **safe action area** (Figure 7.7). Most HD display technologies, and certainly streaming videos on computer and handheld media monitors, do not suffer from this same limitation, but the tradition still applies.

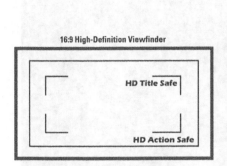
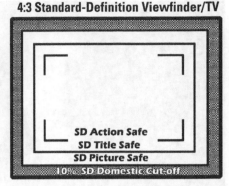

FIGURE 7.7 The safe action area helps to keep important visual information away from the edges of the frame in both 16:9 and 4:3 images.

To help with this, many cameras will have a line, corner marks, or an overlay grid on the viewfinder or monitoring screen that shows where this safe action area exists around the edge of the full image frame. When composing your shots, you should keep in mind that no important information or action should take place in this outer edge of the frame. While taking account of this extra screen area, be aware of appropriately compensated headroom and look room as well. If you record images of signs or other written materials, make sure to place them fully visible within the frame, away from the edges. There are often markings on the viewfinder known as the **safe title area** for just such a purpose. In general, regardless of your camera format, it is good practice to keep all of the important action and composed visual elements well within the safe action area (Figure 7.8). Most video-editing software will also have the option to display similar safe action and safe title grids (overlays) in the playback monitors, so any questionable framing may be double-checked by the editor.

While HD (and other high-resolution formats) may no longer suffer from domestic cutoff on digital displays, it is still best to err on the side of a slightly "looser" framing. This will give the talent just a bit more headroom/look room, etc. An editor could always crop/reframe/resize the shot in post-production to adjust if needed. Overly tight shots cutting off important information cannot be expanded to reveal data that was never captured at the edges. This process gets easier, allowing for more creative reframing and reformatting, when you use very high-resolution image capture devices and software.

7. Safe Action/Safe Title Areas

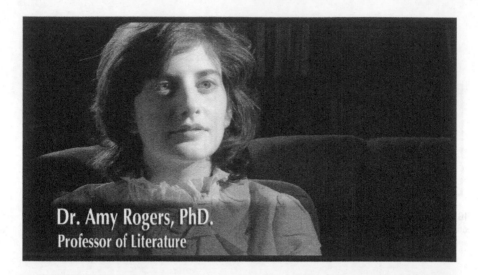

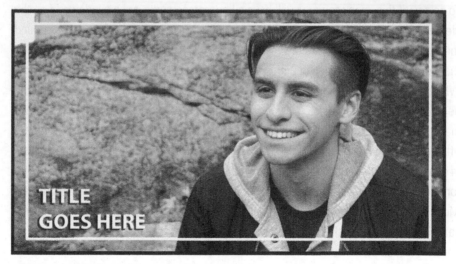

FIGURE 7.8 A lower third title is typically placed just inside the safe action area. (Photo credit: B – Anthony Martel)

8. How to Manually Focus a Zoom Lens

Any auto-focus camera lens should do all of the focusing "on the fly" as you set your shot's framing. If your camera is equipped with a manual focus zoom lens, there is an easy way to achieve best focus on your subject.

The main things to remember are:

- If it has one, check the focus of the camera's eyepiece/viewfinder and verify that it is set to your vision's prescription.

- Select the framing for your shot with subjects in place, etc.
- Set your aperture wide to allow maximum light into the viewfinder system.
- Zoom in on your subject (set the lens to the maximum focal length and magnify the object that you wish to be in sharp focus).
- Set the focus (on the eyes if a human face is your subject).
- Reset the focal length to select the recording frame composition.
- Set the aperture for the desired exposure.

9. Always Have Something in Focus

You will find it beneficial to have something within your frame in focus. The human visual system, when working correctly, always allows you to see some plane of space around you in proper focus. You have the luxury of automatic focus shifting, meaning that you can be focusing on something two inches away from your eye one moment and then focusing on an object very far away the next. Cameras have either manually focused lenses or auto-focus controls that guess at the object that you would like to have in focus. The center-weighted "face recognition" or multi-point auto-focus settings can be helpful when you are first starting out, but controlling your focus manually is usually preferred. It is a skill that you will carry with you from camera device to camera device. You get greater creative control this way regardless of technologies.

The main lesson about focus is to have something important in focus at all times. Humans do not see "out of focus" by design (unless you require prescription corrective lenses and do not wear them). We do not like to watch a blurry image because it goes against our nature. Our eyes and brains try to make it sharp when it cannot be made sharp, and we reject it. That is why a viewer might overlook bad framing or flat lighting, but any out-of-focus (blurry or soft-focus) shot stands out like a sore thumb. Of course, there are special cases and allowances for creative uses of blur. Perhaps the shot is a subjective POV and the camera represents the altered perceptions of an inebriated or semi-conscious character. Music videos, commercials, and experimental films often play with radical focus shifting and blurred imagery as well.

As an example, let us say that your frame has one female character in a close-up shot. If the depth of field of the shot is shallow enough, only the woman is in focus and the background is blurry. Creatively, this helps to keep the attention of the audience on the woman and not on other objects behind her in the frame. However, if the woman fully exits the frame and the focal plane does not alter, then the background will remain blurry

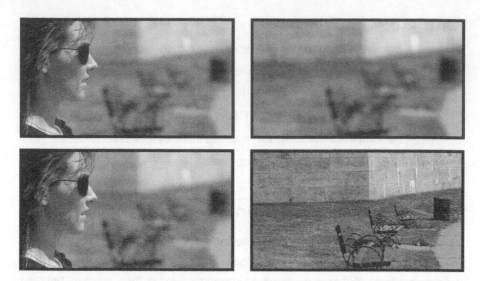

FIGURE 7.9 A series of shots illustrating no focus shift to the background and then a rack focus from the fore-ground subject to the background after the subject's exit from the frame. Typically, the audience should have something in focus to look at on the screen.

and the audience are left watching an empty blurry frame until the next shot cuts onto the screen. It is good practice to rack focus to the background as soon as the character fully exits the frame. This way, the audience are watching the woman (in focus) leave the frame and then their eyes can immediately rest on the background, which has come into sharp focus. There is no awkward feeling or moment of confusion on the part of the viewer. This is critical, especially just before a cut to a new shot or new scene. The quick, smooth shift in the plane of critical focus to the background gives the viewer's eye something to focus on as the shot ends (Figure 7.9).

10. Control Your Depth of Field

You should always be aware of your depth of field (DOF): the range of objects seen to be in acceptable focus within the depth of your shot. The DOF can be controlled (made greater or smaller) and shifted within the film space (moved closer to or further from camera). Remember that the nature of optics will provide you with only one plane of critical focus in front of the camera's lens. Whatever lives exactly at that distance from the camera will be in sharpest focus. The DOF operates around this one plane of critical focus and its depth (in distance from the camera) is segmented into two unequal parts. The first segment (roughly one-third the overall area of good focus) falls before the plane of critical focus, and the second segment (roughly the remaining two-thirds of the good focus depth) falls just behind it.

If you are familiar with the several variables that can affect the DOF, then you will always know how to control it.

- LIGHT – When your set or location is bathed in lots of light, either from the sun or from large film lighting fixtures, you will need to close down the iris of the lens to achieve "proper" exposure. The smaller iris opening (or higher f-stop number) optically causes a larger depth of field. This is why many daylight exterior shots provide you with sharp focus on almost all objects – from very near to the camera out to infinity. **Deep focus** techniques such as this can be used on interior film sets, but you have to bathe the space with very large quantities of light to achieve this.

  When you shoot in very dark spaces, the lens iris must be opened up very wide, letting in as much light as possible in order to capture a properly exposed image. This wider opening of the lens aperture causes a shallow DOF. You must be cautious when shooting in low-light conditions because it is more difficult to keep the important objects within your frame in proper focus, particularly when there is movement toward or away from the lens. If your shooting environment is bright (sunny) and you wish for a more shallow DOF, then you could employ neutral-density filtration (either attached to the lens or digitally in your camera settings) to "knock down" the quantity of light used for exposure and achieve that wider lens aperture.

- FOCAL LENGTH – The optics of the camera lens also play a role in how much DOF you get to use. Wide-angle lenses, or lenses set to a short focal length such as 10mm, will offer a greater DOF. Long-focal-length lenses, set to 75 or 100mm or more, will generate a much more shallow DOF.

- CAMERA-TO-SUBJECT DISTANCE – The DOF increases when your subject (and the plane of critical focus) is far away from the camera. The DOF decreases when your subject (and the plane of critical focus) is very close to the camera. Macro-photography (capturing images of small objects very close to the lens) exhibits this same phenomenon. Your lens may have a macro setting, or you could employ close-up filters (+ diopters or "plus" diopters). Product shots and TV commercial work can use these to great effect.

- SIZE AND SENSITIVITY OF THE RECORDING MEDIUM – The sensitivity of your video camera's digital imager and its size play a factor in the depth of field calculation. A "full-frame" sensor offers more opportunity to play with a shallow DOF, while smaller "cropped" sensors usually yield a larger DOF.

10. Control Your Depth of Field

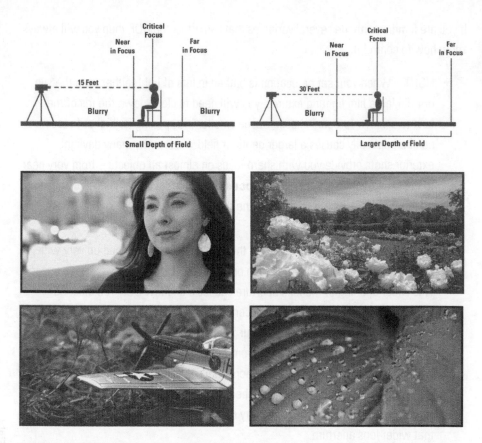

FIGURE 7.10 A shallow depth of field directs the audience to look where the focus is. A larger DOF creates a deeper area within the film space that also appears in sharp focus, allowing the audience to see both near and far. Macro or close-up cinematography can yield a very shallow DOF of just a few millimeters or inches. (Photo credit: F – Brennan Marlow)

It will now be rather simple to imagine a scenario for either a very large DOF or a very narrow one. Placing the camera far away from a subject, with a wide-angle lens setting and lots of light, will generate a very large DOF: a great distance, both near and far from the camera, will be in apparent focus. Placing the camera rather close to your subject, with a long-focal-length lens in very dim lighting, will generate a rather shallow DOF. Use these guidelines when you wish to keep your subject in focus but blur out your foreground or background objects (Figure 7.10).

11. Be Aware of Headroom

An important part of your compositional considerations should always be headroom: how much or how little space you allow at the top of the frame for a person's hair or hat, etc. Too much headroom will force the eyes and face of a subject too low in the frame. Too little headroom will raise them too high in the frame or simply look wrong due to the chopping-off of the forehead, etc. If you have to err in one direction, however, you should have slightly less headroom.

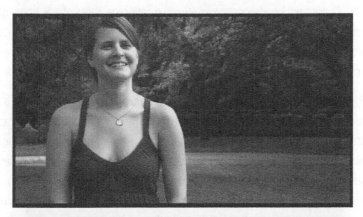

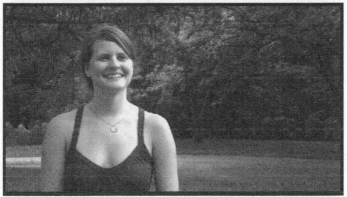

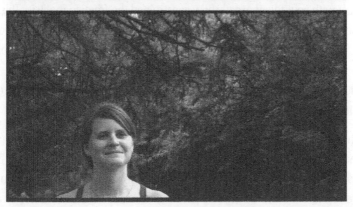

11. Be Aware of Headroom

FIGURE 7.11 Always compose subjects for proper headroom in your shots.

Why? Well, when you give too much and force the face lower in the frame, you also force the mouth and chin lower. As the person speaks, it is very likely that the bottom of the chin and jaw will break below the bottom edge of the frame in a CU shot. The top of the head does not traditionally move, so it is safer to place it above the top edge of the frame. This keeps the chin and jaw fully visible in the frame as the person speaks (Figure 7.11). Consistent headroom across mirrored coverage shots of a fictional narrative dialogue scene is also important. As the editor cuts back and forth between characters, the headroom of each shot will stay relatively consistent, keeping the viewer's eyes engaged roughly at the same height in the frame.

The talking-head subject being interviewed for a documentary also requires a consistent treatment of headroom. While shooting a long question-and-answer session for a documentary, it is important that the camera operator maintains consistent headroom throughout the shoot. The editing may call for shots to be placed in any order, and if there is largely differing headroom among the shots, it may look awkward when they are cut together in the final piece. As a final important tidbit about shooting the talent for a documentary, try not to reframe drastically while the subject is speaking. Very slight pans and tilts may be necessary to keep proper framing as the subject moves around in his or her seat, but you should not drastically alter your focal length, framing, or focus while the subject is giving the answer to a question. If you do, it will most likely make that portion of the visuals unusable for the editor. You should wait until the subject stops speaking and then reframe and adjust focal length and focus.

12. Shooting Tight Close-Ups

If you need to shoot a tight close-up or an extreme close-up of a face, mouth, or hands, be very clear with your talent exactly how constrained the framing really is. This enables them to better judge the limitations of their possible on-camera movements for such a tight shot. A close-up is going to be achieved with either very close camera proximity to the talent or a rather long-focal-length lens on a camera slightly further away. In either case, the resulting frame represents a magnification of the person's face, mouth, or hands, and therefore the entire screen will be filled with that information.

With such extreme magnification, the slightest movements of the talent can "break frame" (move beyond the edges of the established frame border), alter good composition to bad, change critical focus within the depth of field, etc. Typically, your goal would be to have the talent move as little as possible on these very close shots. If action is needed, be very precise about how little movement is really required and communicate

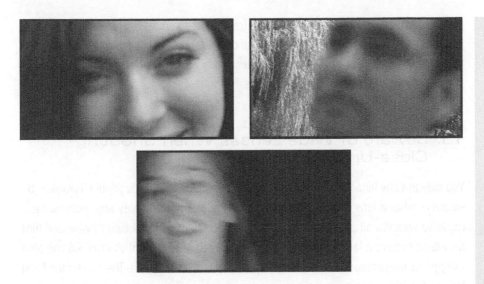

FIGURE 7.12   It is easy to "break frame" or lose focus when dealing with human subjects in BCU and XCU shots. Clearly communicate the limitations of movement inside this tight framing to your subject.

that clearly to the talent. You may even choose to show them physically what you need by demonstrating it yourself.

There is an old expression concerning an actor's performance: "Less is more." This holds very true when photographing the close-up shots. With the entire face filling the frame, slow, subtle movements and minor changes in facial expressions yield a very effective performance. The audience, attuned to watching faces for emotional cues, can make a very powerful connection with the actor in close-up.

Projects destined for television, computer, tablet, or smartphone screens can benefit from having more MS to MCU shots than media distributed for the large cinema screens. The closer shots display more important narrative information and the magnified visual details "read" better on the smaller display screens.

When you are planning your shots for coverage, incorporate the big close-up and XCU shots of "details" with discretion. If they fit your overall visual style for the project, have a place in the narrative, and provide important details to the audience, then they will fit in with your other shot types. If not, they have the potential to be too "big" and run the risk of standing out as visual anomalies within your project.

Documentaries and other non-fiction filmmaking involve many talking-head interview close-up shots. You will find that the MS and the MCU might be the tightest shots you wish to get. A CU or especially a BCU might be too intimate when listening to a scientist or historian discussing factual information (remember the meaning of the implied proximity between the image size and the audience). However, the audience might not mind a very tight close-up in an emotional documentary about a cancer survivor. Here, the personal connection feels more appropriate.

13. Beware of Wide Lenses When Shooting Close-Up Shots

You may use any lens you like if it suits the shot and the story. You should, however, be aware of what a lens will do for your image in both a positive way and, potentially, a negative way. We all understand that wide lenses capture a large field of view and that they tend to have a larger depth of field. The curvature of the optics involved can also exaggerate the perspective when the subject is close to the camera. The shorter the focal length, the more exaggerated the warped perspective. Extreme versions of this optical phenomenon are called fisheye lenses, like you find on wearable action cameras.

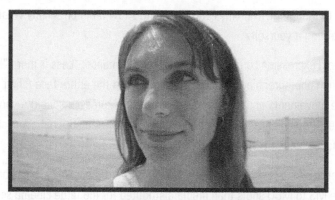

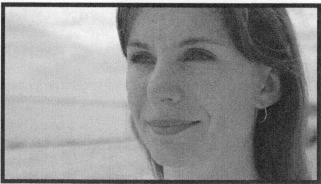

FIGURE 7.13 Wide lenses in close can distort facial features in a CU. A longer focal length from slightly further away can help to keep the "portrait" perspective normal.

If you set your lens to the shortest focal length and reduce the camera-to-subject distance to get a close-up shot, you will most likely encounter this warped perspective exaggeration. The individual's nose will appear larger and perhaps bulbous, almost poking out at the camera, whereas the ears and the remainder of the head will appear to recede from the camera. Background objects, if visible, will also appear much smaller and more distant than they would with longer FLs.

This treatment (the warped perspective) is often used for a comic effect or when you wish to show a "nightmare" state of consciousness. For normal CU work, however, you may be better served by using a longer-focal-length setting on your lens and moving the camera further away from the talent. Much like still photographers who use longer lenses to take portraits, you can reduce the exaggerated perspective of the subject by "flattening" the recorded space. The reduced depth of field of the long FL may also help to isolate the facial features and bring more attention to the CU, while the background blurs (Figure 7.13).

14. Try to Show Both Eyes of Your Subject

The eyes of your subject act as a magnet for the eyes of the viewer and much of the emotional or mental state of the character is conveyed via the eyes in a close-up shot. So, if it fits your story, you would be well served by making sure that the subject's eyes are both visible. This can be easily achieved with a well-lit 3/4 profile shot. The use of the **eye light** or **catch light** for bringing extra attention to the eyes will be discussed later in this chapter.

The 3/4 profile allows the camera lens to see and record both eyes of the subject. This same angle on the subject would work for an over-the-shoulder shot as well, but you may have to play with the physical distance between the actors to get the framing correct. If you wanted to quickly change an over-the-shoulder shot into a clean single close-up in 3/4 profile, you would have to ask the actor whose back is to camera to step backward a few paces in order to clear the edge of the frame. Keeping that now out-of-frame actor nearby will maintain the eye-line of the actor being recorded in the CU (Figure 7.14).

Remember that a straight-to-camera shot will reveal both eyes, and if the eyes remain off the axis of the lens, then you have a clear full-face view of the subject. If the talent looks directly into the lens, then the shot becomes entirely a subjective shot, which is less appropriate for drama and more appropriate for news reporting or hosted programming. A full profile shot is also a specialty shot. Only one side of the subject's face is

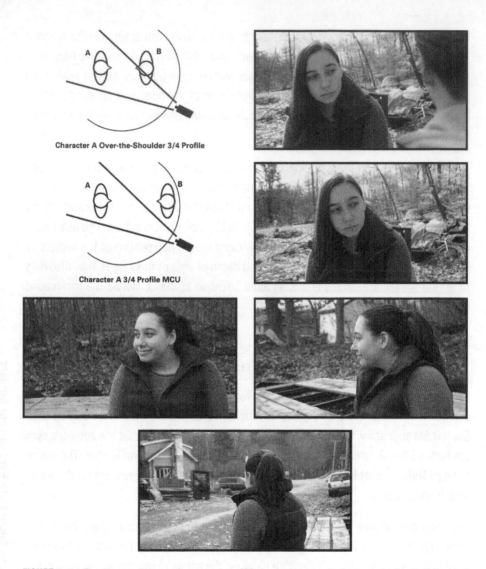

Character A Over-the-Shoulder 3/4 Profile

Character A 3/4 Profile MCU

FIGURE 7.14 The diagrams illustrate how to turn an OTS shot into a clean single shot by having the "shoulder" talent step back and out of the frame. These examples show a 3/4 profile, a full profile, and a full back shot of the subject. Use the most appropriate angle for the shot in your story, but remember to favor your subject's eyes as much as possible. (Photo credits: Zach Benard and Anthony Martel)

visible and the one eye that is visible cannot really be "looked into." The audience stay separated from the subject's thoughts or feelings, but if this framing begins a pan over to what the character is looking at, then the initial profile is a motivator for conveying new visual information to the audience. Of course, you should use any talent position or camera angle that you feel is appropriate to your story, provided it conveys your meaning or makes visible your intended information. The 3/4 profile is just a very solid approach to shooting closer shots and it will not disappoint the audience.

15. Be Aware of Eye-Line Directions in Closer Shots

An eye-line traces across the film space to connect the subject's gaze to some object of interest. Whether the object of interest is another person, a picture frame, a car outside of a window, or a menacing cloud in the sky does not matter. What *does* matter is the direction in which the actor's eyes look when you cover them in a medium shot or closer. Head placement and the resulting direction of the subject's gaze are easy to "fudge" in a wide shot because we have greater context in the film space. Close shots reveal more detail of the subject's head and eye alignment but remove the greater context of the film space, so a keener emphasis on eye-line direction is needed.

Generally, when filmmakers look at the talent through the camera's lens, they will have to gauge how accurate the eye-line of the actor is. Does it match the direction of the eye

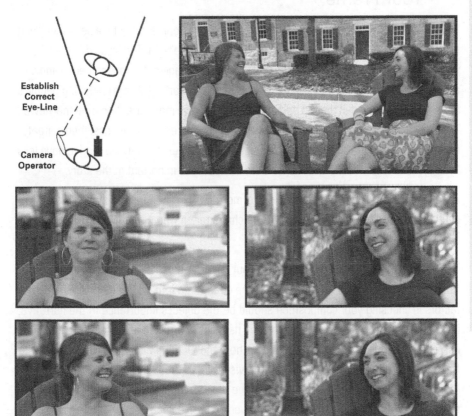

FIGURE 7.15 The talent's eye-line must match from wide shots into closer shots. The eye-line of Character A is first off its "mark" and then corrected. You may have to talk the talent into establishing a new object of interest on set for a better eye-line.

already established in the wider shots? Will it match up with the corresponding shot of the object being "seen" when the reveal shot is edited after? Because close-up shots magnify the features, it may be necessary to modify the actual direction in which an actor is looking. The important thing is to ensure that the eye-lines for all concerned characters match in their individual shots. The angle or direction of the gaze will often just not look correct and you will have to talk the talent into adopting the right eye-line (Figure 7.15). Experienced actors can pick a spot and "hit" their eye-line marks off camera easily. In certain situations, it can be helpful if someone behind or around the camera holds a tracking object, such as his or her closed fist, to get the talent to establish the new and correct eye-line for your closer shots.

16. Place Important Objects in the Top Half of Your Frame

We normally view things from the top down (pages of a book, a website, a person walking toward us, etc.) and, in many cultures, from the left to the right. This is no different when viewing a motion picture. Filmmakers have taken advantage of this phenomenon and created meaning around an object's placement within the frame. Objects (including people's heads) that are placed in the top half of the frame receive more attention from the viewer. The objects are said to have more "weight" or visual presence and are assigned a greater importance within the scene or story. Objects placed lower in the frame tend to have less "weight" and less visual presence, and are seen as less important in the story.

An example is a wide two-shot where a more powerful character stands frame left over the seated figure of the less powerful character on frame right. An up/down power dynamic is created (Figure 7.16).

This does not mean that you should never put important objects in the lower half of your frame, but the top half/bottom half guideline does come into play quite often. Some key factors in choosing your composition should be the object's importance in the narrative, its size (proximity to the camera/audience), its focus and its illumination, and, of course, its position within the frame. Think about how the viewing audience will look at your frame on screen. How will they digest the visual information that you present to them? Many significant objects will be placed at the top, but interesting compositions that use the entire frame can also challenge the viewer. You can compel the viewer's eyes to roam the image looking for that item of interest. You may wish to experiment and put all of the main objects of a story at the bottom of the frame and see what kind of reaction you get from the audience.

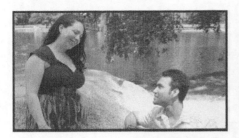
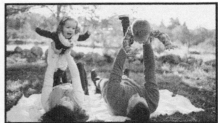

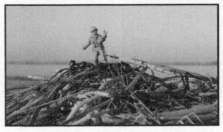

FIGURE 7.16 Objects placed higher in the frame hold more visual "weight" or importance. A viewer's eye is trained to look there first. (Photo credit: B – Amy DeCosta)

17. Keep Distracting Objects out of the Shot

Many of you will have seen a live news report on location when a passer-by waves vigorously at the camera from behind the standing reporter. The out-of-place movements distract our attention away from the main point of the report and the connection to the story is lost. A small crew on a live news report cannot do much to prevent these distractions, but any not-live-to-air shoot should allow for some control over the set. Take the time to verify that the frame is clean and that no objects, either moving or stationary, might prove to be a visual distraction for the viewing audience.

The main goal is to keep the composition strong. Any object that has noticeable movements, bright colors, or an odd shape can compromise the good composition by acting as an "eye magnet" to the viewer. If you shoot a CU of a person's head, make sure that no strange lines, shapes, or objects appear behind the head. This can have a comic effect when done intentionally, but, for the most part, frame these shots so that no distracting objects either obscure the face in the foreground or "grow" out of the head or body from the background. The same can be said for any talking-head interview shot for a documentary. Active TV screens, computer monitors, and even windows to the outside world can draw the viewer's eye away from the main subject. Either do not incorporate these items in the shot, or purposefully overexpose them or blur them out through creating a very shallow depth of field (Figure 7.17).

17. Keep Distracting Objects out of the Shot

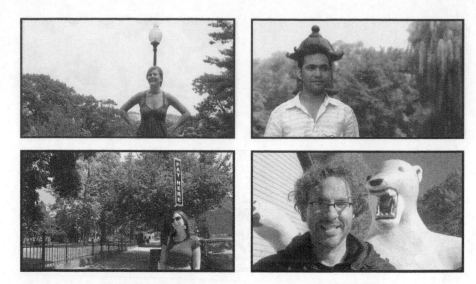

FIGURE 7.17 Try to keep your frame clean and free of distracting objects, especially if they are overly colorful, move too much, or appear awkwardly near the heads of the talent.

18. Use the Depth of the Film Space to Stage Shots with Several People

Simple shots of one or two people allow ample screen space to compose their blocking and placement within the frame. When your shot must contain a larger number of people, you will have to find creative ways to layer the multiple subjects into the depth of the film space. The foreground, middle ground, and near background become a combined zone where persons can be blocked or staged to fit within the frame. As seen through the camera's lens, the bodies of the people will have a slight overlap, but the faces will mostly be clearly visible and discernible.

The actual blocking will depend on the physical space of the set or location, the set dressing or furnishings within the space, and the size of the individuals. For groups of six to ten people, you may need to have some sitting and some standing and all at different distances from the camera's lens. If the group is larger or needs to be a crowd, there will eventually be a point where an overlap of faces will occur and most will not be discernible. In that event, place the most knowable or important people nearer to the camera so that the audience can still see their faces and recognize them for who they are.

It is not often desirable to have one or more characters whose head is turned away from the camera, but you might find that to have all heads facing the same direction (toward the lens) looks awkward, unnatural, or too subjective. When you finally know the

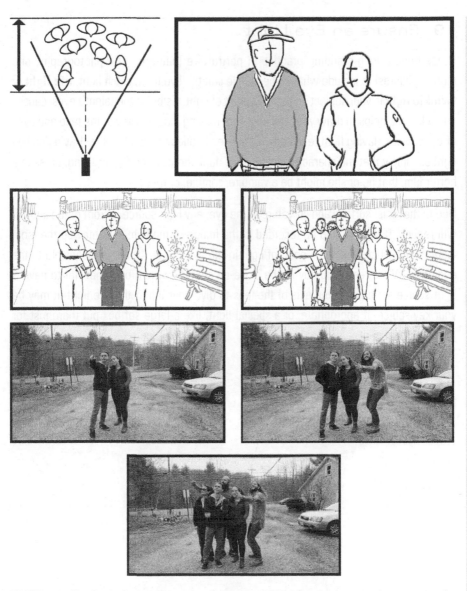

FIGURE 7.18 Use the depth of the film space to help to stage the bodies when more people must occupy the frame. (Photo credits: E–G – Zach Benard and Anthony Martel)

variables on the day of shooting, you should quickly experiment with the best blocking options that take advantage of the depth of the film space. Raising the camera height above the crowd (a slightly higher-angle shot) will also show the staging of bodies deep into the set, and more faces may be seen this way (Figure 7.18).

18. Use the Depth of the Film Space to Stage Shots with Several People

19. Ensure an Eye Light

It has been a long-standing practice in portraiture (painting, still photography, and motion pictures) to include what some people call the eye light, catch light, **life light** or **twinkle light** in your subject's eyes. This point of light, visible in the talent's eyes, causes a twinkle and helps to draw your audience into looking more closely at the face and eyes of the subject. Having light reflected off the eyes implies the spark of life. Having no eye light can imply that the character is dark, evil, duplicitous, or no longer living, or, as in a horror film, that he or she might be a vampire, zombie, or robot.

Due to the moist surface and curvature of the eye, any light source in front of the subject will reflect off the eye and be recorded in the image. A medium shot may be the most distant shot where the small point of light in the eye can be "read" or be visible to the audience. While recording any of the close-up shots, it would be beneficial to have a light source set up near the axis of the lens to give your talent the eye light; it may be your key source, if appropriate, or a special light, like a large softbox put there just for the catch light glint.

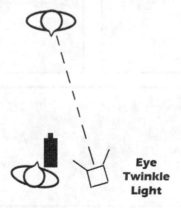

Eye
Twinkle
Light

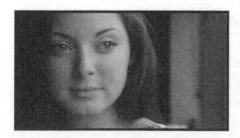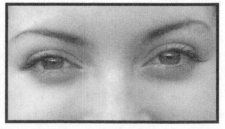

FIGURE 7.19 A light source placed along the axis of the lens will help to generate an eye light or twinkle on the recorded image. These bright dots in the eyes bring life to your subject.

Whether you are using a point source, a soft source, a bounce, or the sun, the important thing is to make sure that the reflection in the eye shows the light source coming from the correct direction of other known light sources in the film world. Because most lighting fixtures in reality and in film worlds are above the head of the people, the reflection would be in the middle to the top hemisphere of the human eye as seen through the camera's lens. In certain instances, as with a desk lamp, smartphone or computer screen, or water reflection, the eye's twinkle light may come from below and be visible in the bottom half of the eye. In the end, because the eyes are so important, it is almost always a good idea to give them as much attention as you can in all of your shots, even just for reasons of good exposure (Figure 7.19).

20. Be Aware of Color and Contrast Choices Made Throughout Your Project

Color choices can be very important to any motion media production. A particular color can take on meaning in your story: red could be a warning or indicate passion, whereas blue could symbolize a cold or uncaring individual, a sterile environment, or even the freedom found in the open air or water. Even if you do not take your color scheme that far into thematic meaning, the color choices that are made for set dressing, costumes, and make-up will have an effect on how the shots get recorded and how visible certain objects might be. For instance, you may not wish to put a subject fully clothed in dark clothing in front of a shadowy or dark-colored wall fearing that she or he will get "lost" in the sea of darkness. Or maybe that is precisely what you wish to do.

There is a science to color and light and there are numerous artistic color theories that you should certainly explore more on your own (see the suggested internet and book references in Appendix A). Just be aware that bright colors and warmer tones will tend to appear closer to a viewer (as though they were popping off the screen), whereas darker colors and cooler tones appear to be further away (as if they were receding into the background). This phenomenon could help you to create particular areas of visual attention in your compositions by juxtaposing bright and dark color areas within your sets and wardrobe (Figure 7.20). An art director or production designer often works on such details and collaborates with the film's director and director of photography to help to establish an overall look.

Beyond the colors of paint and fabrics, you can also apply colored gels to lighting fixtures to create color washes across people and environments – most commonly seen as blue for cool moonlight at night and orange for warm interior night lights. These work especially

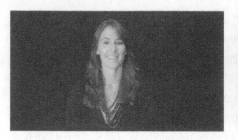 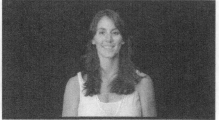

FIGURE 7.20 The colors or tones of wardrobe and set dressing can play a major role in your image creation. Beware of combining dark clothes with dark backgrounds.

well together within the same lighting scheme. There are also color-altering processes that you can use during the post-production phase of a digital video project. These color treatment effects may even include **desaturation,** where you remove much (or maybe all) of the color information from your source material.

21. Allow the Camera More Time to Record Each Shot

We all know that time and money are very important to all motion media projects, no matter what the medium, format, story, or type of event being shot. Most often, the ultimate goal is to pass on all production video to the editing team and have them piece together the final presentation. It is very important that you provide the post-production crew with as much usable visual material as possible, which means making sure that each take of each shot has plenty of start-up time and plenty of completion time.

It is wise to get the camera **rolling** before any critical action happens. This allows all equipment the time required to get up to **operating speed** and it gives the talent and crew time to settle. Rolling the camera (starting the recording process) before "Action!" is called also provides the editor with critical extra frames at the head of the shot. She or he can then potentially use these extra video frames to pad out the timing of the shots during the edit or even create a longer video transition effect in the editing software. It is a common pitfall of new filmmakers to start recording as they call out "Action!" and as a result they often miss some very critical frames at the start of the shot. This holds especially true for tape-based capture but also applies when a camera generates digital media file video.

A similar process should be followed at the end of the shot. As the filmmaker calls "Cut!," the camera should be allowed a few more seconds of recording time. This ensures that all

HOW TO "CALL THE ROLL"

1. "LOCK IT UP!"
2. "EVERYONE SETTLE. THIS IS FOR A TAKE."
3. "ROLL SOUND" - IF RECORDING SEPARATELY
4. "SPEED" - FROM THE SOUND MIXER
5. "ROLL CAMERA"
6. "ROLLING" - FROM CAMERA OPERATOR
7. VOICE / PICTURE SLATE (SCENE & TAKE)
8. "MARKER"
9. CLOSE THE SLATE CLAP STICKS - 'CLACK!'
10. PAUSE A MOMENT OR TWO
11. "ACTION!"
12. ACTION BEGINS
13. ACTION ENDS
14. PAUSE A MOMENT OR TWO
15. "CUT!"
16. STOP DEVICES RECORDING PICTURE/SOUND

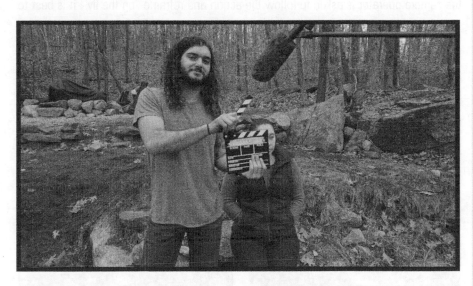

FIGURE 7.21 Rolling the camera early and stopping it late will ensure the capture of the extra "padding" footage often needed during the edit. Slating shots will help to identify them during post-production. If you wish, use this method of "calling the roll" to be thorough. (Photo credit: B – Zach Benard)

necessary action is captured by the camera and also provides that critical extra footage at the tail of the shot for the editor to play with. Getting into the practice of rolling early and cutting a bit late will help you to win friends for life on the editing team (Figure 7.21).

21. Allow the Camera More Time to Record Each Shot

22. Follow Action with a Loose Pan and Tilt Tripod Head

Much of what you record with your shots will involve objects or talent in motion. Whether you are framing a medium shot or a medium close-up, you could run the risk of having the action on screen bump the edges of the frame or even break out beyond the boundaries of your frame – usually left, right, or top. It is best to keep all major action away from the edges of your frame, but there will be times where the action covers more ground on set or location and you will need to follow the movements of your subject. This certainly happens with sports coverage, but it may be as subtle as tilting up slightly when your actor sits up tall in his or her seat when he or she gets a brilliant idea (Figure 7.22).

Most tripod heads (where you mount the camera to the support legs) are equipped with pan and tilt capabilities and therefore pan and tilt locks to help to keep them stable. When the camera operator is asked to follow the action and reframe "on the fly," it is best to

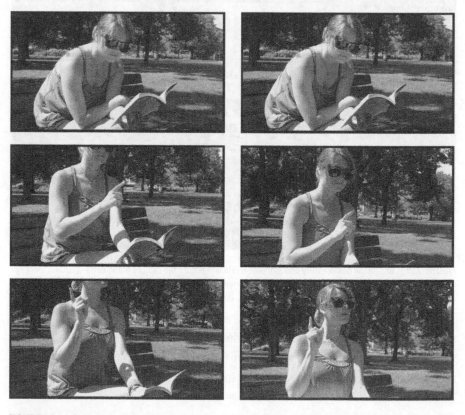

FIGURE 7.22 The camera operator is responsible for maintaining proper composition while recording the subject's performance. Subtle or more substantial movements will require reframing during the take and keeping the tripod's pan and tilt locks loose can help with this.

have a better-quality tripod head and camera support. The more professional equipment allows for smoother and more stable panning and tilting actions.

The goal of the camera operator is to maintain good framing. This is clearly understood if the talent is making substantial movements, such as pacing the floor, playing tennis, or dancing. It may be less intuitive but just as wise to keep the pan and tilt locks loose when you are recording closer shots. This allows for smooth, minor adjustments of the camera angle as the subject gesticulates or makes other small head movements during the take. An operator should be free to recompose as needed because the film frame is rarely a "set-it-and-forget-it" situation. This reframing happens all of the time, either smoothly and unobtrusively or with quick, jerky shifts in composition; the established visual style of the program will often dictate the chosen method.

23. Shooting Overlapping Action for the Edit

Remember that it is your job during production to provide the appropriate shots to the editor so that the visual elements will make sense and cut smoothly in the final product. When you have to shoot an action from two or more angles and you do not have the luxury of operating more than one camera, you will have to make the talent repeat the same action over and over again for each take at each camera position. Overlapping action is the action performed by the talent that is visible from the different camera angles covering the scene. You need to record this overlapping action in each shot so that the editor will have good and varied choices for creating an "action edit" or a "continuity edit." (Learn more about editing practices in the companion text, *Grammar of the Edit.*)

Wide shots and medium shots may call for more overlapping action coverage due to their inclusion of more visual elements. Closer shots will not normally require as much overlapping coverage because they tend to highlight details that are magnified on the screen and not as much movement can be recorded for matching from one shot to the next – although matching the direction and speed of head turns, hand movements, etc. in CU shots is rather important for smooth continuity action edits.

Continuity of Action

Most filmmakers value performance over continuity, and some will encourage their talent to perform similar movements but alter the scripted lines or emote in various ways from shot to shot and take to take. This approach can work well if the performance is there in all coverage shots, but, if not, the continuity mismatches will be a nightmare during the editing process.

Matching Speed of Action

Closer shots of overlapping action may benefit from having the movements performed at a slightly slower speed. For example, your scene calls for a subject to walk up to a closed door, turn the knob, open the door, and walk through into the next room. You decide to cover the action with an MLS and an MCU on one side of the door and an MS on the other. The actions performed by the talent in the MLS and MS should be of similar speeds (walking up to the door and opening the door and walking through). However, there may be a need for a modification to the speed of execution on the part of the actor while performing the close-up shot. A hand traveling into a close-up shot of a doorknob will appear to move much faster across the screen because the screen is only showing the magnified detail of the doorknob and the moving hand. As experienced by the audience, the larger object covers more screen space in a faster time. In wider shots, when more of the comparative film space is visible, the movements of an object or action can appear slower even though the rate of progress is the same. So, for proper continuity, you may wish to shoot the close-up insert shot with slightly slower movement by the talent. At your discretion, perhaps shoot another take at "normal" speed so that the editor will have both choices (Figure 7.23).

Too Much Overlapping Action

There is a danger in shooting too much overlapping action on each camera set-up. For economy of time, money, and energy in both production and post-production, it is

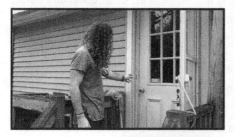
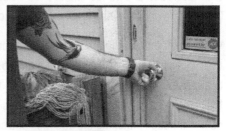
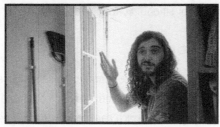

FIGURE 7.23 Talent movements in CU shots should be performed slightly slower so that, when magnified across the entire screen, they appear normal when compared to the rate of movement in the wider shots of continuous action. (Photo credits: Zach Benard)

wise to be judicious with your choices of how much or how little overlapping action will need to be captured from each unique camera angle. Too little will provide the editor with inadequate options for cutting the continuity edit. Too much may allow a greater choice but can come at the added expense of more time and money being spent on getting the extraneous coverage that may never be used during the edit.

24. Frame for Correct Look Room on Shots that Will Edit Together

You need to record a simple scene of two people facing each other having a conversation. In addition to a wide two-shot, your coverage calls for clean singles with medium close-ups. When you compose for the MCU of Character A on the left, you might place A's head along the one-third "line" on frame left, allowing him or her to look across the empty space over to frame right. The "answering" shot of Character B is mirrored in its composition, with B's head on frame right looking across the void to frame left. This composition mimics what the wider two-shot had already established regarding the empty space between the two characters. The eye-lines of the subjects trace back and forth across the empty space between them and, as a result, the audience will do the same when the two MCU shots are edited together. The direction of the "gaze" is maintained and followed across the cut (Figure 5.12).

This same technique can be used between a person and any object at which he or she may look. In one shot, a person frame left may be looking off frame right at an object.

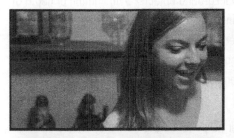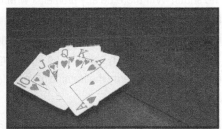
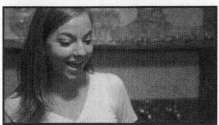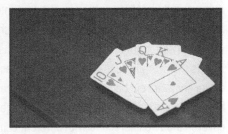

FIGURE 7.24 It is important to follow lines of attention and allow for proper look room space when composing closer shots of people and their objects of desire that will be cut together.

When you record the answering shot, that object should be placed over on frame right to allow the appropriate space for look room. When these two shots are cut together, the eye-line traces across to screen right in Shot 1 and continues that direction in Shot 2 until the viewer's eye rests upon the object of interest. It would be rather awkward to frame people or objects such that when they are cut together they appear to butt up against one another, as in Figure 7.24.

25. Shoot Matching Camera Angles When Covering a Dialogue Scene

With a traditional approach to recording a simple dialogue scene, you would most likely begin by covering the wide or establishing shot. You may then move the camera for a tighter two-shot, then get one character for his or her over-the-shoulder shot and clean single, and finally "turn around" and get the same tighter shots for the other character. Working this way, you set the scene for the audience and also allow the talent to settle in and match their lines and actions better across each take of each shot. Your goal should be to use the same camera distance, camera height, lens focal length, and depth of field, and the same or very similar lighting for each character. The framing and composition of the single close-up shots and any OTS shots should mirror one another.

The important lesson for the new filmmaker to remember is that although close-up shots may be shot last, they should be thought about ahead of time to check how they will be physically set up in that environment. Will there be room for the camera to move to get the shots? Will there be any problems with background objects? Will lighting or depth of field pose any issues? Before you set everything and shoot the wide shot, it can be a good idea to quickly walk through the other camera set-up positions and check for possible "gotchas." With today's small and lightweight cameras, or even your smartphone, it is relatively easy to verify the framing of your planned shots once you, the talent, the lighting, etc. are in place on set.

As usual, how things eventually edit together helps to dictate how they should be originally recorded. When you cover the two individuals talking in this simple scene, their close-up shots and over-the-shoulder shots should match or mirror one another. This way, when the editor gets to cut the scene together, the viewer sees the wide shot and understands the overall scene's lighting and character placement in the film space. Then, when closer shots are cut back to back, the audience are given matching mirrored shots and know how to place these individuals within the larger film space outside the CU frame. If you have covered the two characters with different camera heights, lens focal lengths, or depths of field, or drastically different lighting, then there will be noticeable visual incongruity in the

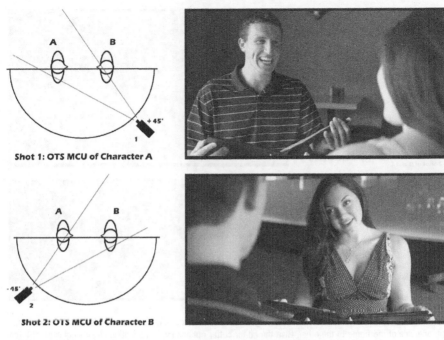

Shot 1: OTS MCU of Character A

Shot 2: OTS MCU of Character B

FIGURE 7.25 Shoot matching shot–reverse–shot coverage for traditional editing choices.

edited scene. Mismatched shots cut in a back-and-forth fashion could confuse and possibly annoy the viewer because the information being presented is not harmonious.

This sequence of mirrored coverage is often called **shot–reverse–shot**. The coverage shots for one character are shot all of the way through into the closest framing and then the camera and lighting can switch over to cover the shots for the remaining character. In our example, the first MCU is shot from +45 degrees around the 180-degree arc and, eventually, the other character is covered in an MCU from –45 degrees (Figure 7.25). You get matching imagery, and the shot–reverse–shot cycle is available for the edit.

26. A Three-Person Dialogue Scene: Matching Two-Shots Can Be Problematic for the Editor

By staging three people standing across the width of the frame in a wide shot, you establish the position and spatial relations among the people. For this example, let us label the person frame left as Character A, the person in the middle as Character B, and the person frame right as Character C. You would normally continue to get coverage of the scene by moving in for the two-shot. In this case, you could get a two-shot of A and B and you could get a two-shot of B and C. The issue arises during the editing session.

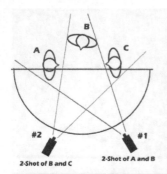

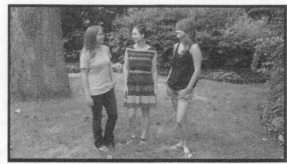

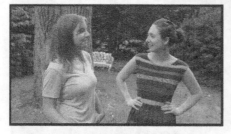

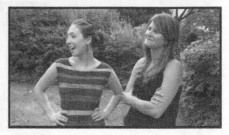

FIGURE 7.26 Two-shots in a three-person dialogue scene will not cut together well as the central figure jumps from one side of the frame to the other. Give the editor better options by also shooting clean singles of all three characters in addition to the wide shot.

In Two-Shot 1, A will be frame left and B will be frame right, but in Two-Shot 2, B will be frame left and C will be frame right. If you cut Two-Shot 1 next to Two-Shot 2, you will clearly see B jump from frame right to frame left (Figure 7.26). This may prove rather distracting to a viewing audience. It could also cause continuity of dialogue and action issues for the editor. Although you should shoot both two-shots mentioned earlier, you may also wish to shoot single close-up shots of all three characters so that the editor will have the best possible shot options when the cutting process begins.

27. Beware of Continuity Traps While Shooting a Scene

A filmmaker needs to be aware of many continuity concerns while shooting coverage for a scene: matching dialogue delivery, action or motion, framing, camera angles, eye-line, etc. There may be many things, however, beyond the basics that can cause a continuity headache. The important thing is to be observant and thorough. Continuity issues can make the post-production process difficult, so try to avoid them during production (Figure 7.27).

Continuity traps tend to be objects on set or around the shooting location that will change over time. Shooting all of the coverage for a particular scene or event can take a long time, so these continuity traps will appear to change (sometimes drastically) from one shot to the next and back again when the coverage is edited together. These secondary continuity errors may not be as noticeable as actor movement or eye-line matching but they are still potential sources of audience annoyance. Any time that the audience are reminded that they are watching an artificially crafted motion picture, you run the risk of losing them and their positive attention.

Continuity traps to watch for:

- Be aware of functional clocks or large watches that could potentially reveal a jumping back and forth through time when the scene is edited.
- The same goes for the movement of the sun. Either bright sunshine or the resulting shadow movement will jump around from shot to shot during the edited piece. You may not have any control over the sunlight, but you could structure your shooting schedule around it or change the framing so that it does not become an issue. Dawn and dusk may bring about issues of streetlights and car headlamps in use when none should be on at that "film time."
- Any background activity, such as a functional TV display, people walking, and cars driving, should be either removed or made to repeat actions in each coverage shot where they may be visible to the camera.
- Finally, audio concerns should be addressed, such as airplanes, automotive vehicle sounds, telephones ringing, refrigeration and HVAC units, and especially music from any source around your location. All of these could potentially pose a threat to smooth audio editing.

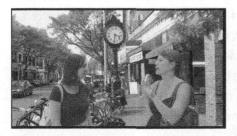
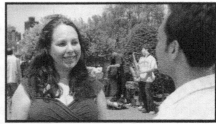

FIGURE 7.27 Be aware of continuity traps (both visible and auditory). The clock and the street musicians may not help your edited shots.

27. Beware of Continuity Traps While Shooting a Scene

28. Ways to Cross the 180-Degree Line Safely

We know that when shooting coverage for a scene, the camera should normally stay on one side of the set or location within the established 180-degree arc. We do this so that when the various shots of that scene's coverage are edited together, the screen direction of movements and the eye-lines of characters match the established spatial relations found in the wider master shot. There may be times when you wish to move the camera around the set and get new angles on action from the opposite or "incorrect" side of the axis of action. This can be done, but there are some special ways to do it without it being jarring to the viewing audience.

Talent movement (blocking changes) within the shot will establish a new axis of action for each new direction in which the subject faces. Once a new line exists, the camera is free to reposition.

If the movement of the talent provides the motivation, then a mobile camera (hand-held, Steadicam™, dolly, etc.) can cross over the action line during the continuous shot. The original 180-degree line is established with the first wide shot, but the line is then changed and updated as the camera moves to follow the movement of the subject and the resulting new action lines.

If you establish the line in the wide shot and then move the camera to the furthest extreme along the arc without going over the line, you will have created a neutral shot for use during the editing process. Because this extreme location along the arc "sits on the fence," you would then be free to fall to the other side of the line and shoot from the new side. The new line is established after the neutral shot and allows the audience to reset their spatial understanding of the film space.

You may also try to use a **cutaway** shot to a related object or person within the same film space. If you provide shots from both sides of the action line, but you have also recorded cutaways or insert shots for the editor, then a cutaway can break the spatial attention of the viewer and the next shot may be shown from the far side of the original axis of action. The majority of the film space and the blocking of the subjects will be established in the wider shot, so the visual break of the cutaway creates an easier transition to the new action line for the audience. You could even record another wide establishing shot of the scene from a different angle (Figure 7.28).

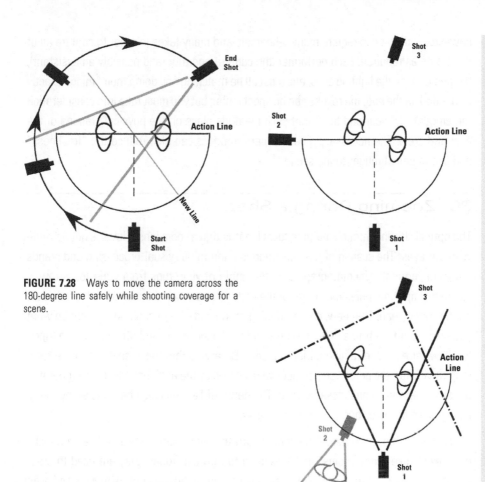

FIGURE 7.28 Ways to move the camera across the 180-degree line safely while shooting coverage for a scene.

29. The Long Take

Today's small, lightweight HD cameras and motion-stabilizing gimbals allow for camera operators to freely move along with the action while recording dynamic scenes in a story. It can be very engaging for the audience to have their camera proxy follow closely along with the characters without the interruption of editing. Traditional coverage for scenes was broken down into the family of shot types and the editor stitched these together to show the "continuous" key events of the scene. The long take – a lengthy, mobile tracking shot – can now take the place of all of those individual coverage shots by recording the unbroken events across continuous time until the scene ends.

On the surface, this technique initially seems like a great way to save all of the time that would normally be devoted to setting up for those multiple coverage shots. This can hold true if every aspect of the shot is performed at 100% on the first take. What you will find, however, is that it can require many rehearsals and many takes in order to capture all of the action as required. Each performer, the camera operator (and possibly an assistant), the audio team, the lighting cues, etc. must all be matching and doing their "thing" exactly as needed. In the end, the results can be spectacular, but you must take into consideration the amount of "wear and tear" that such methods place on the physical stamina of the cast and crew. The necessary repeated performances can also reduce the "freshness" and spontaneity brought to the scene.

30. Zooming During a Shot

The optical shifting through multiple focal lengths that a zoom lens allows is not possible with our eyes. The scaling of magnification is alien to our visual processing and stands out from "normal" cinematography. As the angle of view runs from wide to narrow, a zoom-in simply magnifies the center of the wider frame when the camera is locked down on the tripod head. That new, center framing at the end of your zoom-in may not be what you want your final frame to be, so you should keep loose pan and tilt locks on the tripod to allow for easier reframing during the shot. Be aware that these changes in the focal length will alter the perceived perspective observed by the audience (wide = exaggerated distance, narrow = compressed space). The depth of field will also be affected by the FL changes, so be conscious of your focus marks.

There was a time when zooms in fictional narrative films were considered "amateurish" or "hokey" (like "snap zooms" in 1970s kung fu movies). Today, they are used to great effect in a highly stylized fashion in science fiction and action/adventure movies and even video game "cinematics" animation design. Because of their frequent use by amateurs using camcorders (think of that easy access to the "W/T" toggle switch), zooms are often incorporated into POV videos shot by characters in feature films, TV shows, or music videos. Audiences have also grown quite accustomed to zooming shots when presented in news stories or photojournalistic documentaries where the camera must remain further away from the action for safety reasons.

You may find that a focal length change during a shot with a moving subject is required to maintain your desired composition. Combining the focal length change with a panning or tilting action that follows the moving subject may hide the zoom-in or zoom-out. The camera's reframing helps to cover the more visually distinct optical shift of the zoom factor. You can also "hide" a zoom with its speed of execution. Very, very slow zooms can be incorporated into a very long take, such as an engaging dialogue scene, where the focal length change is so subtle over time that it is not really noticed by the engrossed audience member (Figure 7.29).

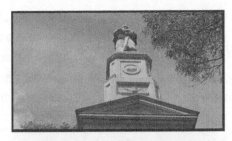

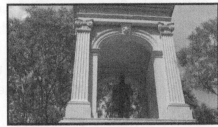

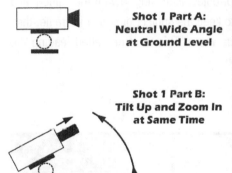

**Shot 1 Part A:
Neutral Wide Angle
at Ground Level**

**Shot 1 Part B:
Tilt Up and Zoom In
at Same Time**

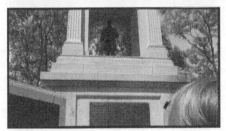

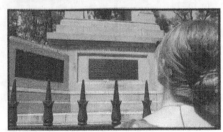

FIGURE 7.29 "Hiding" a zooming lens movement within a pan or tilt is often very effective. Framing and focal length changes are made at the same time to alter composition and perspective. This tilt-up also "hides" a zoom-in.

31. Motivate Your Dolly-In and Dolly-Out Camera Moves

31. Motivate Your Dolly-In and Dolly-Out Camera Moves

It is commonly accepted that camera movement during a shot is motivated by the movements of the subjects, which means that, as things move in the shot, the camera can move along with them. This holds true for dolly shots that either push into a set or pull out of it. This practice is often called tracking or trucking.

Usually, the motion of any object (a rolling ball) or any subject (a baby stroller) is ample motivation to track in. The object moves into the depth of the shot so the camera follows, seeking out more detail and more information. This pushing in and exploring is natural to the audience because it replicates what a human might do to follow the action and see more detail: get closer to the area of concern or keep pace with the moving item. It is an investigative expression of coverage.

Tracking out, however, is a less "natural" movement. The reverse motion of the dolly-out implies a person leaving a scene walking backward – not something people are likely to do on a regular basis. If a subject or object is moving toward the camera and the filmmaker wishes to track out in order to keep the subject or object in frame, then that provides the motivation for the camera move. This is often called leading the subject (Figure 7.30).

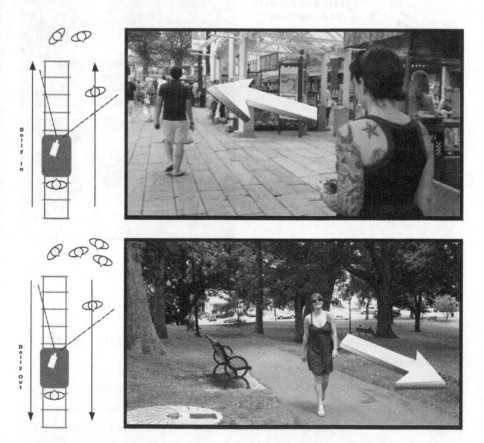

FIGURE 7.30   Talent movement can motivate dolly-in and dolly-out camera moves.

Because a dolly-out usually reveals larger or longer areas of the film space yet to be seen by the audience, it can be a useful tool in creating suspense (where is the character taking us? – what is he seeing behind us?), in relating new story information, and in revealing the consequences of another's actions. Therefore, you are likely to find a dolly-out at the end of a scene or sequence or at the end of an entire motion picture. The track-out provides a visual overview of where a subject has been and sets up a possible reveal for new plot points and visual data.

32. Use Short-Focal-Length Lenses to Reduce Handheld Camera Shake

The field of view or angle of view that a lens provides depends on its focal length. A wide-angle lens – a lens that is set to a short focal length such as 10mm – captures a larger field of view and therefore creates an image that shows more of the environment in front of the camera. When you see more of the environment, objects in that space tend to appear smaller. If the camera were to move or shake slightly while recording a wide shot, as with a handheld camera, the smaller objects in the frame do not travel very far because of the relative distances that they have to traverse in the wider image. The larger distances between objects and their relationship to the horizon line and the edges of the frame will help them to appear more stable if the camera experiences a minor shake or wobble.

Conversely, a lens set to telephoto – a long focal length such as 100mm or more – captures a much narrower field of view. This lens setting magnifies details of a narrow slice of the environment, and the objects within the frame are enlarged. These magnified objects will have less distance to travel around the frame before they hit an edge or leave the frame altogether. Also, a shallow depth of field usually accompanies the long FL, so focus issues become heightened. This is why a handheld camera with a long-focal-length lens is likely to create an extremely shaky and motion-blurred image. Magnified

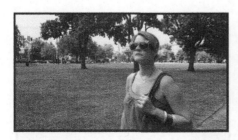 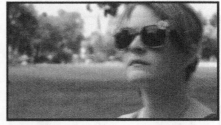

FIGURE 7.31 A wider-angle lens provides more stability if the camera shakes during handheld recording. A longer lens will most likely produce too much image shake on tighter shots.

objects in a narrow field of view make even small movements appear like large shifts in spatial stability. As a result, try to use short focal lengths when you need help stabilizing handheld camera coverage (Figure 7.31).

33. Allow Actions to Complete Before Cutting the Camera

There may be many occasions when this practice is neither possible nor prudent, but, for the most part, it should be followed because it makes a great deal of sense. It is the job of the editor to decide when to cut into a shot and when to cut out of a shot. The production crew should cover all of the action in each shot so that the editor has that footage from which to make his or her best choice while cutting the scene.

If an actor is to walk out of frame, let him or her walk fully out of frame and allow the empty space to be recorded for a short while. The same goes for a car, airplane, dog, etc. Allow the exit action to complete and let the camera run for a bit longer: a second or two. These extra frames can be of particular importance if the editor decides to create a dissolve or fade or some other transition that will imply the passage of time before the next shot. If the action calls for something to fall, a door to close, or a person to round the corner of a building and disappear from view, then let all of those actions complete in the shot before you cut the camera (Figure 7.32). As discussed earlier, the static end frame of a pan or tilt will also provide the opportunity for the recorded action to be completed at the end of the camera move.

You may also occasionally see the camera trail off from an action and move its attention/ framing onto a neutral background. After covering an action fully or partially, perhaps it tilts up to the sky, or down to the ground, or simply comes to a rest on some other nearby but unrelated object or background element in the scene. This treatment implies that the action is ongoing but gives the editor a clean neutral frame to cut away from and into the next shot or scene.

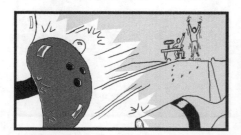 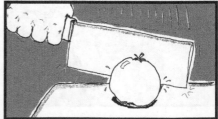

FIGURE 7.32   Allow actions to complete before stopping the camera.

34. Shooting a Chromakey

When you watch a meteorologist deliver the weather report in front of a large radar image showing swirling patterns of cloud movement, you are seeing the result of a **chromakey**. You may be more familiar with the terms "green screen" or "blue screen." These names refer to the same process whereby a certain color (chroma) is "keyed out" or removed from a video image. Post-production software is used to select that particular color (most often, green or blue) and turn it invisible while the remaining pixel data in the image is untouched. This layer of keyed video becomes the foreground element (the weather person) or the top layer in a composite. Then, some other video image (clouds on radar) is placed on the layer below to become the visible background of the new composited video image.

Although you could key any color in your video clips, the colors green and blue are most often used because they are two colors whose ranges of hues are not normally present in the skin or hair of human beings. Be advised that the pupils of people who have green or blue eyes will disappear if you use the same color for your chroma-screen color.

Lighting your foreground object should be done with the same care as you would use when lighting any subject for a motion picture project. Matching the lighting of the composite environment is sometimes desired if you are truly going for that special effect to trick your audience. If at all possible, you should have certain lighting fixtures just to

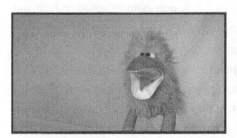
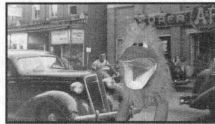
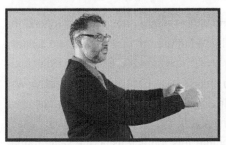
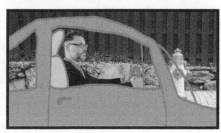

FIGURE 7.33 A simple green sheet (smooth, flat, and evenly lit) can serve as a chromakey screen. Here, the bird host of a kids' show is keyed over an old home movie and his guest host is driving a cartoon automobile. This superimposition is the result of pulling the key in post-production.

use on your talent and another set of dedicated lighting fixtures to illuminate the chroma-screen in the background.

The main things to remember are:

- Keep the screen as smooth and flat as possible.
- Illuminate the chroma-screen with uniform lighting (same light levels) across all of the screen visible in your shot; the screen does not need to be very bright, just uniformly lit.
- Keep your foreground subject far enough in front of the chroma-screen so that there are no shadows of any kind cast on the chroma-screen.
- If using a 16:9 widescreen camera, then you can mount the camera frame vertically to maximize the vertical resolution of the HD imager (shoot with portrait aspect ratio).

35. Shooting B-Roll, 2nd Unit, and Stock Footage

Depending on the genre and budget of your motion picture project, you may have a need for additional visual material beyond the principal photography.

If you are creating a work of non-fiction (especially a documentary, a corporate promotional video, or even a how-to or process video), it is important to schedule time and resources to acquire **B-roll**. B-roll can be any visual material that "shows" something related to the topic of the program that you are constructing. It is often used by the editor of the video to cut away from the main interviews or to pad out the timings between voice-over segments. Examples could be video of a corporation's headquarters, a busy factory's assembly floor, signage, trains pulling into a station, or shoppers in line at a store – whatever may be related to the topic of the main video.

In fictional narrative and long-form non-fiction videos, there often arises the need for visual materials that will be used in the final edit but are not part of the main scenes, interviews, or events recorded by the primary production crew. On films with larger budgets, the **2nd Unit** is another team who go to precise locations to record exterior views, aerial views (helicopter, airplane, or drone), driving shots, etc. This imagery can be used for establishing shots, cutaways, or background plates for process shots or special visual effects shots. It will be very important to acquire this footage using the same format camera, or possibly even a higher-resolution imaging device, to maintain or match the look and quality of the original production video.

Another option available to filmmakers is the acquisition of **stock footage**, archive film, or still photography for use in a new project. As the original material may not be of the same format, it will be important to create a workflow plan so that the copies that you access can be used in your final edit. Often, payment for usage is required, or at least a full credit needs to be given to the organization that contributes the archive materials and possibly holds the copyright.

36. Shooting a Talking-Head Interview

Depending on the genre of and the chosen visual plan for your motion media project, there could be innumerable methods to frame, light, and record an interview subject. If you capture the person saying the things he or she has to say, then the job would appear to be accomplished successfully. Certain basic approaches to covering the talking-head interview for documentaries and other non-fiction programs have worked well for decades, so perhaps you would like to start here and diverge when it suits your story.

A traditional approach is as follows:

- Seat your subject in a quiet room, with few distractions. The chair should not swivel, roll, recline, or squeak.
- If you, the filmmaker, are asking questions, then sit with your head very close to camera lens. The subject's eye-line will go to you consistently, near the lens but not into the lens.
- If you can record two channels of audio, use a body mic (lavalier) for clear, clean subject voice and a boom mic for voice plus ambience.
- Expand the camera-to-subject distance if possible so you can frame a medium shot to medium close-up with a longer focal length. This helps with flattened portrait perspective and a shallower depth of field.
- The subject should be seen in 3/4 front profile composition either frame left or frame right, with appropriate headroom and look/nose room. When interviewing more than one person for the show, stagger some folks along frame left and others along frame right, so that during editing the people who speak are not all facing the same way for the entire viewing experience.
- Allow space at the bottom of the frame for any lower third identification graphic added in post-production.
- A three-point lighting set-up is a good place to start. Try a soft key and fill light, then add a hard kicker back light on the opposite side from the key. Position

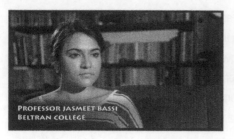 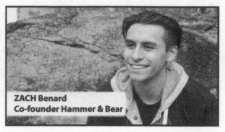

PROFESSOR JASMEET BASSI
BELTRAN COLLEGE

ZACH Benard
Co-founder Hammer & Bear

FIGURE 7.34 A sample frame showing the MCU talking-head composition from a documentary subject's interview. Note the headroom, look room, eye-line, eye catch light, soft-focus background, and the room for a lower-third title at the bottom of the frame. (Photo credit: B – Anthony Martel)

the key side of the face away from the lens. If you do not like it, use whatever lighting you have that is appropriate for your documentary's visual design.

- Exposure should be lower, so a shallow depth of field can help to blur out the background of your "set." The audience then watch the "in-focus" interviewee's face.
- Always ask the interviewee to say and spell his or her full name at the beginning of the recorded interview. Some producers like the interviewee to state the date as well.
- Ask open-ended questions that require explanations and not simply "yes" or "no" answers.

37. During Documentary Filming, Be as Discreet as Possible

When you are on location shooting documentary footage, it can become very challenging to acquire the shots that you need without drawing a lot of attention toward yourself and your crew. You will most likely attain the best results by remaining discreet, being respectful, and working quickly. As a crew member working on any project, you would be wise to remain discreet and efficient, but these working practices might get you more mileage when working in foreign or potentially hostile environments in particular.

You should, first of all, obtain all required permissions, certificates, releases, and waivers so that you can shoot at these locations legally. Your goal is to observe and record, not intrude or stage the events. The more people who are aware of who you are and what your purpose is, the more likely you are to get negative attention or simply have people behave differently than they normally might. Equipment advancements – small digital video and audio recorders – will help you to keep your "footprint" smaller, allowing for more discreet operations. Film emulsion cameras still tend to be a bit bulkier, and their rarity causes more curiosity in onlookers. Remember to obey all local laws and respect the privacy of individuals who do not wish to be a part of your project.

38. Use Visual Metaphors

Easily discernible visual metaphors have a high prominence in motion media commercial advertisements. The rocket-shaped can of soda shooting up to a high altitude conflates the soda brand with having huge amounts of energy. This drink gives you a rocket-sized boost. Visual metaphors can be created by combining two unrelated objects or subjects that are compared to one another or that take on an attribute of the other when presented together. While any motion media piece will have some form of imagery (video, animation, motion graphics, etc.), not every project can or should contain visual metaphors.

It is possible, however, to incorporate visual components and story elements (especially in fiction films or music videos) that, when united on the screen, can conjure associations between the physical content and emotional and/or psychological attributes. Color themes and unique lighting treatments for certain locations or characters can fall under this loose interpretation of visual metaphor. In a cartoon, the blue-skinned, teenaged alien is always sad (he is literally blue in color and "blue" due to sadness). Or you might have the young adventurers walk into a large spider web when they enter the creepy, old mansion where they get trapped. At the end of your movie, the sun dawns brightly on a new day after the heroes go through some harrowing, nocturnal challenges. However subtle or blatant you wish to make the associations, using visual metaphors in video work can provide extra layers of meaning and visual interest to your motion media projects.

39. Aim for a Low Shooting Ratio

It should be clear that not every frame shot during production makes it into the final edit of the project. Bad takes, beginnings and endings of shots, coverage not required, and overlapping actions not used by the editor will end up on the "cutting room floor" (an expression from film-editing days when the unwanted outtakes of the physical plastic strips of emulsion film were tossed on the floor of the editing room).

The **shooting ratio** is the relationship between the amount of visual material recorded during production and the amount of material that makes it into the final edited version. The overall shooting ratio is represented by two numbers separated by a colon (:). As an example, if you used one good take in the final edit, but shot seven different versions of that take, then your shooting ratio for that one shot would be 7:1. People have based this ratio on different criteria (film footage, takes, HD-cam tape stock, etc.) but time is probably the most predominant factor. If you recorded 30 hours of material for a one-hour program, then you have a 30:1 shooting ratio.

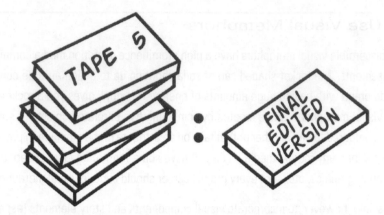

FIGURE 7.35   Five "tapes" of material edited down to one "tape" of that material is an example of a 5:1 shooting ratio. Ratios may be based on footage, time, or media captured against the actual amount of production material used in the final version.

Scripted fictional narratives will often have a lower shooting ratio because each shot should be well planned ahead of time. Documentaries may have a larger shooting ratio due to the lack of traditional scripting for the action and interviews. Wildlife, travel, and especially multi-camera "reality" television shows can have huge shooting ratios. It is not always easy to predict what the shooting ratio of a project will become, but it is a good idea to at least generate a best guess ratio when planning your shoot. Budgets are not always about money. Time is a very important factor during production and post-production, so the fewer takes you have to roll on, the more time is saved all around. A low shooting ratio with a good variety of shot coverage can be a winning combination for everyone (Figure 7.35).

Chapter Seven – Review

1. Storyboards and shot lists help with organization and efficiency during production.
2. Slate the head of your shots with pertinent information and a sync "clack."
3. Help the boom operator to place the microphone.
4. Using two or more video cameras to record multiple shots of coverage can help to save time and preserve continuity of performance and action.
5. Be aware of reflections of lighting fixtures or the camera/crew on polished surfaces around the film set or location.
6. Communicate clearly with the talent before and during production.

7. Frame action within the camera viewfinder's safe action area and frame signage or titling within the safe title area.

8. Manually focus a zoom lens at the longest FL on a subject that you wish to see clearly.

9. Always have something in your frame in focus.

10. Control your depth of field through choices of FL, aperture, and camera-to-subject distance.

11. Be aware of headroom in your frame.

12. Use close-up shots when you want your audience to pay more attention and make either an intellectual or an emotional connection with the subject on screen.

13. Be aware of very wide lens distortion when shooting close-up shots near to the talent.

14. Try to show both eyes of your subject; the 3/4 front profile is a good place to start.

15. Be aware of eye-line directions in closer shots.

16. Place important objects in the top half of your frame.

17. Keep distracting objects out of the shot and away from the talent's head.

18. Use the depth of the film space to stage shots with several people.

19. It is most often appropriate to place an eye light or catch light so that your talent's eyes glint.

20. Be aware of the color and contrast choices made throughout your project.

21. Allow the camera more time to record each shot at the head and the tail.

22. Follow action with a loose pan and tilt tripod head.

23. Record some overlapping actions during each coverage shot so that the editor may cut on action movements within the frame during a scene.

24. Action may be the movement of human subjects or of machines or animals, etc. and efforts should be made to capture similar actions from each camera set-up.

25. Matching speed of action will aid the editor's ability to create smooth continuity edits on action.

26. Overlapping too much action in each camera set-up can waste time and talent energy.

27. Frame for the correct look room across the cut on shots that will edit together.

28. Shoot matching camera angles of subjects when covering dialogue for a scene.

29. In a three-person dialogue scene, matching two-shots can be problematic for the editor. Record clean single close-up shots of each character as well.

30. Be aware of continuity traps while recording coverage for a scene.

31. Plan accordingly to cross the 180-degree line safely when shooting coverage for a scene.

32. Finding moments in the script where coverage for a scene can be long and continuous allows for greater flow of talent energy and performance. The long take covers a great deal of action without cutting.

33. Understand when and how to perform a zoom during a shot.

34. Motivate your dolly-in and dolly-out camera moves.

35. Use short-focal-length lenses to smooth out handheld camera movements.

36. Allow all actions to complete before cutting the camera.

37. Light chromakeys with even illumination, no shadows, and no matching hue in the FG.

38. Be aware that while out in the field during production, it can be very advantageous to record a fair amount of B-roll, insert shots, and cutaways.

39. In order to get the interview subject comfortable and relaxed, it is important to keep him or her in a private, quiet space with appropriate lighting and good sound quality. Have him or her address the director or producer and not look directly into the camera's lens. Three-point lighting, MS to MCU, and 3/4 front profile offer a good start to creating a traditional talking-head interview.

40. During documentary shooting, be as discreet as possible.

41. Find creative ways to incorporate visual metaphors into your motion media work.

42. Be aware of your shooting ratio to save time and money.

Chapter Seven – Exercises

1. Practice recording close-up shots of non-human subjects: signs, cars, plants, books, chairs, etc. Make sure that you account for "headroom" and "look room" and maintain all items of interest within the safe action/safe title areas.

2. If your video camera has a zoom lens, practice zoom–pans, zoom–tilts, and zoom–pan–tilts. Does it make a difference if the focal length change is motivated or unmotivated? Could you achieve a similar effect by moving the camera instead?

3. Go to a friend's house or take him or her to some public space in your community. Ask the friend questions about himself or herself and how he or she relates

to the space where you are. Take note of the responses and then, after the interview, go and record B-roll and inserts that will be useful for the editing process of this interview footage.

4. Using a handheld camera (with a wider focal length), practice following a moving subject from the back, leading from the front, and crabbing along from the side in profile. Which is easiest/most difficult to accomplish and why? Think of scenarios when you might wish to use each type of handheld dolly. (Safety Note: always have a spotter moving with you when operating the camera by hand so no one falls or gets hurt – especially if you are walking backward or sideways).

Chapter Seven – Quiz Yourself

1. What documents can you prepare during pre-production that will help you to set up the necessary shots quickly on the given shoot day?

2. Describe two ways in which you can "cross the line" safely when recording coverage for a dialogue scene.

3. What are the key visual cues that let you know a shot is achieved with a zoom and not a dolly move?

4. Why is it suggested to run the camera before calling "Action" and for a few seconds after calling "Cut?" Who will thank you the most for doing this on all takes?

5. What is the process of "calling the roll?"

6. How can you effectively control the depth of field for your camera/lens while recording on your own film set?

7. What is the danger in recording a tight close-up with the camera very near to the subject's face when the lens is set to its shortest focal length and, therefore, its widest angle?

8. What might it mean, thematically in the story, if one character's head is placed in the upper half of the film frame and the other character's head is placed along the lower portion of the film frame?

9. What are two methods for alleviating a lighting fixture's reflection on a film set that don't involve turning off the light?

10. True or false: it is the subject's hard-edged, well-defined shadow cast upon the chromakey backdrop that allows for the green screen to become invisible in composite editing.

Chapter Eight
Concluding Thoughts

- Know the Rules Before You Break the Rules
- The Reason for Shooting Is Editing
- Your Shots Should Enhance the Entire Story
- Involve the Viewer as Much as Possible
- Take Pride in the Quality of Your Work
- Practice Proper Set Etiquette
- Know Your Equipment
- Be Familiar with Your Subject Matter
- Understand Lighting – Both Natural and Artificial
- Study What Has Already Been Done

This book has presented some of the basic principles of visual grammar in filmmaking, described a number of different shot types, and offered some common working practices. None of this material is carved in stone and much of it is open to interpretation. Different people may call things by different names or choose to approach things in slightly different ways. Elaboration, experimentation, and blatant subversion have given rise over the years to many new and interesting approaches to creating and conveying entertainment and information programming. However, no matter what the technology or material to be presented, underneath all of the innovation would still lie the basic guidelines of accepted visual communication in motion media and cinematic language.

This final chapter offers some additional food for thought and advice.

Know the Rules Before You Break the Rules

Contrary to popular belief, not all rules were made to be broken. Just as there are rules to sporting games, we have discovered in this book that there are rules that govern the production of motion pictures. The grammar of the shot – the film language – has evolved over the last 100-plus years but the basic tenets and guidelines have remained the same. As a result of this standardization of imagery, creators the world over are able to tell stories – or show stories – that are understood by a very wide audience. As with a written language, you can read the images and comprehend what is going on in the motion picture presentation.

You can imagine, then, that if the rules of written language were not followed, there would be many people who could not read and comprehend what the words on the page were supposed to mean. The same holds true for the motion picture. Follow the established rules and guidelines of film grammar and you should find that the widest possible audience will understand the imagery and comprehend what you are attempting to convey via the visual elements of the story – regardless of whether it is a fictional narrative, a documentary, an informational video, or an animated cartoon.

There is always room for experimentation and innovation; just be judicious with when, how much, and on which type of motion media project you let it loose. When you break the rules before you know the rules, you are taking certain risks with the project. If the show is entirely your own, then go for it, but if you are using other people's money, time, and resources, it might be wise to start from an informed base of cinematic conventions. When you start with the basic rules and guidelines and build on them in creative ways, you will most likely meet with more acceptance and success, but you won't know until you start to do it for yourself. So get out there and put them into practice. Learn more by doing more.

The Reason for Shooting Is Editing

Unless you are shooting coverage at a live telecast, your goal in recording motion images will be to pass along the best possible visual material to the editor. The raw visual pieces are generated during film production but the real story isn't told until the final cut is made. If you create excellent individual shots at the expense of the story's editorial needs, then you have done a great disservice to the entire motion picture project. If it does not cut, then the problems started much earlier than post-production.

The film production process, no matter how simple or how elaborate, is never an easy undertaking. The potential for mistakes is always present. Numerous stresses, unplanned events, or last-minute changes can always happen. A good solution for alleviating as many of these potential headaches as possible is solid pre-production planning. Shot lists, storyboards, set/location overhead floor plans, and, of course, a strong understanding of film language will go a long way in helping you to generate visually interesting and informative imagery that serves your story.

Well beyond talent performance, you must also make sure that your shots are technically acceptable for the edit.

- Have you matched angles, camera distances/heights, focal lengths, and lighting schemes on your coverage for a scene?

- Have you followed the action until it completes?
- Is there good focus on all of the right planes within the complex shot?

Many aspects of the overall project must be planned and executed correctly for the final product to be as good as it possibly can be. So remember to think about what you are shooting and understand how it will be used during the edit.

Please don't use the expression, "We'll fix it in post" as an excuse for bad preparation and shoddy work during production.

Your Shots Should Enhance the Entire Story

The basic shot types discussed in this book will be able to provide you with the basic building blocks for shooting coverage of any motion picture event. Even if you do not move beyond the visual basics for recording a news report, a sporting event, or a documentary, then you may still show your audience a worthwhile experience. The simple film language provides all of the visual information necessary to clearly show the story's factual content.

It has traditionally been the scripted fictional narrative film that allows for more experimentation in the imagery. Your shot compositions, talent blocking, lens choices, camera angles and movement, etc. have the potential to support, underscore, and enhance the story being told. These visual aspects can highlight, in special ways, the characters that populate that story. The filmmaker may find more freedom in creating visual expressions that stimulate and engage the audience. The images should be used to augment the narrative and the characterizations.

As a quick and easy example, let's say that two roommates have just found out that the third did not pay the rent on time. The wide establishing shot shows all three characters (A, B, and C) standing together. The characters, location, and scene are set from this first shot. Then you move in for the coverage. You record a clean single CU of Character A, but only one MCU two-shot for both B and C to appear on screen together. As we experience tensions between A and the team of B and C, then the cutting between shots of A by herself and B and C grouped together can enhance the narrative by physically showing A as a loner/outsider and B and C together as a unified team "against" their roommate (Figure 6.1).

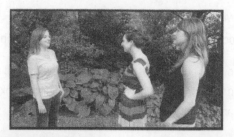

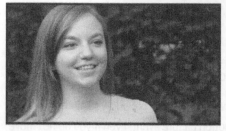

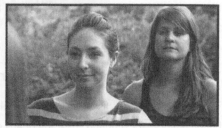

FIGURE 8.1 The single close-up shot of Character A keeps her isolated from the pair of Characters B and C in their overlapping close-up two-shot. The imagery reinforces the themes of the narrative.

Involve the Viewer as Much as Possible

Motion pictures really are a participatory experience. It might seem as though most people just sit and watch, but what usually happens when they are viewing good material is that they are actively engaged on many levels. Certainly, they should follow the story, but they will also experience many emotions and have physical reactions and responses to the actions viewed on the screen. What you show to the audience, how you choose to show it, and when it gets shown are rather important factors in the success of a motion picture.

One of the main goals of most visual works of storytelling is to keep the viewer engaged. There should always be a need to pay attention. If there is no direct involvement for the majority of a motion picture, then it is more likely to be seen as boring by the disinterested viewer. Of course, everyone has different tastes, and different stories call for different treatments of picture, sound, and pacing in the edit. All works should have a way to involve the viewer's senses, brain, and emotions. The visual elements are all within your control as a filmmaker, so at least make a concerted effort to cover all of the important information — and figure out a way to do it creatively.

Remember that, on the most basic level, when you show a new shot to the audience, they are going to scan it for information and, if given time by the editing, they are going to appreciate it for all of the aesthetic qualities incorporated into its frame: composition, lighting, color, focus, movement, etc. Most modern audiences are very well acquainted with the visual grammar of film language. They can comprehend the important facts presented in the visuals very quickly. From one shot to the next, they are constantly scanning for, observing, and digesting visual information, which generates a sense of expectation within them. If you fail to provide the audience with the appropriate information when they expect to see it, then you run the risk of losing them.

Motivating your shots is extremely important as well. There has to be a reason for the shot to exist. What information does it convey? Can an image tell the viewing audience more about the story than spoken words? This is the meaning behind the old filmmaking expression, "Show, don't tell." Find a way to make your pictures express information and emotion rather than using dialogue or narration to do so.

As an example, let's consider the following scenario. A wide shot shows a college graduation ceremony in progress. A medium shot shows a young woman accepting her college degree on the stage. She expectantly looks out to the parents in the audience. A close-up of her father shows that his eyes are tearing up with pride and happiness. The wide shot sets the scene and motivates the exploration of who is getting the degree. The medium shot of the young woman answers that question. Then, her eye-line out to the crowd motivates the CU of the father. His CU reveals new data about his emotional state. Each shot conveys new information, helps to progress the narrative, and motivates each successive shot as well.

Take Pride in the Quality of Your Work

To paraphrase an old expression, if something is worth doing at all, it is worth doing well. Whether you are working on a group exercise for a video production class, recording a motovlog for your YouTube channel, or producing a multi-million-dollar indie feature, you should always take pride in your work and strive to deliver the best product possible. This holds especially true for when you are creating projects for clients — particularly if you are taking their money in exchange for your expertise and labor. Every production — no matter how small, frustrating, or perfectly awesome — should receive the same amount of focus, energy, and thoughtful attention from you.

No one should expect you to know everything, but people will have expectations that you know something and are willing to learn more by finding solutions to problems encountered along the way. If you are just starting out, you may find that your handheld shots are too shaky, your horizon lines are always a bit askew, the focus is off just a bit on the main object of interest, your dolly moves are filled with bumps and jiggles, or your zooms are not smooth, etc. This is okay. As with so many things in life, you get better with practice. That is why you should view each camera set-up, each lighting design, each rack focus, etc. as an opportunity to learn new skills, try new techniques, and improve your understanding of the filmmaking craft.

If everything you do for a production needs to be top quality according to your own high standards, then it is only natural that that effort and care will come across to others — whether they are another crew member, a paying client, or a paying audience member.

Practice Proper Set Etiquette

As a filmmaker, it is very important for you to exhibit a high level of professional behavior. On any size production, you may be dealing with coworkers, talent, agents, police, location managers, business owners, equipment rental firms, or even curious on-lookers. Treat everyone with respect. If you communicate your needs clearly and to the point, then, typically, you will reach your goals more quickly. Do not assume that everyone "knows" what you are thinking. Understand that not everyone will share your vision and that not all aspects of your production will go according to plan. Handle each step with the attention that it deserves and offer your best professional courtesy to all involved with the project — no matter how large or how small a role they are playing.

When it comes to doing your actual job on set, be aware that you are an important member of a team. On larger productions, everyone has a job to do, and even if it looks like they are not doing much of anything, trust that they are and do not disturb them. Ask for help when you need it, but be aware of the appropriate times and people to ask for that help. On small productions, be ready to offer help to those in need because there are so few of you on hand to get the show done. Keep a cool head and get the shot; once you get it, move on. A good shooting pace keeps your talent and crew fresh and motivated to work hard. Don't blame others if you encounter problems, but work together to find a quick solution. Try not to schedule very long shoot days. You need to keep your "behind-the-lens" actions and movements to a minimum during shooting. You could wear dark clothing to help to blend in (be less visible in reflective surfaces) and not be a distraction to the talent performing in the scene. If you have an exterior shoot planned and the weather turns foul, you should have an alternative interior shoot ready to go as a back-up; some call this a "cover set."

We are at a social and technological generational shift in our production crew make-up, meaning that there is not just a blend of older, more experienced crew members and an influx of younger, eager newbies; that's always been the case. No, what we have happening around us now is a situation where the technologies have changed (advanced) rapidly and the nature of the motion media "industry" is evolving. The kinds of projects being made, how they are captured and edited, and how they are being disseminated out to the world for consumption have evolved rather quickly. There are many motion media producers now who have literally grown up with these new digital technologies. These workers use digital tools (like smartphones, tablets, wireless controllers, apps, social media, cloud-based sharing, etc.) rather adeptly for many aspects of the phases of motion media production.

This reliance upon digital tools (especially smartphones, which are really highly capable mini-computers) means that we all run the risk of becoming distracted while we work. Just because a smartphone or an internet-connected computer can help us to do our work does not mean that we should allow ourselves to get sidetracked by its other capabilities, such as texting, Instagram, Snapchat, web surfing, etc. Use the tools as tools and put them away when done. Live in the moment. Experience each aspect of production with your full attention. Observe, absorb, and be ready to do anything that is necessary. A professional demeanor, a low profile, and an efficient working style will go a long way toward sustaining positive results on the shooting set, regardless of age, experience, or technological understanding.

Know Your Equipment

It is imperative that the members of a film crew are well acquainted with the required equipment. Lighting, grip, audio, and camera are some of the key areas of concern during production. Whether it is the latest high-resolution digital video camera, an action cam, a drone, or a smartphone, the camera operator and other members of the camera department crew must know as much as possible about the device and all of its accessories. Experience is a great help here, but if you are a newer user, then reading the manuals will be a good first step. Be ready to ask questions of other, more knowledgeable users of the equipment. Before the first day of shooting, you should make time to play with the equipment, build it, take it apart, and handle it so you know how it feels, sounds, moves, and responds. Shooting tests for image quality and walking the media through a post-production workflow will be very informative.

Preparation goes beyond just being familiar with the equipment. You should be accountable for all of the parts as well. Make sure that you have all of the pieces of gear that you need and that they are functional and clean. Charge all batteries the night before your first shoot day and remember to pack them when you leave for the job. Know your lenses. Understand their capabilities and make sure that they are clean. Have all required cables, filters, memory cards, and any extra tools or supplies organized and ready to go. When you are in a studio or, especially, on location, designate an area strictly for camera department equipment and ask other personnel to stay clear. Keep your camera gear organized and in its cases whenever possible so that you know exactly where to go when you need something. On film sets, there is very little tolerance for time and money lost to easily avoided errors.

Be Familiar with Your Subject Matter

As someone new to filmmaking, you should make the time to familiarize yourself with the material in the project during pre-production. Whether it is a documentary being made, a fictional narrative story being told, or a music video being shot, you should know the subject matter, the people involved, and what the goals of the production will be. Read the entire script if you can get your hands on a copy. Understand the tone of the piece: dark, heavy, light, joyful, etc. Be as familiar as possible with the locations, perhaps through a "tech scout" where you examine the location for access, electrical supply, sun passage, sound issues, etc. Anticipate the needs of crew members and performers while watching for opportunities to make the entire production better. Good preparation of this kind will put you more at ease while shooting and allow you to work more efficiently should something go amiss.

Understand Lighting – Both Natural and Artificial

Anyone involved in creating good visuals for a motion picture project, whether it is something for television, movies, or the internet, should have a solid understanding of lighting and how to best use it for shooting. You can spend a lifetime mastering the science behind light and color and also the nuances behind manipulating then correctly for use on film sets. Everybody starts somewhere in that learning process, so you should not delay your own training. Composing great shots or pulling off wild dolly moves is certainly a positive thing, but without the appropriate lighting, all of it could be moot.

It is essential that you understand the basics of lighting: hard light, soft light, motivated light, bounced lighting, top lighting, practical set lighting, etc. You need to understand that there is lighting used just to get exposure (enough to record your image) and there is lighting for creative purposes. You may highlight certain characters or keep others in silhouette. Have overall high-key flat lighting, or create strong chiaroscuro with low-key lighting. You may also wish to use certain colors that have particular meanings for your story. With all of this light around your film set, it is very important to check your camera lens for light flares: lights that have their beams pointing into the lens. This errant light falling into your lens can cause flares or flashing on the image. This can be done creatively, but you will most often not wish for this to happen by accident.

When sunlight can be used, it can often save a great deal of time and money. However, as we all know, the sun is always moving. Throughout the day, the sun arcs across the sky. This results in an ever-changing play of light and shadow across the world. When you are using natural sunlight as your primary light source, you should be aware that it will be different in just a matter of minutes to a few hours, depending on the time of year and your geographic location. No matter where you are shooting, you should take some time to familiarize yourself with the availability of sunlight and the course that the sun will take across the sky — and, yes, there is an app for that. Part of your responsibility is to plan the best locations and best times of day when the sun can be used to its best illuminative and cinematic advantage. It might be mid-morning, noon, or the **golden hour**. Knowing about light and lighting is a critical part of anyone's motion picture training.

Study What Has Already Been Done

A large part of learning how to make motion pictures is knowing that you should really study what has already been done. Conducting research is an easy, informative, and entertaining way to prepare for almost any shoot. You may watch movies, television programming of all kinds (sitcoms, documentaries, cartoons, dramas, news shows, music videos, reality programs, etc.), experimental or avant-garde films, and even animations and video games. The web is a great resource for video clips that are available whenever you wish, as are pay services like Netflix and Amazon Prime. Your goal is not to replicate precisely what others have already achieved, but to find inspiration and create new approaches to visual communication for yourself.

Many visually creative people (filmmakers, graphic designers, illustrators, screenwriters, etc.) also turn to art history for ideas, inspiration, and education in particular practices. Paintings, especially, can be a very rich source of compositional studies, color schemes, uses of light and shadow, focus, texture, etc. As everyone working on the motion picture could see a print of a particular painting or review a series of paintings from a particular artist, the works become a very visual way to relate ideas about color palettes, mood, or subject matter. Sculpture, photography, architecture, textiles, etc. become excellent resources and references for the many people involved in creating the numerous visual elements that go into the making of a motion picture. Studying these art forms and sharing your findings with others will lead to a successful collaboration on the film set. (See some suggested art and film history websites in Appendix A.)

Conclusion

The key lesson in all of this material about "the shot" is that recording motion images, whether with a high-end digital video camera or a smartphone, is not always a matter of simply pointing and shooting. Of course, you can take that approach and it may do well for recording birthday parties and holidays or even a particular kind of "informal" program. However, any professional-grade project that is worth doing is worth doing well, which means that you may have to employ a fair amount of proven cinematic language.

This book has introduced you to many of the basic practices, techniques, and guidelines for creating effective imagery that can build a solid motion picture experience for the audience. As you work on projects, you will become more knowledgeable. You will get better at selecting the parts of this special language that suit your needs and the needs of your particular characters and story. Not every shot type, camera move, or lens angle will fit into the visual style that you plan for each project. Your goal over time is to develop an ever-expanding tool set and an ever-growing collection of references and resources, so that you move from being a person with an idea in your head to an artful and effective visual communicator using the full power of film language in all of your works.

The grammar of your shots will tell the story. Thank you.

Appendix A
Helpful Resources for the New Filmmaker

Websites

www.artoftheguillotine.com

www.cinema5d.com

www.cinematography.com

www.cinematography.net

www.colorgradingcentral.com

www.dofmaster.com

www.filmcontracts.net

www.filmmakeriq.com

www.googleartproject.com

www.joyoffilmediting.com

www.lightsfilmschool.com/blog

www.newsshooter.com

www.precinemahistory.net

www.premiumbeat.com/blog

www.theasc.com

www.videomaker.com

www.wga.hu/index1.html

(All website URLs accessed on May 1, 2017.)

Books

Cinematography: Theory and Practice
Image Making for Cinematographers and Directors, 3rd Edition
By Blain Brown
(Focal Press, 2017)

Voice & Vision
A Creative Approach to Narrative Film and DV Production, 2nd Edition
By Mick Hurbis-Cherrier
(Focal Press, 2011)

DSLR Cinema
Crafting the Film Look with Video, 2nd Edition
By Kurt Lancaster
(Focal Press, 2013)

The Visual Story
Creating the Visual Structure of Film, TV, and Digital Media, 2nd Edition
By Bruce Block
(Focal Press, 2008)

Motion Picture and Video Lighting
2nd Edition
By Blain Brown
(Focal Press, 2007)

Light: Science and Magic
An Introduction to Photographic Lighting, 4th Edition
By Fil Hunter, Paul Fuqua, and Steven Biver
(Focal Press, 2011)

The Art Direction Handbook for Film & Television
2nd Edition
By Michael Rizzo
(Focal Press, 2014)

If It's Purple, Someone's Gonna Die
The Power of Color in Visual Storytelling
By Patti Bellantoni
(Focal Press, 2005)

The Screenwriter's Roadmap
21 Ways to Jumpstart Your Story
By Neil Landau
(Focal Press, 2012)

Directing
Film Techniques and Aesthetics, 5th Edition
By Michael Rabiger and Mick Hurbis-Cherrier
(Focal Press, 2013)

Changing Direction
A Practical Approach to Directing Actors in Film and Theatre
By Lenore DeKoven
(Focal Press, 2006)

Directing the Story
Professional Storytelling and Storyboarding Techniques for Live Action and Animation
By Francis Glebas
(Focal Press, 2008)

Grammar of the Edit
4th Edition
By Christopher J. Bowen
(Routledge, 2018)

The Technique of Film and Video Editing
History, Theory, and Practice, 5th Edition
By Ken Dancyger
(Focal Press, 2010)

FilmCraft: Editing
By Justin Chang
(Focal Press, 2011)

Make the Cut
A Guide to Becoming a Successful Assistant Editor in Film and TV
By Lori Coleman and Diana Friedberg
(Focal Press, 2010)

The Camera Assistant's Manual
6th Edition
By David E. Elkins
(Focal Press, 2013)

Experimental Filmmaking
Break the Machine
By Kathryn Ramey
(Focal Press, 2016)

Appendix B
Crew Members Commonly Needed for Motion Picture Production

Assistant Director (AD) – Responsible for setting and maintaining the production schedule. The assistant director will verify with all departments that they are ready for a take, call the actors to the set for the director, and call the roll to begin the recording process for a take.

Boom Operator – In charge of holding or rigging a microphone from a boom pole (a telescoping rod that supports the sensitive microphone suspended over the actors as they speak). Works with the sound mixer and camera operator to find the best placement of microphones for sound levels and picture integrity.

Camera Assistant (AC) – Technician responsible for all camera equipment (bodies, lenses, accessories, batteries, media, etc.). Ensures that everything is clean, cabled, and running correctly. During the take, usually controls the follow focus apparatus. Also often the keeper of the camera report and logs. On smaller productions, the camera assistant may also do the head slating of each take for picture and sound.

Camera Operator – In charge of running the camera. Responsible for ensuring proper framing and double-checking focus during a shot. Sometimes starts and stops the recording process of the camera as well.

Digital Imaging Technician/Data Wrangler/Media Wrangler (DIT) – On productions exclusively using digital video cameras that generate media files, the digital imaging technician is the person in charge of calibrating the digital imaging sensors of the cameras and doing on-set color grading in cooperation with the director of photography. The data wrangler also copies media from camera memory cards, backs them up, and transports them to the hard drives of the post-production team. Without film or tape original sources, these media files are extremely important and their careful replication and preservation is paramount.

Director – In charge of interpreting the written words of the screenplay story and turning them into viewable motion pictures. Responsible for selecting shots and working with actors to achieve desired characterizations. Collaborates with many other members of the production and post-production teams to help to realize her or his overall vision for the piece.

Director of Photography/Cinematographer (DP or DOP) – Responsible for creating the overall look of the film. Chief member of the camera department. Works with the director to select the shots. Creates the lighting scheme for each set-up. Collaborates with the electric, grip, and art department heads. Often consults on color correction and grading during post-production.

Dolly Grip – A grip specifically assigned to build, maintain, and move the camera dolly around the film set. May set up and level any tracks or rail needed for the dolly move.

Editor – The person, during post-production, responsible for editing picture and sound elements into the final story that will be experienced by the audience. Depending on the project, the editor may also occasionally be on set during production to edit together scenes from the digital "dailies" made each day.

Electric – Responsible for running the power lines of electricity to all departments on a film set.

Gaffer – Chief electric in charge of the entire electric department. In consultation with the director of photography, chooses and sets the lighting fixtures that illuminate the film's sets or locations. Responsible for achieving the desired look and levels of light for exposure.

Grip – Member of the grip department. Grips have many responsibilities and are capable of performing many tasks on a film set that involve moving and supporting things.

Key Grip – Chief grip in charge of all grips on the crew. Works closely with the director of photography and gaffer to get the necessary support equipment (for camera and lighting) placed for each shot.

Lighting Technician – Hoists, strikes, and angles the film lights on set.

Production Designer – In charge of the design elements of a film's overall look. Generates the concepts for and oversees set design, costuming, make-up, etc. Collaborates closely with the director, director of photography, and art director.

Screenwriter – Writes the screenplay, which is either an original idea or an adaptation of an existing property. Not typically involved during the production or post-production phases of the project.

Script Supervisor – Responsible for monitoring each take during production and noting how closely it follows the written script. Takes notes on all significant aspects of the set, props, actions, line delivery, etc. Keeps track of scene and take numbers and provides that data to the camera and sound departments for the organization of slate information.

Sound Recordist/Sound Mixer – Audio technician in charge of running any audio-recording equipment on set. Maintains good levels of sound during recording. Coordinates the best microphone placement with the set boom operator.

Glossary

4K – A shorthand reference to the 4096 x 2160 pixel image of digital cinema projection.

4:3 – The aspect ratio for standard-definition television. Four units wide by three units tall – more square in its visual presentation than the widescreen high-definition 16:9 video display.

16:9 – The aspect ratio for high-definition video. Sixteen units wide by nine units tall – a widescreen display.

30-Degree Rule – A cousin to the 180-degree rule, this rule suggests that when recording coverage for a scene from differing camera angles within the film set, the camera should be moved around the 180-degree arc by at least 30 degrees from one shot to the next to create enough variation on the angle on action so that the two different shots will edit together and appear different enough in their framing. A focal length change between set-ups will also help.

50–50 – A profile two-shot, typically in a medium shot or closer, where both subjects look across the screen at one another. Used especially in dialogue scenes.

180-Degree Line/Action Line/Axis of Action/Imaginary Line – The imaginary line established by the sight lines of subjects within a shot that determines where the 180-degree arc of safe shooting is set up for the camera coverage of that scene. Traditionally, the camera should not be moved to the opposite side of this action line because it will cause a reversal in the established screen direction when the shots are edited together. See also 180-Degree Rule, Sight Line.

180-Degree Rule – In filmmaking, an imaginary 180-degree arc, or half-circle, is established on one side of the shooting set once the camera first records an angle on the action in that space. All subsequent shots should be made from within that same semi-circle. As screen direction, left and right, for the entire scene is already established, the camera cannot photograph the subject from the other side of the circle without causing a reversal in the screen direction.

Act (noun) – Much as in stage plays, in long-form programming (feature films or episodic television, etc.), the story is broken down into several major sections known as acts. In fictional narrative filmmaking, a story will traditionally have three acts, loosely termed the set-up, the confrontation, and the resolution.

Action – What the director calls out to signify that the acting for the shot being recorded should begin.

Aesthetics – A way of creating and analyzing art and art forms for their beauty.

Angle of Incidence – The angle from which incident light falls upon a film set. A single lighting fixture directly overhead will have a 90-degree (from horizon) angle of incidence.

Angle of View – The field of view encompassed by the light-gathering power of a camera's lens. A wide-angle lens has a wide angle of view. A telephoto lens has a narrower angle of view on the world.

Angle on Action – The angle from which a camera views the action on the film set.

Aperture – In motion picture equipment terms, the aperture refers to the iris or flexible opening of the camera lens that controls how much or how little light is used to expose the image inside the camera. A wide aperture or iris setting lets in a larger amount of light. A smaller aperture lets in less light. On some camera lenses, the aperture can also be fully "stopped down" or closed all of the way for total darkness on the image.

Artificial Light – Any light generated by a manmade device such as a film light, a desk lamp, or a neon sign.

Aspect Ratio – The numerical relationship between the dimensions of width and height for any given visual recording medium. In the example 16:9, the first number, 16, represents the units of measure across the width of a high-definition video frame. The second number, 9, represents the same units of measure for the height of the same frame.

Atmospherics – Any particulates suspended in the air around a film set or location, such as fog, mist, or dust, which will cumulatively obscure the distant background or "catch" and "show" the light in the air.

Attention – The direction in which a subject looks within the film space. The attention of a subject may be drawn by another subject, an inanimate object, or anything that attracts his or her gaze. An imaginary line connects the eyes of the subject and the object of his or her attention, and, most often, the audience will trace this line to also see what the subject is observing. See also Sight Line.

Background – The zone within a filmed frame that shows the deep space further away from the camera. The background is often out of focus, but serves to generate the ambience of the location.

Back Light – A light used on a film set placed behind an object but pointed at its back side. It generally serves to help to separate the object from the background by providing a rim or halo of light around the edges of the body, head, and hair. It may also illuminate the reflective surfaces around the subject such as wet pavement or polished floors.

Binocular Vision (human visual system) – Having two eyes located at the front of the head. The slight distance between the two eyes causes humans to see nearby objects from two distinct vantage points. The brain then combines the two distinct images into one picture where the overlapping elements take on a 3D aspect.

Blocking – The planned movement of subjects within the film space and the corresponding movement, if any, of the camera to follow the actions of the moving subjects.

Boom Arm – Deriving its name from the armature on a sailing ship's mast, a boom arm is used to swivel and extend the camera's placement to get sweeping shots or keep the camera buoyant without a tripod directly beneath it.

Break Frame – When an object being recorded accidentally moves to the edge of the frame and falls outside the visible area of the image.

B-Roll – Any visual material acquired for a project (especially news, documentary, and reality) that visually supports the main topic of discussion but does not include important human subjects. Often used to "mask" edits in an interviewee's answers or commentary when used as a cutaway on the picture track.

Camera Angle – The angle at which a camera views a particular scene. Camera angles can be based on horizontal camera positioning around the subject or vertical camera positioning below or above the subject.

Camera Person/Camera Operator – The person who physically handles the camera during the shooting, whose main responsibility is to maintain proper framing and composition and to verify good focus.

Camera Set-Up – A place on the film set where a camera is positioned to record a shot. Each time the camera is physically moved to a new position, it is considered a new camera set-up. The camera set-up is often associated with a particular shot from the shot list for scene coverage.

Camera Support – Any device or piece of film equipment that is used to support the motion picture camera. Tripods, dollies, and car mounts are all examples of various kinds of camera support.

Charge-Coupled Device (CCD) – The electronic light sensor built into many video cameras that turns light wave energy into electronic voltages. These voltages get recorded as brightness and color values on a tape, hard drive, or memory card in the camera.

Chiaroscuro – Italian for light/dark, this term is used in the visual arts to talk about the high contrast ratio between light and dark areas of a frame. Filmmakers, as well as painters, use this technique to show or hide certain visual elements within their frames.

Clean Single – A medium shot to a close-up that contains body parts of only one person even though other characters may be part of the scene being recorded.

Close-Up – Any detail shot where the object of interest being photographed takes up the majority of the frame. Details will be magnified. When photographing a human being, the bottom of the frame will just graze the top part of the shoulders and the top of the frame may just cut off the top part of the head or hair.

Color Temperature – Often referenced on the degrees Kelvin scale, color temperature is a measurement of a light's perceived color when compared to the color of light emitted from a "perfect black body" exposed to increasing levels of heat. The color temperature for tungsten film lighting is generally accepted as around 3200 degrees Kelvin. Noontime sunlight is generally accepted as around 5600 degrees Kelvin. The lower numbers appear "warm" orange/amber when compared to white, and the higher numbers appear "cool" blue.

Complementary Metal Oxide Semiconductor (CMOS) – A type of image sensor used in many smaller devices such as smartphones and in both consumer- and professional-grade digital video cameras.

Composition – In motion picture terms, the artful design employed to place objects of importance within and around the recorded frame.

Continuity – In motion picture production terms: (1) having actors repeat the same script lines in the same way while performing similar physical actions across multiple takes; (2) making sure that screen direction is followed from one camera set-up to the next; (3) in post-production, matching physical action across a cut point between two shots of coverage for a scene.

Contrast – The range of dark and light tonalities within a film frame.

Contrast Ratio – The level of delineation between strong areas of dark and strong areas of light within a film frame, as represented in a ratio of two numbers: key+fill:fill.

Coverage – Shooting the same action from multiple angles with different framing at each camera set-up. Example: A dialogue scene between two people may require a wide, establishing shot of the room; a tighter two-shot of both subjects; clean singles of each actor; reciprocal over-the-shoulder shots favoring each actor; cutaways of hands moving or the clock on the wall, etc.

Crane – Much like the large, heavy machinery used in construction, a crane on a film set may raise and move the camera or have large lighting units mounted to it from high above the set.

Critical Focus – As with the human eye, there can be only one plane or physical slice of reality that is in sharpest focus for the motion picture camera. The plane of critical focus is this slice of space in front of the lens, at a particular distance, that will show any object within that plane to be in true focus. Example: When recording a person's face in a medium close-up, his or her eyes should be in sharpest focus, in which case the plane of critical focus is the same distance away from the lens as the actor's eyes.

Cutaway – Any shot recorded that allows a break from the main action within a scene. The editor may place a cutaway into an edited scene of shots when a visual break is necessary or when two other shots from the primary coverage will not edit together smoothly.

Daylight Balance – Emulsion film stock and video cameras may be biased toward seeing the color temperature of daylight as "white" light. When they are set this way, they have a daylight balance of approximately 5500 degrees Kelvin.

Degrees Kelvin – The scale used to indicate a light source's color temperature, ranging roughly from 1000 to 20,000 degrees. Red/orange/amber-colored light falls from 1000 to 4000 and bluish light falls from 4500 to 20,000.

Depth – The distance from the camera receding into the background of the set or location. The illusion of 3D deep space on the 2D film plane.

Depth of Field (DOF) – In filmmaking terms, the DOF refers to a zone, some distance from the camera lens, where any object will appear to be in acceptable focus to the viewing audience. The DOF lives around the plane of critical focus, appearing one-third in front of and two-thirds behind the plane of critical focus instead of being centered equally. Any object outside the DOF will appear blurry to the viewer. The DOF may be altered or controlled by changing the camera-to-subject distance or by adding light to or subtracting light from the subject and adjusting the lens iris accordingly.

Desaturation – In filmmaking, the removal of colors (hues) from an image such that only gray-scale values (blacks, grays, whites) are left in the pixels of the image.

Digital Zoom – A camera lens function that digitally enlarges an image, based on a magnification of the existing pixel data by the camera's processor. The result is often blurry or "pixelated" due to this expansion of limited picture information. A digital zoom is a digital blow-up, and differs from an optical zoom, which uses glass lenses to record an actual magnified image of a distant object.

Direct Address – A subjective style of recording motion pictures where the subject looks (and speaks) directly into the camera lens. Used in news reporting, talk shows, game shows, etc.

Director of Photography (DP, DOP) – The person on the film crew who is responsible for the overall look of a motion picture project's recorded image. He or she primarily creates the lighting scheme but may also help in planning the angles, composition, and movement of the camera as well as design details such as color palettes and object textures.

Dirty Single – A medium shot to a close-up that contains the main person of interest for the shot but also contains some visible segment of another character who is also part of the same scene. The clean single is made "dirty" by having this sliver of another's body part in the frame.

Dolly – Traditionally, any wheeled device used to move a motion picture camera around a film set, either while recording or between takes. A dolly may be three or four wheeled; travel on the floor, or roll (with special wheels) along straight or curved tracks; or have a telescoping or booming arm that lifts and lowers the camera.

Domestic Cutoff – The outer 10% of analog-transmitted picture information that is cut off at the outside edges of a cathode ray tube television set and not viewable by the in-home audience. Although not as common in the digital age, this phenomenon should be taken into account when composing shots for a project that will be broadcast on television or viewed as a standard-definition DVD. Videos encoded for web playback will display full frame.

Dutch Angle/Dutch Tilt/Canted Angle/Oblique Angle – In filmmaking terms, any shot where the camera is canted or not level with the actual horizon line. The Dutch angle is often used to represent a view of objects or actions that are not quite right, underhanded, diabolical, or disquieting. All horizontal lines within the frame go slightly askew diagonally and, as a result, any true vertical lines will tip in the same direction.

End Frame – Any time that the camera has been moving to follow action, the camera should come to a stop before the recorded action ceases. This clean, static frame may be used by the editor to cut away from the moving shot to any other shot that would come next. In a filmed sequence, viewing moving frames cut to static frames can be a jarring visual cut, and this static end frame may help to prevent this visual glitch.

Establishing Shot – Traditionally, the first shot of a new scene in a motion picture. It is a wide shot that reveals the location where the immediately following action will take place. The audience may quickly learn place, rough time of day, rough time of year, weather conditions, historical era, etc. by seeing this shot.

Exposure – In motion picture camera terms, the light needed to create an image on the recording medium (either emulsion film or a video light sensor). If you do not have enough light, you will underexpose your image and it will appear too dark. If you have too much light, you will overexpose your image and it will appear too bright.

Exterior – In film terms, any shot that has to take place outside.

Eye Light/Catch Light/Life Light – A light source placed somewhere in front of the talent that reflects off the moist and curved surface of the eye. This eye twinkle brings out the sparkle in the eye and often informs the audience that the character is alive and vibrant. Absence of the eye light can mean that a character is no longer living or is hiding something, etc.

Eye-Line – The invisible line of attention that emanates from a subject's eyes and goes to the object of interest. The eye-line can inform a filmmaker about how to angle the coverage of the reveal shot, insert shot, or cutaway that will follow.

Eye-Line Match – The attention line from a subject (eye-line) should match in direction and angle to the object of interest in the reveal shot. Example: When shooting clean single coverage for a two-person dialogue scene, the eyes of each character should be looking out of the frame in the direction of where the other character's head or face would be. Even though the actors may not be sitting next to one another as they were in the wider two-shot, the eye-line of each "looking" at the other must match from shot to shot so that there is consistency in the edited scene.

Fill Light – A light, of lesser intensity than the key light, used to help to control contrast on a set but most often on a person's face. It "fills" in the shadows caused by the dominant key light.

Film Gauge – In the world of emulsion film motion pictures, the physical width of the plastic film strip is measured in millimeters (e.g., 16mm, 35mm). This measurement of film width is also referred to as the film's gauge.

Film Noir – A term generated by French film critics of the late 1940s to describe the visually and thematically dark motion pictures created in Hollywood from the early 1940s to the late 1950s. Meaning "black film," the term typically applied to black-and-white, gritty crime-dramas that used a very low-key lighting design.

Film Space – The world within the film, both that which is currently presented on screen and that which is "known" to exist within the film's manufactured reality.

Fisheye Lens – A camera lens whose front optical element is so convex (or bulbous, like the eye of a fish) that it can gather light rays from a very wide area around the front of the camera. The resulting image formed when using such a lens often shows a distortion in the exaggerated expansion of physical space, object sizes, and perspective – especially with subjects close to the camera.

Focal Length – The angle of view that a particular lens can record. It is a number, traditionally measured in millimeters (mm), that represents a camera lens' capacity to gather and focus light. A lower focal length number (e.g., 10mm) indicates a wide angle of view. A higher focal length number (e.g., 200mm) indicates a narrower field of view where objects further from the camera appear to be magnified and fill more of the frame.

Focus – The state where objects being viewed by the camera appear to be sharply edged and well defined, and show clear detail. Anything out of focus is said to be blurry.

Following Focus – If a subject moves closer to or further away from the camera but stays within the film frame, often the camera assistant or camera operator must manually control the focus of the recording lens to keep the moving subject in clear, crisp focus. If a subject at the plane of critical focus moves away from that plane and outside the corresponding depth of field, he or she will get blurry unless the camera assistant follows focus and shifts the DOF.

Foreground – The zone within a filmed frame that starts near the camera's lens but ends before it reaches a more distant zone where the main action may be occurring. Any object that exists in the foreground of the recorded frame will obscure anything in the more distant zones out to the infinity point that would normally have been visible behind it.

Foreshortening – In the visual arts, it is a way that 3D objects get represented on the 2D plane. When pictured from a certain view or perspective, the object may appear compressed and/or distorted from its actual shape: the closer end will appear larger and the further end will appear smaller or tapered.

Fourth Wall – In fictional narrative filmmaking, this term means the place from which the camera objectively observes the action on the film set. Because it is possible for the camera to record only three of the four walls within a film set without moving, the fourth wall is the space on set where the camera lives and it is from that privileged place that it observes the action. "Breaking the fourth wall" means that the actor has directly addressed the camera lens and therefore the audience.

Frame – The entire rectangular area of the recorded image with zones of top, bottom, left, right, center, and depth.

Front Lighting – Any lighting scheme where lights come from above and almost directly behind the camera recording the scene. The talent, when facing toward the camera, will have an overall even lighting, which often causes flatness to their features but may also smooth out surface imperfections.

Geared Head – A professional piece of camera support used on dollies, cranes, and tripods that has two spinning geared wheels that allow for very fluid vertical and horizontal movements of the camera. The camera operator must crank each gear wheel manually to maintain the appropriate framing during tilts or pans.

Gel – Heat-resistant sheet of flexible, thin plastic that contains a uniform color. Used to add a "wash" of color on a film set. Example: If the feeling of sunset is required for a shot, an orange/yellow gel can be placed between the lights and the set to give the impression of a warmer sunset color.

Genre – A French term meaning a category within some larger group. In film, the term applies to types of movies such as comedy, drama, action, musical, etc.

Golden Hour/Magic Hour – The moments just after actual sunset but before the ambient light in the sky fades to night-time darkness. Filmmakers often appreciate the visual quality that the soft top light of dusk creates on exterior scenes.

Grip – A film crew member whose job is to move, place, and tweak any of the various pieces of film equipment used for the support of camera and lighting units, or devices used to block light, among other duties. A special dolly grip may be used to rig the dolly tracks and push or pull the dolly or camera during the recording of a shot.

Handheld – Operating the motion picture camera while it is supported in the hands or propped upon the shoulder of the camera operator. The human body acts as the key support device for the camera and is responsible for all movement achieved by the camera during the recording process.

Hard Light – A quality of light defined by the presence of strong, parallel rays being emitted by the light source. Well-defined, dark shadows are created by hard light.

Head – A common film term for the beginning of a shot, especially during the post-production editing process.

Headroom – The free space at the top of the recorded frame above the head of the subject. Any object may have headroom. Too much headroom will waste valuable space in the frame, and not enough may cause your subject to appear cut off or truncated at the top.

High-Angle Shot – Any shot where the camera records the action from a vertical position higher than most objects being recorded. Example: The camera, looking out of the third-floor window of an apartment house, records a car pulling into the driveway down below.

High Definition (HD) – A reference to the increased image quality and wider frame size (16:9) of the digital video format, compared to the standard-definition format used for television in the 20th century. The increase in vertical line resolution per frame (720 or 1080) increases the sharpness and color intensity of the playback image. All HD formats use square pixels.

High-Key Lighting – A lighting style in which a low contrast ratio exists between the brightly lit areas and the dark areas of the frame. Overall, even lighting gives proper exposure to most of the set and characters within it. There are no real dark shadow regions and no real overly bright regions.

HMI – A film lighting fixture in which the internal lamp burns in such a way as to emit light that matches daylight/sunlight in color temperature (5500–6000 degrees Kelvin).

Hood Mount – A device used to mount a tripod head and camera to the hood of a motor vehicle such that the occupants of the vehicle may be recorded while the vehicle is in motion. Often a large suction cup is employed to help to secure the camera rig to the hood.

Horizon Line – The distant line that cuts across a film frame horizontally. It is used to help to establish the scope of the film space and to define the top and bottom of the film world.

Interior – In film terms, any shot that has to take place inside.

Iris – In motion picture equipment terms, the iris refers to the aperture or flexible opening of the camera lens that controls how much or how little light is used to expose the image inside the camera. Some modern video cameras use an electronic iris that controls the amount of light automatically. Most high-end HD and emulsion film lenses use an iris of sliding metal blades that overlap to make the aperture smaller or wider. A marked ring on the lens barrel can manually control the size of the opening.

Jib Arm – A piece of motion picture camera support equipment that allows the camera to move around a central fulcrum point, left/right/up/down/diagonally. It may be mounted onto tripod legs or on a dolly.

Jump Cut – An anomaly of the edited film when two very similar shots of the same subject are cut together and played. A "jump" in space or time appears to have occurred, which often interrupts the viewer's appreciation of the story.

Jump the Line/Cross the Line – Based on the concept inherent to the action line or 180-degree rule, this expression refers to moving the camera across the line and recording coverage for a scene that will not match the established screen direction when edited together.

Key Light – The main light source around which the remaining lighting plan is built. Traditionally, on film sets, it is the brightest light that helps to illuminate and expose the main subject of the shot.

Kicker Light – Any light that hits the talent from a 3/4 backside placement. It often rims just one side of the hair, shoulder, or jawline.

Legs – An alternative name for a camera tripod.

Lens Axis – In motion picture camera terms, the central path cutting through the middle of the circular glass found in the camera's lens. Light traveling parallel to the lens axis is collected by the lens and brought into the camera, exposing the recording medium. You can trace an imaginary straight line out of the camera's lens (like a laser pointer) and have it fall on the subject being recorded. That subject is now placed along the axis of the lens.

Light Meter – A device designed to read and measure the quantity of light falling on a scene or being emitted from it. Often used to help to set the level of exposure on the film set and, consequently, the setting on the camera's iris.

Line of Attention – The imaginary line that connects a subject's gaze to the object of interest being viewed by that subject. Example: A man, standing in the entryway of an apartment building, looks at the nameplate on the door buzzer. The "line" would be traced from the man's eyes to the nameplate on the wall. The next shot may be a close-up of the nameplate itself, giving the audience an answer to the question, "What is he looking at?"

Locked Off – The description of a shot where the tripod head pan and tilt controls are locked tight so that there will be no movement of the camera. If there were a need to make adjustments to the frame during shooting, the pan and tilt locks would be loosened slightly for smooth movement.

Long Shot/Wide Shot – When photographing a standing human subject, his or her entire body is visible within the frame and a large amount of the surrounding environment is also visible around him or her.

Look Room/Looking Room/Nose Room – When photographing a person, it is the space between his or her face and the furthest edge of the film frame. If a person is positioned frame left and is looking across empty space at frame right, then that empty space is considered the look room or nose room.

Low-Angle Shot – Any shot where the camera records the action from a vertical position lower than most objects being recorded. Example: The camera, on a city sidewalk, points up to the tenth floor of an office building to record two men, suspended with rigging, cleaning the windows.

Lower Thirds – A title or graphic that appears as a superimposed visual element across the bottom lower third of the screen. Usually used to identify a person or place in a factual news piece or a documentary interview.

Low-Key Lighting – A lighting style in which a large contrast ratio exists between the brightly lit areas and the dark areas of the frame. Example: Film noir used low-key lighting to create deep, dark shadows and single-source key lighting for exposure of the principal subjects of importance.

Matching Shots/Reciprocating Imagery/Answering Shots – When shooting coverage for a scene, each camera set-up favoring each character being covered should be very similar if not identical. You should match the framing, camera height, focal length, lighting, etc. When edited together, the matching shots will balance one another and keep the information presented about each character consistent.

Medium Shot – When photographing a standing human subject, the bottom of the frame will cut off the person around the waist.

Middle Ground – The zone within the depth of a filmed frame where, typically, the majority of the important visual action will take place. Objects in the middle ground may be obscured by other objects in the foreground, but middle-ground objects may then also obscure objects far away from the camera in the background.

Monocular Vision (camera lens) – A visual system in which only one lens takes in and records all data. The 3D aspect of human binocular vision is not present in the monocular vision of the film or video camera.

MOS – A term applied to shots recorded without sound. It should be noted on the clap slate and on the camera report and camera log. Although originating in the early days of sync sound emulsion film production, it may be used on any project where a camera records the visual images and a separate device records the audio signal. The post-production team know not to search for a sync sound clip that corresponds to that MOS picture clip.

Motivated Light – Light, seen on a film set, that appears to be coming from a light source within the film's pretend world.

Natural Light – Any light that is made by a non-manmade source, such as the sun or fire.

Negative Space – An artistic concept wherein unoccupied or empty space within a composition or arrangement of objects also has mass, weight, and importance, and is worth attention. Used to help to balance actual objects within the frame.

Neutral-Density (ND) Filter – A device that reduces the amount of light entering a camera (density), but does not alter the color temperature of that light (neutral). It is either a glass filter that you can apply to the front of the camera lens or, with many

Glossary

video cameras, a setting within the camera's electronics that replicates the reduced light effect of neutral-density glass lens filters.

Normal Lens – A camera lens whose focal length closely replicates what the field of view and perspective might be on certain objects if those same objects were seen with human eyes.

Objective Shooting – A style of filmmaking where the subjects never address the existence of the camera. The camera is a neutral observer, not actively participating in the recorded event but simply acting as a viewer of the event for the benefit of the audience.

Overexposed – A state of an image where the bright regions contain no discernible visual data but appear as glowing white areas. The overall tonality of this image may also be lacking in true "black" values so that everything seems gray to white in luminance.

Overheads – Drawings or diagrams of the film set, as seen from above like a bird's-eye view, that show the placement of the camera, lighting equipment, talent, and any set furnishings, etc. These overheads will act as a map for each department to place the necessary equipment in those roughed-out regions of the set.

Overlapping Action – While shooting coverage for a particular scene, certain actions made by the talent will have to be repeated from different camera angles and framings. When cutting the film together, the editor will benefit from having the talent making these repeated movements, or overlapping actions, in multiple shots so that when the cut is made, it can be made on the matching movement of the action across the two shots.

Over-the-Shoulder (OTS) Shot – A shot used in filmmaking where the back of a character's head and one of his or her shoulders create an "L" shape in the left/bottom or right/bottom foreground and act as a "frame" for the full face of another character standing or seated in the middle ground opposite the first character. This shot is often used when recording a dialogue scene between two people.

Pan – Short for "panoramic," this is the horizontal movement of the camera, from left to right or right to left, while it is recording action. If you are using a tripod for camera support, the pan is achieved by loosening the pan lock on the tripod head and using the pan handle to swivel the camera around the central pivot point of the tripod to follow the action or reveal the recorded environment.

Pan Handle – A tripod head with a horizontal pivot axis allows for the panning action of the camera, either left or right. The pan handle is a stick or length of metal tubing that extends off the tripod head and allows the camera operator to control the rate of movement of the camera pan by physically pushing or pulling it around the central axis of the tripod.

Point of View (POV) – In filmmaking terms, any shot that takes on a subjective vantage point. The camera records exactly what one of the characters is seeing. The camera sits in place of the talent, and what it shows to the viewing audience is supposed to represent what the character is actually seeing in the story. It can help the audience to relate to that character because they are placed in that character's position.

Point Source – A light source derived from a specific, localized instance of light generation/emission. A non-diffused light source.

Post-Production – The period of work on a motion picture project that occurs after all of the action is recorded with a camera (also known as production). Post-production can include picture and sound editing, title and graphics creation, motion effects rendering, color correction, musical scoring and mixing, etc.

Practical – A functional, on-set lighting fixture visible in the recorded shot's frame that may actually help to illuminate the set for exposure. Example: A shot of a man sitting down at a desk at night. Upon the desk is a lamp whose light illuminates the face of the man.

Pre-Production – The period of work on a motion picture project that occurs prior to the start of principal photography (also known as production). Story development, script writing, storyboards, casting, etc. all happen during this phase.

Prime Lens – A type of lens that has only one focal length.

Principal Photography – The recording of motion images that involve the major talent of a production during the primary dialogue and/or action scenes contained in the script.

Production – The period of work on a motion picture project that occurs while the scenes are being recorded on film or video. This could be as short as a single day for a commercial or music video or last several months for a feature film.

Proscenium Style – In theater as well as motion pictures, a way to stage the action such that it is seen from only one direction. The audience or, for the film, the camera view and record the action from only one angle.

Pulling Focus – Camera lenses that have manual controls for the focus will allow a camera assistant or camera operator to move the plane of critical focus closer to the camera, therefore shifting the distance of the zone that appears to be in sharp focus within the depth of the frame. This is often done to shift focus from an object further in the frame to one closer within the frame.

Punch-In – When two or more separate shots of differing frame sizes cover the same subject along the same camera axis.

Pushing Focus – Camera lenses that have manual controls for the focus will allow a camera assistant or camera operator to move the plane of critical focus further away from the camera, therefore shifting the distance of the zone that appears to be in sharp focus within the depth of the frame. This is often done to shift focus from an object near in the frame to one further away within the frame.

Racking Focus – During the recording of a shot that has a shallow depth of field, the camera assistant or camera operator may need to shift focus from one subject in the frame to another. This shifting of planes of critical focus from one distance away from the camera to another is called racking focus.

Reveal – Any time that the filmmaker shows new, important, or startling visual information on the screen through camera movement, talent blocking, or edited shots in post-production. The reveal of information is the pay-off after a suspenseful expectation has been established within the story.

Rim Light – Any light source whose rays rim or halo the edges of a subject or an object on the film set, often placed somewhere behind the subject but directed at him or her.

Rule of Thirds – A commonly used guideline of film frame composition where an imaginary grid of lines falls across the frame, both vertically and horizontally, at the mark of thirds. Placing objects along these lines or at the cross points of two of these lines is considered part of the tried and true composition of film images.

Safe Action Area – Related to the domestic cutoff phenomenon, the safe action area is found on many camera viewfinders and is used to keep the important action composed more toward the inner region of the frame. This prevents important action from being cut off.

Scene – A segment of a motion picture that takes place at one location. A scene may be composed of many shots from different camera angles or just one shot from one camera set-up.

Screen Direction – The direction in which a subject moves across or out of the frame. Example: A person standing at the center of the frame suddenly walks out of frame left. The movement to the left is the established screen direction. When the next shot is cut together for the story, the same person should enter the frame from frame right, continuing his or her journey in the same screen direction – from right to left.

Shooting Ratio – The amount of material that you shoot for a project compared to the amount of material that makes it into the final edit. Example: You shoot 14 takes of one actor saying a line, but only use one of those takes in the final movie. You have a 14:1 shooting ratio for that one line of dialogue.

Shot – One action or event that is recorded by one camera at one time. A shot is the smallest building block used to construct a motion picture.

Shot List – A list of shots, usually prepared by the director during pre-production, that acts as a guide for what shots are required for best coverage of a scene in a motion picture project. It should show the shot type and may follow a number and letter naming scheme (e.g., Scene 4, Shot C, or simply 4C).

Shot–Reverse–Shot – A term applied to an editing style where one shot of a particular type (e.g., medium close-up) is used on one character and then the same type of shot is edited next in the sequence to show the other character in the scene. You see the shot, "reverse" the camera angle, and see a matching shot of the other character.

Side Lighting – A method of applying light to a subject or film set where the lights come from the side, not above or below.

Sight Line/Line of Attention – The imaginary line that traces the direction in which a subject is looking on screen. The sight line also establishes the line of action and sets up the 180-degree arc for shooting coverage of a scene. See also 180-Degree Line.

Silhouette – A special way of exposing a shot where the brighter background is correct in its exposure but the subject (in the middle ground or foreground) is underexposed and appears as a black shape with no detail but the hard edge "cut out."

Slate (noun) – The clapboard used to identify the shot being recorded. Often, the name of the production, director, and director of photography, the shooting scene, and the date are written on the slate.

Slate (verb) – Using the clapboard sticks to make a "clapping" sound, which serves as a synchronization point of picture and sound tracks during the editing process.

Slider — A short, metal track with a small, rolling plate to which you attach a tripod head or camera directly. The camera slides up and down this short track, creating very smooth/gliding visuals — especially for closer shots of people or, more often, objects.

Soft Light — Any light that has diffused, non-parallel rays. Strong shadows are very rare if you use soft light to illuminate the talent.

Spreader — The three legs of a tripod are often attached to a spreader, a rubber or metal device to keep them from splaying too far apart while the heavy camera sits atop the tripod head. This three-branched brace allows for greater stability, especially as the tripod legs are spread further and further apart to get the camera lower to the ground.

Staging — The placement of set dressings and objects within the film set.

Standard Definition (SD) — A reference to the normal image quality and frame size of most televisions around the world during the 20th century. Limitations in broadcast bandwidth, among other technological reasons, required a low-resolution image (525-line NTSC or 576-line PAL) of the 4:3 aspect ratio for television reception in the home.

Start Frame — Any time that the camera needs to move to follow action, the camera should begin recording, stay stationary for a few moments while the action begins, and then start to move to follow the action. The start frame can be useful to the editor of the film so that the shot will have a static frame to start on at the beginning of the cut. Static frames cut to moving frames can be a jarring visual experience and this static start frame may help to prevent this visual glitch.

Sticks — (1) An alternative name for a camera tripod; (2) the clapboard or slate used to mark the synchronization point of picture and sound being recorded.

Storyboards — Drawings often done during pre-production of a motion picture that represent the best guess of what the ultimate framing and movement of camera shots will be when the film goes into production. These comic-book-like illustrations act as a template for the creative team when principal photography begins.

Subjective Shooting — A style of filmmaking where the subjects address the camera straight into the lens (as in news broadcasting) or when the camera records exactly what a character is observing in a fictional narrative, as with the point-of-view shot.

Tail — The common film term for the end of a shot, especially during the post-production editing process.

Tail Slate – Often used while recording documentary footage, a tail slate is the process of identifying the shot and "clapping" the slate after the action has been recorded but before the camera stops rolling. The slate is physically held upside down to visually indicate a tail slate.

Take – Each action, event, or line of dialogue recorded in a shot may need to be repeated until its technical and creative aspects are done to the satisfaction of the filmmakers. Each of the times that the camera rolls to record this repeated event is called a take. Takes are traditionally numbered, starting at one.

Taking Lens – The active lens on a motion picture or video camera that is actually collecting, focusing, and controlling the light for the recording of the image. On certain models of emulsion film motion picture cameras, there can be more than one lens mounted to the camera body. Most video cameras have only one lens, which would be the taking lens.

Talking Head – Any medium close-up shot or closer that frames one person's head and shoulders. Usually associated with documentaries, news, and interview footage.

Three-Point Lighting Method – A basic but widely used lighting method where a key light is employed for main exposure on one side of the talent, a fill light for contrast control on the opposite side, and a back light for subject/background separation.

Tilt – The vertical movement of the camera, either down/up or up/down, while it is recording action. If you are using a tripod for camera support, the tilt is achieved by loosening the tilt lock on the tripod head and using the pan handle to swing the camera lens up or down to follow the vertical action or reveal the recorded environment.

Timecode – A counting scheme based on hours, minutes, seconds, and frames that is used to keep track of image and sound placement on videotapes, digital media files, and editing software.

Tracking In/Trucking In – Moving the camera into the set, usually atop a dolly on tracks.

Tracking Out/Trucking Out – Pulling the camera out of the set, usually atop a dolly on tracks.

Tracks/Rail – Much like railroad tracks, these small-scale metal rails are used to smoothly roll a dolly across surfaces, either inside or outside, to get a moving shot.

Tripod – A three-legged device, often with telescoping legs, used to support and steady the camera for motion picture shooting. The camera attaches to a device capable of vertical and horizontal axis movements called the tripod head, which sits atop the balancing legs.

Tungsten Balance – Film and video cameras may be biased toward seeing the color temperature of tungsten lamps (also known as film lights) as "white" light. When they are set this way, they have a tungsten balance at approximately 3200 degrees Kelvin.

Two-Shot/2-Shot – Any shot that contains the bodies (or body parts) of two people.

Ultra High Definition (UHD) – Video industry term used to reference a display screen with a resolution of 3840 x 2160 pixels.

Underexposed – A state of an image where the dark regions contain no discernible visual data but appear as deep black areas. The overall tonality of this image may also be lacking in true "white" values so that everything seems gray down to black in luminance.

Vanishing Point – A long-established technique in the visual arts where opposing diagonal lines converge at the horizon line to indicate the inclusion of a great distance in the image's environment. It is an illusion used to help to represent 3D space on a 2D surface.

Video Format – A video combines recorded electronic voltage fluctuations or digital bit data that represent picture and sound information. Video cameras are manufactured to record that data onto a tape or memory card in a particular way. The shape, amount of data, frame rate, color information, etc. that get recorded are determined by the technologies inside the video camera. Examples include NTSC-525 line, PAL, HD-1080i, and HD-720p.

Visible Spectrum – The zone in electromagnetic energy waves that appears to our eyes and brains as colored light.

Voice Slate – A practice used at the head of a shot after the camera is rolling and before the director calls "Action." Often, a camera assistant will verbally say the scene and take number so as to identify audio data that may be recorded separately from the picture.

Workflow – A plan or methodology that maps the flow of picture and sound data from production through numerous post-production phases and ultimately to a finished product that is distributed for viewing. Managing a clear digital media file workflow is very important to the efficient completion of any project.

Zoom Lens – A camera lens with a multiple glass lens element construction and tele-scoping barrel design, allowing it to gather light from a wide range or field of view and also from a very narrow (more magnified) field of view. The focal length of the lens is altered by changing the distances of the optical elements contained within the lens barrel itself. Most modern video cameras have built-in optical zoom lenses that can be adjusted from wide to telephoto with the touch of a button or a twist of the focal length ring on the lens barrel.

Index